THE DETECTIVE IN FILM

William K. Everson

THE CITADEL PRESS

Secaucus, New Jersey

First edition
Copyright © 1972 by William K. Everson
All rights reserved
Published by Citadel Press, Inc.
A subsidiary of Lyle Stuart, Inc.
120 Enterprise Ave., Secaucus, N.J.
In Canada: George J. McLeod Limited
73 Bathurst St., Toronto 2B, Ontario
Manufactured in the United States of America

Designed by A. Christopher Simon

Library of Congress catalog card number: 72-85523

ISBN 0-8065-0298-3

ACKNOWLEDGEMENTS

Especially grateful thanks are extended to Alex Gordon of Twentieth Century-Fox for his generous help in providing both screening facilities and rare stills, and to Jacques Ledoux, curator of the Royal Film Archive of Belgium, James Barfoed of the Danish Film Museum, and Ken Wlaschin of the British Film Institute, for similar help.

To James Card, curator of George Eastman House, Rochester, N.Y., and Charles Turner, of the Audio-Visual Department of Greenwich Public Library, appreciation for their extreme generosity in the supplying of many rare stills.

To Alan Barbour, Spencer Berger, Richard Gordon, Herbert Graf, and William Kenly of Paramount Pictures, thanks for their kind help in the supplying of stills.

I am much indebted also to Charles Shibuk and Edward Connor, whose extensive and authoritative writing on detective fiction and the mystery movie provided some extremely useful short cuts.

Finally, my thanks to Bowling Green University Popular Press for their permission to reprint (and expand on) my notes on "The Kennel Murder Case" included in their publication *The Mystery Writer's Art*.

WILLIAM K. EVERSON

CONTENTS

1 INTRODUCTION

THE MALTESE FALCON: Humphrey Bogart, Peter Lorre, Mary Astor, and Sydney Greenstreet.

Few books attempting to trace the history of any filmic genre face as thankless a task as this one. Obviously, the musical has clearly defined boundaries and, in addition, is perforce almost entirely limited to the sound period. While there may be no exact definition of the horror film, and it may encompass the science-fiction movie as well as the more sophisticated suspense story, at least the writer can fall back on the common denominator of themes that try to evoke the emotion of fear in their audiences. The western, while no longer the exclu-

sive domain of Hollywood, is the product of a specific geographic locale and an equally specific period of history. And, while the comedy is necessarily ambiguous and varied in style and content, at least there are guidelines.

But the detective story, already confusing and defiant of categorizing in the literary field, presents an ever greater morass to the motion picture scholar. Obviously, there is no debate where the filmed adventures of the great detectives of fiction are concerned: the "official" detectives—from Sherlock Holmes through Philo Vance,

Charlie Chan, and Sam Spade up to Mike Hammer—*belong*. But what, then, of the comic strip or boys' dime novel heroes—from Britain's Sexton Blake and Dick Barton to America's Dick Tracy? And where does one draw the line between a Dick Tracy and a superhero like Batman, who certainly uses the superficial paraphernalia of the classic scientific detective, even if his deductions are mainly a matter of the scriptwriters feeding him the right inspiration at precisely the right moment. For that matter, many of the more "respectable" detectives of film and fiction—including those British stalwarts, Sir Nayland Smith (Fu Manchu's perennial nemesis) and James Bond—are likewise men of action first and sleuths second, operating on infallible intuition and on anticipating, and outguessing, the next moves of their opponents.

Admittedly, there are many "rules of the game" where the whodunit is concerned, but they are of little help in establishing a workable form in which to encase the detective film. Many of the screen's finest mystery movies provide the requisite complicated crimes, red herrings, neatly worked out solutions—but, in so doing, thoughtlessly leave out one key ingredient, the detective himself, placing his functions in the hands of a comic hero, a plucky heroine, or the traditional scoop-hunting newspaper reporter.

In an effort to break away from cliché, many "B" westerns have adopted the detective story formula and, with the exception of the underplayed rangeland surroundings, have been quite orthodox mysteries. Tim McCoy in his Columbia series of the early thirties was very fond of this ploy; so was William Boyd in the last of his Hopalong Cassidy westerns, where films like *The Dead Don't Dream* and *Unexpected Guests* literally dispensed with outdoor chases to become equivalents of *The Cat and the Canary*. Chaplin excepted, every major comic (or comedy team) has somewhere in his career ventured into a spoof of the detective genre, and even the animated cartoons have satirized them. Several of the leading movie detectives—Sherlock Holmes, Philo Vance, Bulldog Drummond among them—have been mercilessly but often quite amusingly lampooned.

There is a vast filmic area in which the movie detective operates quite separately from heroics, action, or detection: the plodding, methodical drudgery as exemplified by Barton MacLane and Ward Bond in *The Maltese Falcon*; the business-like, typecast professionals like Thomas Jackson, whose very entrance and appearance tells experienced audiences that he is a detective, and whose function seems to be primarily to place legal stumbling blocks in the way of the brighter but less orthodox hero; the colorless officials of the Fritz Lang thrillers, who bring the miscreants to justice but without any personal sense of triumph; and, of course, the "dumb" detectives (usually,

inexplicably, with a rating of sergeant or higher) whose main function is to jump to the wrong conclusions and arrest all the wrong suspects, thereby making our hero the amateur sleuth seem all the brighter.

Since crime, in one form or another, is a more constant motivating factor in movies than any other, and since it has to be opposed and defeated by an amateur or professional detective, it is not surprising that the detective film has thus spilled over into virtually every *other* genre of film: the western, the horror film, the comedy, the musical, the love story, and all the various subcategories. What *is* surprising, however, is that so few really classic detective movies have resulted. Perhaps the two arts are too far apart. The detective story is essentially a contemplative and nonvisual art. The good ones are so structured that the reader can go back and restudy the case in light of later knowledge. The essential information is conveyed not by action, but by extended dialogue conversations, and by meticulous description—sometimes, as in the case of Raymond Chandler, description of such minute detail that it is self-defeating and the reader is tempted to skip it and get back to the plot! The film, of course, does not allow for the luxury of either extended detail or protracted examination; at best, it occasionally allows, via flashbacks or other devices, for the rescrutiny of important sequences. And the viewer has no option: he is reshown only what the writer or director chooses.

In one other important regard, the book has an edge over the movie. The reader cannot question what the author writes, but he is free to exercise his imagination. Given a facial description of a character, it is safe to say that no two readers will conjure up an identical image. But with film there is no such leeway. Stories revolving around deception and disguises invariably give themselves away (Tod Browning's *Miracles for Sale* being a good case in point) because few disguises—and fewer actors—are camera-proof.

Moreover, through the years, audiences have become used to the "rules" and typecasting methods of the movie mystery. By now, they know that the totally disinterested, motiveless, charming, and exceptionally cooperative secretary or best friend will automatically be revealed as the murderer in the last-reel denouement. The presence in the cast of a well-known actor, seemingly given no more to do than a bit player, is a further dead giveaway. Curiously, the movies have seldom exploited the public's familiarity with the clichés of the detective formula. Anticipating the audience reaction to a given set of circumstances—leading them astray—giving them credit for tumbling to the deception and carrying it a step further—this is the kind of gambit thinking that *could* have made the movie mystery an entertainment form quite separate from the detective *story*. But few directors (or writers) have ever chosen to play with their audiences like that. Alfred Hitchcock is a notable exception, and that is not the least of the reasons why his movie mysteries are so engrossing. Knowing that audiences have the tendency to accept blindly the story premises given them from the screen, he led us beautifully up the garden path in *Stage Fright*. At one point early in the story, Richard Todd relates a series of events in flashback—and acceptance of those flashbacks as the truth neatly pointed the audience in the wrong direction. Many were later outraged to find that Hitchcock—and Todd—had lied in those flashbacks, which were pure fabrications. It was against all the "rules"—but why not?

Hitchcock excepted, however, the movies on the whole have not done well by the detective story *if* one accepts the literary form as the original and the model. Most movie mysteries have supplanted the novel's shared hard work of detection by action, excitement, and the suavity or quaintness of the detective hero. They have assumed that audiences like the formula more than the content. Despite the admitted entertainment value of literally thousands of movie mysteries, barely a handful have really matched the skill, cunning, and meticulous construction of their source novels. The British *Green for Danger* was one that did; so did an early Philo Vance talkie, *The Kennel Murder Case,* a model of its kind, and the best of the Philip Marlowe mysteries, *Murder My Sweet.* The rest have entertained us, excited us—but rarely fooled us.

However, while enthusiasms naturally overlap, the detective *novel* and the detective *movie* appeal to entirely separate bands of fanatical devotees. Students of the literary form possess all of the perceptive powers and photographic memories of their fictional heroes. Perusal of such notable journals as *The Armchair Detective* (devoted to reviews, analyses, exchanges of opinion, checklists of authors and/or detectives) is an almost frightening experience. Its readers have absorbed and remembered every nuance of a detective's mannerisms, every clue in specific cases, every interrelationship and crossed path. To a non-detective-fiction addict, such erudite devotion is not only staggering in its efficiency, but also a little hard to understand. Conversely, to *them,* it probably seems equally inconceivable that students of the film can look at a crowd scene and identify just about all the extras or, more insane still, remember the individual plot-lines of five hundred "B" westerns with interchangeable titles!

Given the enormous scope and range of the detective movie (and, like the western, it is as old as the movies themselves) the highly critical and exacting requirements of the detective novel *aficionados,* and the entirely different standards applied by those who care little for fidelity to a literary school as long as Basil Rathbone is Sher-

lock Holmes and William Powell is Philo Vance, this book can obviously hope to satisfy no one faction thoroughly. Devotion to detective fiction is a life's work in itself, as is devotion to the movies. Perhaps one day independently wealthy representatives of both fraternities—men who do not have to worry about such mundane problems as earning a living—can get together and jointly produce an encyclopedic reference work on the detective film. In the meantime this volume is intended as an affectionate and, I hope, reliable, but certainly not comprehensive, introduction to the field, done with an admitted bias in favor of the film and a merely casual familiarity with the untold volume of novels and short stories from which they derive.

Nigel Bruce as Dr. Watson and Basil Rathbone as Sherlock Holmes.

2 THE MASTER

Basil Rathbone and Nigel Bruce as Holmes and Watson on Grimpen Mire in THE HOUND OF THE BASKERVILLES (1939).

Perhaps it is only appropriate that this survey should begin with Sherlock Holmes, not only because Sir Arthur Conan Doyle's creation is virtually the prototype of the investigator involved in the art of detection for its own sake, but also because Holmes was the *first* detective to be transferred to the screen (as early as 1903). Furthermore, the usage of Holmes on the screen has tended to reflect the movies' fluctuating interest in detective films generally. In the silent period, where the screen detective labored under the difficulty of not being able to conduct prolonged interrogations or oral deductions, he usually found himself shunted into the two-reeler or used in vehicles where the stress was on mystery or physical action rather than on literary-derived sleuthings. Certainly, Holmes fell into this pattern and, since dialogue and the enjoyable mixture of brilliance and the arrogant awareness of that brilliance are key factors in appreciating Holmes at work, it is not surprising that none of his forays into the silent film were markedly successful. In the sound period, Holmes twice reappeared as a kind of bird of good omen—once in 1929, and again in 1939—hovering in the celluloid heavens in the forefront of prolific cycles of detective films, reestablishing the genre as a popular entertainment, and then withdrawing gracefully and allowing his disciples—from Charlie Chan and Philo Vance to Sam Spade and Nick Charles—to take over and carry on.

Sir Arthur Conan Doyle created Holmes in 1887, giving him a Baker Street address which in itself was a kind of tipoff to the kind of man that he wanted Holmes to be. While Baker Street was doubtless more fashionable in the eighteen-hundreds than it is today, at the same time it never represented the *height* of fashion. It was and is a kind of outskirt, boasting a railway station leading to the suburbs and close proximity to the London Zoo and Madame Tussaud's Wax Museum. It is close enough to the theatrical and business centers of London—and to the museums, universities, and hospitals—to be quite convenient, and yet just sufficiently far removed for an inhabitant, if he so wished, to consider himself "in" London without being "of" London. In other words, the perfect location from which a dilettante like Holmes, withdrawn from the bustle of central London, could devote himself to the art of deductive reasoning. Ostensibly, Doyle built the character of Holmes around that of one of his former teachers, and it is the character—rather than the plots—that has made Holmes both a legend and a "problem" to cast. Holmesian students—and such international groups as the Baker Street Irregulars—"know" Holmes as a very real person with specifically designated physical characteristics and mental attitudes which to date have never been totally fulfilled by any one actor, though certainly Arthur Wontner and Basil Rathbone have come close.

None of the earliest attempts to transfer Holmes to the screen appear to have survived, but it is interesting that America and Scandinavia realized his commercial possibilities before Britain did. The first known Holmes film was *Sherlock Holmes Baffled,* made by the American Biograph Company, and since it was copyrighted in February of 1903, the chances are that it was made at the end of 1902. While story films did exist before 1903's *The Great Train Robbery,* Biograph, in its pre–D. W. Griffith days, showed little evidence of interest in dramatic structure. It is likely that this early Holmes effort was little more than a series of tableaux of a melodramatic nature without any real continuity; or, like many other Biograph half-reelers of that period, it may have been little more than an excuse to show exterior views of the city—although, in view of the enormous popularity of the then fifteen-year-old Holmes, a New York or New Jersey location might have been just too incongruous for even such an infant industry. Since Biograph did not begin

The first Sherlock Holmes film from Denmark's Nordisk Films Company: SHERLOCK HOLMES IN DEATHLY DANGER (1908), starring Holger-Madsen (left) as Holmes.

The third Danish Holmes film: THE SECRET DOCUMENT (1908).

Otto Lagoni as Holmes in the 1910 Danish SHERLOCK HOLMES CAPTURED.

5

SHERLOCK HOLMES (1922): Gustav von Seyffertitz as Moriarty vs John Barrymore as Holmes.

Eille Norwood, the British Holmes of the early twenties.

Arthur Wontner, best of the British Holmes interpreters.

to use recognizable actors until much later, it is probable that Holmes was played by a studio employee or relative who happened to look like the traditional image of the detective. In late 1905, Vitagraph made a second Holmes film which, since it carried two titles (*The Adventures of Sherlock Holmes* and *Held for a Ransom*), clearly had a specific story line and must have been a considerable advance on the previous film, even though it was still too early a film to warrant our entertaining any thoughts about it as a valuable contribution to Holmesian lore of the screen.

Three years later, another Holmes film—by the Crescent Company, one of a number of the rapidly proliferating but generally short-lived independent companies—made its bow. Its title was *Sherlock Holmes and the Great Murder Mystery,* and the one traceable review was good, although it should be stressed that critical standards of such an early date cannot be regarded as too reliable. Its plot, involving murder by a gorilla, seems to incline more toward Edgar Allan Poe than toward Doyle!

Also, in 1908, the Nordisk Company of Denmark embarked on a whole series of Sherlock Holmes films directed by F. Holger-Madsen, who also played the role of Holmes. Unfortunately, a recent sojourn at both the

Swedish and Danish Film Archives failed to turn up any surviving copies of the dozen or so films (all approximately a reel and a half in length) made in this series and, presumably, they have been lost for some time since they are not even represented in the compilation films that the Scandinavian film industries have put together to record their early film history. This is a particularly sad loss, since the Scandinavian cinema of pre–World War I years was extremely advanced, turning out films comparable to (and, in the case of early feature-length productions, superior to) American films of the same period. Records indicate that the films had well-staged physical action, a good deal of exterior shooting, and certainly no little showmanship. Apart from the utilization of Professor Moriarty as Holmes' enemy in some of the films, others brought him face to face with Raffles, the débonair cracksman created by E. W. Hornung in 1899. Presumably, Raffles was depicted more in a criminal than in an heroic light. Film makers in those days were none too scrupulous about recognizing the still vague copyright laws or about using a character's name but changing his image entirely. (Thus, in America, O. Henry's Cisco Kid made his first bow in an early western as a thoroughly despicable villain, and not as the good-badman cavalier.) The Danish Holmes films were made over a three-year period. Alwin Neuss was cast as Dr. Watson.

Thereafter, Holmes began to appear with rather more regularity. In 1910 Germany made two Holmes films—with Arsene Lupin replacing Moriarty as Sherlock's sparring partner. Allegedly, Conan Doyle was personally involved in a 1912 series of Anglo-French two-reelers. The French also made a series of one-reelers in the same period which, from their titles (*The Speckled Band, The Copper Beeches, Silver Blaze*), did seem to be relying to a degree on the Doyle originals. One very battered print of *The Copper Beeches* surfaced quite recently, too shrunken to risk projection, and viewable only via the ultra-small image on a hand-cranked 35-mm. viewer. Apart from having the distinction of being the earliest known extant Holmes film, it was a tedious and dull production, though it was difficult to assess its photographic and other production qualities under such circumstances. The French also made *A Study in Scarlet* and *The Hound of the Baskervilles* in 1914–15 before abandoning the character and turning instead to their own native mystery specialists, *Fantomas* and *Judex.*

Oddly enough, it was a British equivalent of Fantomas and Judex—Ultus—who dominated the mystery field in Britain at the same time. The several Ultus films directed by George Pearson took the limelight away from Britain's first two six-reel Holmes features: *A Study in Scarlet* (1914, with Fred Paul) and *Valley of Fear* (1916). Since they were both produced by G. B. Samuelson,

a noted British pioneer whose work was well above the admittedly not very high standards of the day (production expansion was very much curtailed by the war), one must assume that they were respectable little films, yet their sucess must have been modest since there were no follow-ups until 1922's *The Hound of the Baskervilles.*

Frankly, it was hardly an auspicious return for the master detective. This time Holmes was played by Eille Norwood, and his effectiveness was minimized by the fact that his Dr. Watson was of the same build and general appearance. Indeed, in the rather gray and washed-out print that has survived, it is often difficult to tell them apart! The plot stuck fairly closely to Doyle's original and would seem to have been foolproof—yet it is amazing how often this much-filmed Holmes adventure has come acropper because of uninspired direction. The director in this case was Maurice Elvey, a reliable workhorse who turned out films with astonishing regularity between 1913 and 1957, tackling everything from historical pageantry and slapstick comedy to Dickens, war films, and science fiction. With a good plot, capable actors, and impressive sets, he could make thoroughly professional films—as, for example, the 1935 *Transatlantic Tunnel*—but he wasn't an imaginative enough director to evoke mood or to create atmosphere or menace from a script that didn't tell him how. *The Hound of the Baskervilles,* of all films, needs *mood* far more than it needs logic or action, and mood is the one thing that this version consistently lacks.

Baskerville Hall, never seen in relation to its supposedly bleak surroundings, looks exactly like what it probably was—a London suburb townhouse belonging to someone of above-average but by no means spectacular wealth. The few forays on to Grimpen Mire suggest cheerful parkland, or possibly Hampstead Heath, but one never has the sense of desolation, of sweeping moorlands and treacherous quicksands. Not even miniatures or fog effects are pressed into service to heighten the feeling of natural menace and, undoubtedly aware of the shortcomings of his exteriors, Elvey keeps most of his action indoors. The one solitary touch of showmanship: the hound was tinted or hand-painted with a luminous glow, so that its infrequent appearances did carry a token shock value.

Quite coincidentally, *The Hound of the Baskervilles* had also been made in Germany (in 1917) by a director, Richard Oswald, who was an exact equivalent of Maurice Elvey. His work was literal, stodgy, unimaginative—and tremendously popular in his own country. It is perhaps unfair to criticize a film that is not available for reappraisal, but many of Oswald's German films (silent and sound) *are* still extant and, apart from occasional pleasing camera compositions, none live up to their potential or generate much excitement. Oswald, who had a penchant

Raymond Massey: THE SPECKLED BAND (1931).

for remaking his big commercial hits, redid *The Hound of the Baskervilles* in 1929, still as a silent, with Carlyle Blackwell singularly miscast as Holmes.

Although the 1922 British *Hound* had not been a marked success, Eille Norwood had been. With Maurice Elvey continuing as producer-director (and scenarist) and Hubert Willis cast as Dr. Watson throughout, Norwood played in close to fifty Holmes films. Some were two-reelers, others longer features, and they must have literally saturated the market since all were made over a three-year period. If the quality of *The Hound of the Baskervilles* is typical, then it is not surprising that the British promptly retired Holmes until the coming of sound!

Back in America, the first feature-length Holmes film was made in 1916. Titled just *Sherlock Holmes,* it was based on the play written as a vehicle for himself by William Gillette. He had been playing the role on stage for some seventeen years and was the logical choice to star in the film version as well. (At this time, many stage personalities were being brought to Hollywood to re-create their famous theatrical roles and, incidentally, to bring a little prestige and respectability to what was still considered a bastard art. Many were too old to photograph well or convincingly; others could not adapt to movie technique. Only Douglas Fairbanks and John Barrymore

were totally successful.) Although Essanay productions had a certain crudity, they were usually well photographed and generous with their closeups. Their films, though well below the standards set by Vitagraph and Fine Arts, did provide useful showcases for actors. *Sherlock Holmes,* directed by Arthur Berthelet, was probably a valuable, if frustratingly mute, record of a famous actor in his finest role. It is tragic that this theatrically important record is apparently lost, while destiny has seen fit to preserve *The Count of Monte Cristo* as a record of James O'Neill's most famous stage role, but a film so primitive that one never gets a single closeup of the actor, and all we have to judge him by is a series of long-shot charades!

The same Gillette play formed the basis for the first really elaborate Holmes film: 1922's *Sherlock Holmes,* produced by Sam Goldwyn and starring John Barrymore. Although Goldwyn was already very much concerned with prestige and production gloss, he was also a show-man. His films of that period—and they included some of the very best Lon Chaney vehicles—were full of rich melodrama, giving the paying audiences what they wanted, but with added bonuses of directorial flair and production values that they possibly didn't expect. Though *Sherlock Holmes* was criticized for its hokum, for being more of a Barrymore than a Holmes vehicle, it was immensely popular. (Barrymore's film career had started slowly in light comedy in 1915, established itself more firmly with *Dr. Jekyll and Mr. Hyde* in 1920, but was now solidly entrenched with the presold role of Holmes and a romantic flavoring to boot.) Exquisitely lit photography made the most of the classic Barrymore profile *and* of his love of the bizarre, as in the scenes where he masquerades—convincingly—as Moriarty, and in one se-quence meets him face to face. Moriarty was played by the satanic-featured Gustav von Seyffertitz, perhaps too wholly evil and physically grotesque to be perfectly cast as Doyle's criminal genius. But he made an ideal facial foil and counterpart to Barrymore, who used him in a similar way (likewise involving a masquerade) in the later *Don Juan.* One of the most enjoyable aspects of the film was its extensive location shooting in London: not just in the obvious "scenic" spots such as the Embank-ment by the Thames, but also in the quiet back streets of Kensington, or amid the bustle of a Piccadilly Circus that still had a goodly percentage of horse-drawn vehicles among the proud new automobiles and double-decker buses.

Tragically, this enchanting film is also (at least partially) a lost work, and attempts to reconstruct it have taken on all of the characteristics of a Holmesian puzzle. Would that the Master himself were on hand to assist in the work! Rochester's George Eastman House, America's foremost film archive, some years ago was able to salvage several cans of negative of the film, each can consisting of short unconnected rolls. They were printed up, spliced together for viewing purposes, and found to be most intriguing but virtually incomprehensible. There was a little of everything—but not very much of anything. Some scenes ran but a few seconds; others would reappear with variations at regular intervals. One method of assuring longer film preservation is the removal of all the subtitles (which tend to decompose first) and, except for a single reference frame for each title, which sped by far too quickly to be read, there were no titles in the film.

Further adding to the puzzle, both Roland Young and Reginald Denny appeared with mustaches in some scenes, without them in others! (Later, it became apparent that the hairless scenes belonged in a prologue or flashback to their younger days, while the mustaches represented a passage of time.) William Powell sneaked menacingly in and out of the proceedings, stealing all of the non-Barrymore scenes with ease even when one wasn't quite sure what he was doing. Anders Randolf, Carol Dempster, David Torrence, and Louis Wolheim made but token appearances, and Roland Young's Watson seemed to make few real contributions. All told, there were about 50 minutes of surviving footage, seemingly representing most of the sequences, but only about half of the total. The first move was to put it all in some semblance of order, so that it could be screened without becoming a surrealist nightmare. The second move was to screen it in London for the film's director, veteran Albert Parker (then an agent and married to actress Margaret Johnston), in the hopes that he could shed light on missing scenes and help to restore the continuity.

Also present at that screening in late 1970 were Clive Brook and British historian and film maker Kevin Brown-

Clive Brook: THE RETURN OF SHERLOCK HOLMES (1929).

Robert Rendell battles Reginald Bach in THE HOUND OF THE BASKERVILLES (1931).

THE RETURN OF SHERLOCK HOLMES: H. Reeves Smith as Dr. Watson, with Clive Brook.

SHERLOCK HOLMES (1932), with Clive Brook as Holmes, Reginald Owen (soon to play Holmes himself) as Dr. Watson.

releasing the film in Britain under the title *Moriarty!*

Barrymore's Holmes had been a youthful one, and the next major Holmes was to maintain the tradition. Clive Brook was introduced to the role in 1929's *The Return of Sherlock Holmes* and thus became the first Holmes to talk on the screen. The film was limited in its action, most of it taking place aboard an ocean liner, but the concentration on talk was what audiences wanted then— or, at least, what the executive offices *thought* they wanted. Brook's excellent diction made him vocally a fine choice, though his rather humorless acting style in that period tended to make Holmes unnecessarily priggish. The film was directed by Basil Dean, a commercially successful but never very enterprising British director, who was then not only a newcomer to films generally but a total novice in sound films. The film, with a contemporary setting, adapted from two Doyle stories ("The Dying Detective" and "His Last Bow"), offered Harry T. Morey as an effective Moriarty (using such colorful gimmicks as a cigarette case with a poisoned needle that was brought

low. Brook, who later played Holmes three times himself, had mellowed gracefully and serenely into the kind of person that one would hope and expect that Brook—and Holmes—would become at age eighty (though Brook's handsome face and spry wit belied those years). Not a great deal was learned about the film at that initial screening, but unexpectedly—and most amusingly—Brook and Parker slid unwittingly and quite naturally into the Holmes and Watson roles (Brook sardonically pointing out the superiority of his version, Parker, forgetful and a little confused, assuming the Nigel Bruce interpretation of Dr. Watson).

It was a delightful evening and one wishes it could have been recorded on film but, apart from a few clues, it brought us no nearer to solving the puzzle of this jigsaw of a film. In the subsequent years, however, Kevin Brownlow—poring over the fragments of film, matching up minute scene numbers printed on to the celluloid, shooting and inserting stills to bridge gaps, restoring titles— has completed the major part of the reassembly process. If *Sherlock Holmes* is gone in its totality, at least a coherent and representative cross-section of it will shortly be available for archival study. One hopes that at its initial rescreening Brownlow will have the wit to deprecate all much-deserved congratulations with an underplayed "Elementary!"

Quite incidentally, although there may have been legal reasons for it, it seems more likely that the mediocrity of so many earlier Holmes films was the deciding factor in

Ernest Torrence, the superb Professor Moriarty of the 1932 SHERLOCK HOLMES.

The second Rathbone-Bruce film: THE ADVENTURES OF SHERLOCK HOLMES (1939).

An albatross provides a clue in THE ADVENTURES OF SHERLOCK HOLMES: Basil Rathbone, Ida Lupino.

ADVENTURES OF SHERLOCK HOLMES: Cameraman Leon Shamroy (extreme right) sets up a shot with Rathbone, Bruce and Ida Lupino.

ADVENTURES OF SHERLOCK HOLMES: A closeup of the props used for Holmes' desk.

into play when the opening spring was pressed) and H. Reeves-Smith as Dr. Watson. It's odd that a property of such comparative importance, with an established star such as Clive Brook, should have been entrusted to a minor British director but, presumably, the thinking was that a man with British stage experience would be the best choice for such a British-oriented dialogue film. Although it was a Paramount release officially shot in Paramount's large Long Island studios, Brook recalls the film as having been shot very quickly and cheaply with few facilities. Some of the shipboard footage was shot on a trip from England to New York, while Brook describes the studio work as done at a small, cramped studio in midtown Manhattan.

That same year Clive Brook made a second appearance as Holmes in the studio's contribution to the all-star musical revue cycle, *Paramount on Parade.* The Holmes skit introduced three of Paramount's leading stars and characters—Brook as Holmes, William Powell as Philo Vance, Warner Oland as Fu Manchu—and, after some informal off-screen banter, let them loose in a wild-and-woolly satire of their own specialties, with all three killed off one by one by a mysterious assailant. (This is a minor historic footnote, since it represents the only time that Holmes died on screen!) It was all rather arch and not as funny as its writers and players thought it was, but it did have pace and a feeling of spontaneity and the atmospheric set

was quite impressive. Coming very early in the film, it remained a highlight in a musical revue that was rather better and more spirited than the competitive entries from Warner's, Fox, and MGM.

Brook's final appearance as Holmes took place in 1932's *Sherlock Holmes* for Fox, one of the most enjoyable and stylish of all Holmes films, though possibly a big disappointment for true Doyle devotees. Officially, it was based on the Gillette play once again but, apart from its similar emphasis on a deliberate confrontation between Holmes and Moriarty, there was little relationship. Oddly enough, even the official studio synopsis bears little similarity to the finished film, written by Bertram Millhauser (who would reappear later as one of the perennial writers on Universal's Holmes series), updated to a contemporary thirties setting and drawing its basic inspiration from Doyle's "The Red Headed League." A hangover from the Gillette play was Holmes' romantic involvement with Alice Faulkner (played by Miriam Jordan) and his retirement to wedded bliss at the film's end. The contemporary setting was given added stress by having Moriarty import saloon bombings and other gangster methods from the States. Holmes was given virtually no opportunity for verbal reasoning and deductions, and the famous "Elementary, my dear Watson!" was used more as a joke following moments of quite ordinary observations. Watson himself, played by Reginald Owen, made but fleeting appearances; in fact, in the cast list Owen was billed *below* Herbert Mundin, who had a small and not very important character-comedy role.

But if the film was disappointing Doyle, it was still a first-class melodrama. William K. Howard, who directed, was a master of slick polished thrillers, his highlight sequences always well composed and angled, edited with pace and precision, and prone to Germanic lighting and set design. The first reel of the film is a model of how to combine theatrical bravura with real cinematic sense. In a series of strikingly lit silhouette and gauze shots, Moriarty (beautifully played by Ernest Torrence, who delivered every line with relish and an effective mock humility) is brought into court, sentenced to death, and in his address to the jury promises that the rope that can hang him has not yet been made—and that Holmes, the judge, and all others responsible for his sentence will precede him in death.

After a stately return to his cell—again in silhouette, and backed by the somber chimes of Big Ben—we cut away to Holmes' laboratory. Mainly as an excuse to utilize some of the impressive Frankensteinian lab machinery that Fox had concocted for a number of science-fiction films of the period. Holmes is shown dabbling with some elaborate electrical gadgetry and demonstrating his new ray with which police can knock out the automobile motors of escaping crooks. It is his parting gift to Scotland Yard, and is accompanied by a neat little speech about the deadly weapon for crime that the automobile has become. Alice Faulkner, Little Billy (rather obnoxiously affected and unconvincingly British, as played by Howard Leeds), and Watson are introduced for some pleasantries, and then we are back to the prison. Chaos; turmoil; guards running; whistles; hooters. George Barnes' smoothly flowing camera follows the prison guards as they race through the grim corridors and Howard cuts rapidly from the muscular figures of prisoners, straining close to the bars to see what is going on, to a detail shot of a whistle hanging from the still fingers of a murdered guard. Finally, the camera tracks along the walls of a cell

SHERLOCK HOLMES FACES DEATH (1943): Halliwell Hobbes, Rathbone, Bruce.

THE SCARLET CLAW (1944): Rathbone, Gerald Hamer.

Lionel Atwill as Moriarty with Rathbone in SHERLOCK HOLMES AND THE SECRET WEAPON (1942).

block, coming to rest on an open door and a message scrawled on the wall: "Tell Holmes I'm OUT—Moriarty!"

It would be difficult for any thriller to match the visual flair and excitement of these opening scenes and *Sherlock Holmes* doesn't quite make it. But it's a surprisingly short film and thus is able to keep its pace fairly taut, while its plot (involving Moriarty's revenge and his plan to force Holmes into a murder and thence to the gallows) is a good one. The bank robbery climax returns to the powerful visual style of the opening scenes, and the only really weak moment in the film is Holmes' totally unconvincing masquerade as a prissy maiden aunt. It's an amusing sequence, but that the disguise should fool the cunning Moriarty is a little hard to accept.

Despite his physical "rightness" for the role and an undeniable screen "presence," Clive Brook fell somewhat short of being the ideal movie Holmes. His diction was fine, the detached imperturbability just right, and yet there was an air of condescension to his interpretation, as though the role wasn't quite worth taking seriously. Some directors (especially Josef von Sternberg with *Shanghai Express*) were able to take this acting trait and turn it to the advantage of the role, while Brook himself dispensed with it for roles that he really believed in (as, for example, with Noel Coward's *Cavalcade*). Nevertheless, his 1932 *Sherlock Holmes* stands as one of the most interesting of a sudden plethora of Holmes films in 1930–33, most of them from Britain. Hollywood's only immediate follow-up was the independently made *A Study in Scarlet* (1933), with Reginald Owen graduating from the Watson role to the least-effective-ever Holmes interpretation. The story took nothing from the book and, apart from an exceptionally strong cast for a small company like World-Wide (Anna May Wong, Alan Dinehart, and Warburton Gamble as Watson), the talkative and tedious film had little to recommend it.

Back in Britain in 1930, the Twickenham Studios introduced the best movie Holmes to that date—and, in fact, still one of the best—in Arthur Wontner. Although his movie career was a long one and he was a fine and sensitive actor (witness the poignancy he brought to his brief scene as the elderly admirer of the antique automobile in *Genevieve*) who had been in films since 1915 —and on the stage before that—he was best known for his interpretation of Holmes in five films of the early thirties. Preceded by their reputation, based largely on the excellence of Wontner's performances, these films tend to disappoint audiences seeing them for the first time today. They are all "modern" versions of the Doyle stories, although since they stick largely to selling the stories by dialogue, with a maximum of interiors, the contemporary settings are not stressed and as the years go by they take on more and more the patina of a "period" background. Twickenham was an ambitious independent company, but it was still an independent, and the lack of really elaborate production values (especially in the early thirties, when there was a big gap between the polish of British films and those of Hollywood) was readily apparent. Moreover, all of the Wontner films were directed by competent, journeyman directors, none of whom were able to do much in the way of creating mood and atmosphere from rather talkative scripts. The films *did* lack pace.

Nevertheless, in their concentration of the characterizations of Holmes and Watson, and in the general faithfulness of their story adaptations, they had an integrity that most of the other Holmes films lacked. Wontner was not only physically right as Holmes, but he also managed to achieve the right mixture of dedication and aloofness without sacrificing warmth and wry humor. Likewise, Ian Fleming (a familiar British character actor, not to be confused with the author of the James Bond stories) made a fine Watson—an intelligent, good-looking man whose intellect was admittedly not called upon too often, but who was at least no mere foil designed to emphasize Holmes' brilliance, the role that so many Watsons (and especially Nigel Bruce) seemed destined to play.

The first of the Wontner films was 1930's *The Sleeping Cardinal*, released in the United States under the title *Sherlock Holmes' Fatal Hour*, and based on two Doyle stories, "The Empty House" and "The Final Problem." It was the longest of the Wontner films, the slowest paced, and by current standards the most dated, yet it was in many ways the best. Its leisurely pacing allowed for ample examples of Holmes' deductive reasoning, all arising naturally out of the plot and the clues and not dragged in merely for their own sake. Although the bulk of the plot line was developed on an intimate level, with Holmes trying to ferret out the identity of the elusive Moriarty from a small group of society friends, it was played against the larger background of Moriarty's world-wide crime organization, with an opening bank robbery sequence containing operational details suspiciously kin to those employed in Fritz Lang's *The Testament of Dr. Mabuse* two years later. The only disappointing aspect of the film was that since Moriarty was acting in the open, as one of a group of above-suspicion citizens, he could not be portrayed by a bravura villian. Norman McKinnell, playing the role, thus had only two real opportunities to display his perfidy during the film: once when, heavily disguised, he confronts Holmes (and inadvertently reveals his identity when Holmes notices a peculiarity of his upper left molar!) and in the final showdown when his plans to murder Holmes are thwarted.

Despite the film's slow pace, it did have some enjoyable moments and highlight sequences reminiscent (in terms of content and photographic style) of the silent German cinema, still a fashionable model for British directors of that period. Moreover, its plot was well constructed; audiences were neither *ahead* of the game nor did they have their intelligence underestimated by sudden and illogical marshaling of facts and deductions that the film had not substantiated.

Wontner's second Holmes film (with Ian Hunter temporarily taking over as Watson) was *The Sign of the Four* in 1932. Again, it was a faithful adaptation. Curiously, many U.S. reviews criticized the film for substandard photography. Since the film had the most professional technical crew of any of the Wontner films—Hollywood's Rowland V. Lee producing; a good British veteran, Graham Cutts, directing; and *two* cameramen, including Hollywood's Robert deGrasse—this seems hard to accept. Possibly, since the American release was handled by an independent, second-rate laboratory work or an inadequate dupe negative may have been to blame.

Ian Fleming returned as Watson in *The Missing Rembrandt,* a good mystery with a good cast (Miles Mander, Francis L. Sullivan) and in 1935 Wontner and Fleming teamed again for *The Triumph of Sherlock Holmes.* Based on "The Valley of Fear," is set a good deal of its action—energetically, if not too convincingly—in America's West. Its main attribute was one of Britain's best villains: Lyn Harding as Moriarty. Harding, a big, bluff, hearty man, somewhat resembling a bearded Gibson Gowland, was a much underrated actor who, despite his bulk, could deliver dialogue with intelligence and subtlety yet play for full-blooded melodrama when the occasion demanded. There has been a higher percentage of successful Moriartys than there has been of successful Holmses—and Harding was one of the best. The last Wontner-Fleming film was *Silver Blaze,* the mildest and the weakest of their series, though still distinguished by their teamwork and by the skill of Lyn Harding.

However, the plot to keep a horse out of the big race seemed unworthy of the talents of Moriarty, whose time would have been better spent in crime of a much broader scope, and equally unworthy of the attention of England's finest detective. Frankie Darro and Kane Richmond could have handled the case just as well. Too, the film showed its less imposing budget (Twickenham was then in its last days as a producer-distributor, although the studio itself is still in use) and rarely got away from cramped interior sets. Even the horse spent most of its time in studio "exteriors." While others of the Wontner films were released in America soon after their British showings, *Silver Blaze* was considered unworthy of importing. It did show up

finally in the early forties, under the title of *Murder at the Baskervilles.* Fortunately, much of the action had taken place at Baskerville Hall, and the new title none too subtly suggested a relationship to *The Hound of the Baskervilles,* which had just successfully launched Basil Rathbone's association with the Holmes saga.

Two other negligible Holmes films had come out of Britain in the early thirties, worthy of note only because of the actors playing the lead. *The Speckled Band* (1931) had Raymond Massey enacting Holmes as though he knew that he would one day also play Lincoln. Athole Stewart was an adequate Watson. The year 1932 saw yet another remake of *The Hound of the Baskervilles,* with Robert Rendell as Holmes, Fred Lloyd as Watson, and Heather Angel as the heroine. Edgar Wallace worked on the scenario. Like other versions of the tale, it had a quite elaborate reconstruction of the Baskerville legend, done this time as a prologue. Oddly enough, only the picture negative of this film seems to have survived, and in recent years it has been impossible to see the film with sound. Thus one cannot be on reliably firm ground in commenting on Robert Rendell's performance but, excellent actor though he was, he would seem to be quite inappropriate as the master detective. Short and alert, he suggests intellect certainly, but not a man of contemplative deduction. One would expect calm reasoning from such a man—but also quick decisions and swift action. Rendell was well cast in wartime films as the naval official in situations where he has the responsibility of making immediate decisions that also have to be the right ones. But as Holmes, while his performance was thoughtful and free of frivolity, he seemed badly miscast.

Hollywood gave Sherlock Holmes a spectacular comeback in 1939 with *The Hound of the Baskervilles.* This was a year in which many formerly popular genres were dusted off and given elaborate revivals, but in new formats which sought to combine the old values in slicker and glossier packages. Thus the gangster cycle was brought back, bigger and noisier than ever via *The Roaring Twenties; Stagecoach* revitalized a western format that had grown somewhat stale, while *Son of Frankenstein,* the longest and most expensive horror film to date, launched a new cycle of chillers. The detective film, which had fallen into a rut of formularized "B" pictures, could hardly have had a more stylish and impressive showcase than *The Hound of the Baskervilles,* with which Twentieth Century-Fox initiated the inspired casting of Basil Rathbone as Holmes and the equally shrewd (though less effectively written) utilization of Nigel Bruce as Watson. The best of the many versions of *The Hound of the Baskervilles,* it remains an impressive, handsomely mounted and certainly "respectful" treatment of Doyle, even if a little too measured in its pacing and never quite makes the most of its excitement potential.

Certainly, one of its shortcomings was the lack of an inspired director, for Sidney Lanfield (a specialist in light modern comedy) was no more suited to the subject than Britain's Maurice Elvey or Germany's Richard Oswald had been. With that cast and such a literate script, an imaginative director could have made of this the definitive Holmes essay. James Whale, for example, would have been a superb choice, or even such a lesser stylist as John Brahm. In fact, one of Brahm's minor horror films for Twentieth Century-Fox—*The Undying Monsters,* with its similar period, location, and even an overlapping plot line—provides a concrete example of just what cinematic wonders Brahm could work with such material, while his more elaborate *The Lodger,* a Jack the Ripper story, confirmed that increasing Brahm's budget increased the thrills proportionately.

The Hound of the Baskervilles also suffered from a surprising lack of background music. Since the thriller depends for its effect on the manipulation of audience fears, and since the use of music (and, at the same time, the dramatic use of silence) is a key factor in involving that audience, the lack of music (even in the alleged interests of realism) can reduce the thriller's impact considerably.

The London scenes, calling as they do on Fox's then remarkable array of standing sets, are totally convincing, but the bulk of the film, set at Baskerville Hall and its environs, does have a rather studio-bound quality. Studio "exteriors" had become a fine art in the thirties, particularly in the well-lit black-and-white cinematography of the day. (To see how much has been lost of this art, especially with the widespread usage of color film, one has only to compare the exteriors in this film with those in the later Hammer films *The Mummy* and *Curse of the Mummy's Tomb,* where color only emphasizes all the blank space and lack of real design.) When well done, studio exteriors can enhance rather than minimize the power of a scene, and certainly James Whale's studio exteriors in his horror films had a stylistic power that shooting in natural locations couldn't have duplicated.

But if you're going to build Dartmoor and Grimpen Mire in a studio, no matter how artfully you design it, you're not going to succeed unless you create an atmosphere of awesome desolation. *Son of Frankenstein,* which didn't really rely on outdoor sets, created that atmosphere via a few dead trees. Cunning and handsome as the moor sets are in *The Hound of the Baskervilles* —and they are enhanced by some barely perceptive use of gauzes over the lens—one never once has the feeling of boundless space, of being cut off from all help. One is all too aware that victim, pursuer, and rescuers are all carefully running around one basic set, with visibility minimized by the dry-ice created mists and rocks stra-tegically placed to allow for a good variety of camera angles.

But to carp is perhaps unfair in the face of such an otherwise satisfying film. For one thing, it restored Holmes to his original period; it warrants respect and admiration not only for that, but for being about the most faithful to its source novel. The changes are minor: the butler, extremely well played by John Carradine and named Barrymore in the novel, was rechristened Barryman for obvious reasons. The villain's *wife* in the novel became his sister in the movie without any notable change in her character although, presumably, the change made her more acceptable as a romantic partner for Sir Henry Baskerville. A seance *not* in the novel was written in, probably out of deference to Doyle's well-publicized interest in spiritualism, and the villain (seldom has there been less doubt about the identity of a "mystery" villain!) quite definitely meets his end in Grimpen Mire in the novel while the film leaves it open to conjecture. Despite its slowness and the artificiality of its sets, the film's mounting and hand-picked cast make it solidly enjoyable throughout, though one rather resents the studio's newest romantic lead, Richard Greene, getting billing over Rathbone.

Lionel Atwill, bearded once more and wearing thick eyeglasses so sinister in appearance that he obviously *cannot* be the guilty party, plays another marvelous red herring role, is favored with some fine low-key closeups, and launches into his lines with special enthusiasm when he has something particularly unpleasant to report. His final tribute to Holmes, however, is a sincere, underplayed scene, that reminds us what a good actor Atwill could be when given the material. Basil Rathbone, who often tended to overact (and did so outrageously in later Holmes films) here keeps his interpretation well in check—colorful yet sober, making his detailed deductions with pride and self-assurance, yet without smugness, and attacking his "disguise" scenes with relish. Nigel Bruce, a physically suitable choice as Watson, is presented as a loyal but none-too-bright aide. Unfortunately, Bruce's role was to be played more and more for comic pomposity in later films. One of the best sequences in *The Hound of the Baskervilles* was its recapitulation of the old legend, this time not done as a prologue but as a flashback, the story being shown over the turning pages of an old manuscript, in the course of its being related to Holmes by Lionel Atwill. A further pleasant surprise was that, while this film was a product of the conservative Production Code-dominated years, we were still permitted to hear Holmes ask Watson for the needle as his graceful curtain line!

The film's success prompted an immediate sequel, *The Adventures of Sherlock Holmes,* this time with Rathbone and Bruce getting the top billing they deserved. Although officially based—again—on the Gillette play, it bore no resemblance to it, or to the earlier Barrymore and Brook "adaptations" of the play. Again, its only similarity was in the dominance of the personal Holmes-Moriarty conflict. Holmes' romantic interest was removed too. The plot was a wild and woolly affair dealing with Moriarty's attempts to steal the Crown Jewels from the Tower of London. It's a pity that the story line was less impressive than that of *The Hound of the Baskervilles,* for in all other respects it was a superior product. Alfred Werker was a much better director than Sidney Lanfield and got much more out of his material; the pace and action were much faster; the concentration on a London locale ensured the continuing use of Fox's substantial standing sets and avoided the claustrophobic artifice of moorland or other exterior sets.

And, in George Zucco, we had one of the movies' best Moriartys. Zucco's face not only had the ability to suggest intellectual superiority, but it also had the happy facility of being able to light itself up with satanic glee at his own perfidy. Obviously, his Moriarty enjoyed villainy for its own sake as well as for the rewards it brought. Moreover, being British himself and possessed of clear diction that had the same kind of built-in smugness and suavity that also characterized Rathbone's speech, he made a perfect vocal as well as physical foil for Rathbone. Although, occasionally, Zucco was to play Scotland Yard detectives himself (as in such films as *Moss Rose*), clearly, he was temperamentally much better equipped to exist on the wrong side of the law. He was to cross swords with Rathbone on other occasions: in a later Holmes adventure, and especially effectively in *International Lady,* a wartime spy thriller in which Zucco's espionage agent was defeated by Rathbone's Scotland Yard detective with a penchant for Holmesian disguises.

The quality of Fox's two Holmes films was such that under ordinary circumstances a series would have been a foregone conclusion. But by the end of 1939 World War II was upon us; spies and saboteurs were much more topical than purloiners of the Crown Jewels and films like Hitchcock's *Foreign Correspondent* took the master criminal from his own environments and dropped him into the arena of political intrigue. And, a year later, the unexpected success of the John Huston—Humphrey Bogart *The Maltese Falcon* suddenly gave new and greater impetus to the "private eye" detective thriller. With such opposition, Holmes and Watson must have seemed out of step with the times indeed. Probably, Fox saw them as a dubious commercial proposition for continuance on the same budgetary level, and too important (and too costly) to relegate to their "B" mystery series. Although Fox had abandoned Mr. Moto in 1939, they still had Charlie Chan on their "B" payroll and Michael Shayne, private

detective, in the person of Lloyd Nolan, would go to work for them too by the end of 1940.

Sherlock Holmes' position as an anachronism was somewhat confirmed when, in 1942, Universal put Rathbone and Bruce into a new series of twelve Holmes adventures —all updated, and the initial ones with a contemporary wartime setting that pitted Holmes against the Axis, and occasionally had Professor Moriarty lending his ingenious talents to the Nazi cause. There was some outcry at first from the purist Holmes devotees—especially as the films, though slick and streamlined, had none of the careful production values of the two Fox predecessors. Rathbone's fondness for overacting was a failing that he indulged in more and more as the series progressed and, presumably, he was trying to find some outlet for his personal boredom. Rathbone's bravura acting was often a definite asset in his costumers and swashbucklers, and some directors (notably, Rowland V. Lee in *Love from a Stranger* and *Son of Frankenstein*) were able to harness his excess energy to the benefit of roles calling for neurosis and hysteria. But, in time, the increasingly frank "ham" of Rathbone's Holmes and the equally increasing stereotype fashioned for Watson began to work against the series.

The first films made at least a token attempt to retain recognizable plot elements from Doyle's stories and the second, and one of the best of the series, *Sherlock Holmes and the Secret Weapon* benefited not only by its casual inspiration from *The Dancing Men* but, most spectacularly, from the inspired casting of Lionel Atwill as Moriarty. (Rathbone and Atwill, another Englishman, worked together as felicitously as Rathbone and Zucco, and had opposed each other in the past in *Son of Frankenstein* and *The Sun Never Sets.*) The macabre climax found Holmes playing for time by submitting to an operation whereby Moriarty systematically drains all the blood from his body. As the operation reaches its climax and Holmes is looking understandably pale and wan, Moriarty chortles that one more drop of blood will do the trick. But there is the inevitable timely interruption and, with astonishing energy for a man in his condition, Holmes gives vigorous chase to the disgruntled Moriarty, who falls to his death through a trapdoor.

Sherlock Holmes in Washington, which followed, was rather tamer and brought back Bertram Millhauser (scenarist for the '32 Fox film) who was to become a regular fixture on the series. Increasingly, his stories were "originals," with fleeting references, if any, to Doyle themes. After two years, Holmes' name was dropped from the titles of the films, which (via such titles as *The Scarlet Claw* and *The Spider Woman*) tried to lure the horror devotees as well as the Holmes aficionados. In fact, Gale Sondergaard's Spider Woman and Rondo Hatton's

ADVENTURES OF SHERLOCK HOLMES: George Zucco as Professor Moriarty.

Creeper (from *The Pearl of Death*) spun off into negligible "B" horror careers on their own.

Among the best of the Holmes series were two from the midway point: *The Scarlet Claw* (1944), a genuinely eerie chiller with some echoes of *The Hound of the Baskervilles,* and 1945's *The House of Fear.* As always, however, with any "B" series of this type, eventually, the inspiration, the interest (and the money allocated) were drastically reduced.

The last three (*Pursuit to Algiers, Terror by Night,* and *Dressed to Kill*), made in 1945–46, were tedious and unexciting, with no recognizable link to any Doyle stories. The later entries were all much below the already none-too-exacting standards of the earlier ones, although they did eschew the sometimes patronizing and embarrassing hands-across-the-seas propaganda with which Holmes bombarded us in the wartime productions, mainly via stirring quotations from Churchill's speeches. The single highlight of the later films in the series was the unexpected reappearance of Professor Moriarty, in the capable hands of Henry Daniell in picture number nine, *The Woman in Green.* Toward the start of the series, Rathbone and Nigel Bruce had also parodied themselves via a brief and heavy-handed guest bit in the Olsen and Johnson musical, *Crazy House.* Dennis Hoey appeared as Inspector Lestrade in six of the films though, like Watson, he was less bright than Doyle had intended.

When considerably more than a decade had passed and it seemed time to trot Sherlock Holmes out again, the always reliable *The Hound of the Baskervilles* was chosen as the trial balloon. This time production was in England; Hammer Films produced, Terence Fisher directed, the film was back to its correct period and in color. Hammer having by this time (1959) carved themselves a profitable niche as producers of horror films, the grislier aspects of Doyle's story were emphasized. Peter Cushing was hardly an ideal Holmes; his earlier work as Van Helsing in the Dracula tales had set him up as a man of learning and meditation, with an appropriate professorial stance. But as a man of action as well, on whom the fates of so many in the Grimpen Mire area depended, he inspired little confidence. Andre Morell, however, a fine British character actor, was a perfect realization of Doyle's conception of Dr. Watson. He was also taller and sturdier than Cushing and tended to seem the dominating half of the duo.

Curiously, Cushing's cohort at Hammer, Christopher Lee, also essayed the Holmes role at this time (none too successfully) in a lurid German thriller, more reminiscent of Sax Rohmer than Conan Doyle, titled *Sherlock Holmes and the Deadly Necklace.* A final British entry, *A Study in Terror,* made virtually no impression.

For the time being, Holmes seemed to have been given

the *coup de grâce* by Billy Wilder's quite charming and unappreciated *The Private Life of Sherlock Holmes* in 1970. Wilder was in a difficult position at that time: his reputation for black comedy and the risqué had been all but stifled by the increasing permissiveness of the screen, in which far more outrageous things than had ever been in his once-notorious films were now not only the order of the day, but were themselves being constantly eclipsed. With the Sherlock Holmes theme by no means assured boxoffice—an earlier Broadway musical had not been a success—Wilder felt he had to pad out his extremely handsome and literate film with a number of "with it" ingredients. These turned out to include undue stress on Holmesian fondnesses for drugs and homosexuality. Not only did these subthemes introduce a note of vulgarity into what was otherwise a tasteful and affectionate film, but they also proved insufficiently strong to have the desired effect. The film was drastically shortened in an effort to streamline its episodic story, but all to no avail. It was a boxoffice flop and disappeared all too quickly—hopefully, to share the fate of another misunderstood satire, John Huston's *Beat the Devil,* and to reappear to a more receptive audience in a few years. Ronald Stephens was a generally uninteresting Holmes but an unexpected bonus was Peter Cushing's extremely funny performance as the detective's brother—a most pleasant surprise after his disappointing showing as the Master some ten years earlier.

Since, in the seventies, the detective film was more and more emphasizing speed, action, violence, sex, and the kind of ultramodern and flashy directorial techniques that would inevitably be alien to a faithful and effective filming of Doyle, it is not surprising that Mr. Holmes bade the movies farewell. The other media, however, more prone to the traditional, continued to find Sherlock Holmes useful. On radio, there had been a long string of Holmes impersonators, Rathbone and Tom Conway among them. British television in the mid-fifties had made a long-running series of placid, comfortable, but quite enjoyable Holmes mysteries. Ronald Howard, son of Leslie, and unfortunately one of those perennially youthful actors who seems out of place in anything but light romantic comedy (where he has been a convincing juvenile for the past twenty-five years), had neither the looks nor the presence to play Holmes. Howard Marion Crawford was typecast as Watson, so that the team generated few sparks.

Holmes' first television spectacular was, however, held back until 1972 when, with stunning originality, Universal selected as a "prestige" thriller—*The Hound of the Baskervilles!* Probable *initial* intentions to use it as the launching pad for a new series of Holmes TV films were scotched by extremely lukewarm reviews. The principal shortcom-

Henry Daniell as Moriarty with Rathbone in THE WOMAN IN GREEN (1945).

ing was its incredible cheapness: not only was it entirely studio-made, but standing sets were not even given a cursory reworking to adapt them to Holmes' England. Florid Spanish architecture stood out like a sore thumb in a street exterior. The script was confusing and unexciting though, reportedly, the initial script had had some considerable novelty values which had vanished either prior to the shooting or during the editing. The only favorable comment one could make of this television enterprise is that at least its makers *did* take it seriously and didn't see the need to "camp" it up, and that Stewart Granger (as Holmes) and Bernard Fox (as Watson) were both quite good, although Granger's whitening hair seemed inappropriate. Curiously, Holmes was off-screen a good deal of the time, and by actual footage count Watson probably had more to do. It was a thorough disappointment, leaving Rathbone's version still out in the

lead, though still not quite good enough in itself to rule out the possibility that this hardy old chestnut will one day provide the definitive Sherlock Holmes film.

In view of the dearth of really good Holmes films and the total absence of even one that could be termed a classic or a definitive filmic treatment, the amount of space herein devoted to Mr. Holmes might seem inappropriately generous. But, apart from the fact that he has attracted the attention of some outstanding actors and interesting directors from at least five countries and has been the only movie detective to span virtually the entire history of film, Holmes' influence (literary and filmic) on other detectives has been considerable. Britain's Sexton Blake is clearly a juvenile-level carbon copy, missing Dr. Watson admittedly, but with Tinker substituting for the Little Billy of the Gillette play, and a protective landlady-housekeeper to fill the role of Doyle's Mrs. Hudson.

20

The basic Holmesian costume props—deerstalker cap, pipe, and magnifying glass—were adopted very quickly, perhaps *because* of their incongruity, by most movies spoofing the detective genre. Mack Sennett's very early *A Desperate Lover* starred Sennett himself, accoutered in such a manner, scouring the Hollywood hills for clues. One of the silent Mutt and Jeff animated cartoons, *Slick Sleuths,* fell back on those costuming devices, as did actors as diverse as Michael Redgrave and Huntz Hall, and such comedy teams as Laurel and Hardy and Abbott and Costello. Even the name "Sherlock" rapidly became absorbed into filmic language as one of the words most used in the titles of detective satires: *Sherlock Junior, Miss Sherlock Holmes, Sherlock Brown, Shivering Sherlocks.*

And while in recent years there has been a general tendency to filmic lampoon of more modern detective *types* such as Sam Spade and James Bond, it is still Sherlock Holmes that has inspired the *specified* satires. One of the most enjoyable was a German spoof of the mid-thirties entitled *The Man Who Was Sherlock Holmes* in which Hans Albers and Heinz Ruhmann, in order to boost their unsuccessful private detective business, assume the

Peter Cushing as Holmes in THE HOUND OF THE BASKERVILLES (1958).

21

identities of Holmes and Watson, one of the film's best running jokes being their frequent encounters with an excessively British type who refuses to take them seriously, and is ultimately revealed to be Conan Doyle. Much heavier-handed but similar in intent was an American comedy of the seventies, *They Might Be Giants,* in which George C. Scott believes himself to be Holmes against the incongruous background of contemporary New York.

However, it is difficult to satirize the Holmes films successfully. There is little to parody in them apart from the man himself—or men, if we extend the parody to include Watson and Moriarty. Comedy, to be effective, needs a certain amount of speed, and to manipulate the Holmes stories so as to provide faster pacing and physical action is to distort those basic contemplative elements which made them so unique and so popular. Parodies of Holmes usually turn out to be parodies of a *genre* with Holmes as an interchangeable key figure. Satires of more conventional mystery forms—the Bulldog Drummond adventures, or the "old house-sliding panel" thrillers—have tended to be far more successful because they retain the ingredients to be good examples of the genre they are kidding even while they are simultaneously satires. The British *Bulldog Jack,* referred to later, is a prime example of this.

There has never been a deliberate parody of the Bible —though DeMille and Sam Katzman have unwittingly come quite close at times—and with the modern trend to shock, outrage, and extreme antiestablishmentarianism, perhaps a biblical parody is inevitable. (*Jesus Christ, Superstar* suggests that it may well be.) But thus far, taste, decorum—and creative stumbling blocks—have prevented it. Since Sherlock Holmes is in a sense the Bible of all detective fiction and since Billy Wilder has already had his little joke at Sherlock's expense, perhaps the Master will remain immune, aloof—and a constant challenge.

THE PRIVATE LIFE OF SHERLOCK HOLMES (1970): Ronald Stephens as Holmes; with Irene Handl.

3 THE SILENT PERIOD

THE MILLION DOLLAR MYSTERY: James Cruze and Margaret Snow in a scene from episode 11.

During the screen's silent years—roughly speaking, the first twenty-eight years of the twentieth century—the detective was a familiar enough figure in film, but never really entrenched himself as a genre hero as did the cowboy. The whole language and construction of the silent film worked against a figure who needed conversation and interrogation. In the earlier days of film, the stress was on action or at least physical *movement,* often backed up by lengthy explanatory subtitles. In the twenties, when the movies rapidly achieved increasing sophis-tication, the pace slowed, meaning was expressed via visual subtleties, and the title was used less and less. Neither period made the detective an easy character to handle.

Basically, he found himself shunted into one of four categories. First, *some* silent films *were* built around famous detective heroes. But their number was small and usually—John Barrymore's *Sherlock Holmes* being a classic example—they were based on plays or stories where the emphasis was on melodrama and action rather than on traditional sleuthing.

Second, the detective hero was a useful figure for shorts: Sherlock Holmes in the pre-nineteen-twenties, Nick Carter in the twenties. Audiences knew these characters in advance, so no time had to be wasted in establishing footage. Time-wasting sleuthing was kept to a minimum, on the theory that audiences would accept their lightning deductions on the basis of their prior reputations. The mystery story was also the dominant theme of the silent serial, its combined elements of the unmasking of a hidden villain, the amassing of clues, the gradual discovery of the hiding place of a secret formula or buried treasure being particularly suited to the methodical and often exotic construction of the chapter play. Mysteries were far and away the most popular type of silent serial, though in the sound period, when the value of the serial lessened and it was designed more and more for juvenile audiences, the mystery story dropped almost to the bottom rung of the popularity ladder, replaced by the western, the jungle film, and other genres that could concentrate on fast physical action.

In the silent period, 1915's *The Exploits of Elaine* (based on the Arthur B. Reeve stories) best illustrates the serial's use of the detective, with scientific criminologist Craig Kennedy pitted against the master criminal known as The Clutching Hand. *The Exploits of Elaine* was an extremely sophisticated and inventive serial for such a comparatively early date, and a remarkable improvement on its immediate predecessor, *The Perils of Pauline* (likewise a Pearl White vehicle) of only the year before. Although Arnold Daly was a rather stolid (and semibald) Craig Kennedy, the character itself was an interesting one, his methods a unique blend of solid deductions, intuitions, and scientific gadgetry. He also possessed the unemotional dedication of the true investigator. In one episode The Clutching Hand warns Kennedy that unless he gives up the case, he will unleash a reign of terror with his new Death Ray and will start the ball rolling outside Kennedy's apartment at a given hour. Kennedy takes up a vantage point by his window at the appointed time, and only when innocent passers-by in the street begin dropping like flies does he send word to his opponent that he will acquiesce to his wishes. (It's a trick, of course, and he's soon on the trail once more, taking a rather cavalier chance on the lives of more potential Death Ray victims!)

The Exploits of Elaine had less physical action than *The Perils of Pauline* and an even slimmer plot, limited to Kennedy's attempts to learn the identity of The Clutching Hand, and continuously unsuccessful attempts on the lives of Kennedy and Elaine. Pearl White, kept relatively in the background in the earlier portions of the serial, came into her own at the midway point, with the action constructed more around her than around Kennedy. She had improved considerably since *The Perils of Pau-line* and was a graceful and relaxed actress as well as an attractive one, in some ways a kind of feminine counterpart to Fairbanks although his first film did not come until 1916. *Elaine* is well scripted, with some quite remarkable ingenuity displayed on both sides, although it's incredible that Elaine (so bright in other ways) shouldn't guess the quite obvious identity of The Hand in episode one.

In many ways, *The Exploits of Elaine* parallels that superb (and slightly later) French serial *Les Vampires*, not only in the imagination of individual episodes, but also in that it is constructed far more like a feature than a serial. Despite an elaborate telephonic electrocution scene and an intriguing false fingerprints episode, Chapter 1 is fairly tame and not likely to inspire particular audience excitement—something that later serials strove for in their initial episode. Other early chapters tend to establish characters and incidents in a fairly orderly fashion. Although The Clutching Hand is unenterprising enough to do most of his own dirty work, he does have a vast network of minions who identify themselves by clawing at the air with their left hands, and he rates a nod of approval for being the very first of the uncomfortably masked, disguised, and stooped serial Mystery Men!

Although the pace is seldom frenetic, the often bizarre flavor more than compensates. A room which has been soaked in arsenic and which gives off poisonous fumes when the heating system is turned on is a really enterprising idea. The Hand's "amnesia drug" for which Kennedy has a ready antidote somewhat foreshadows the resourcefulness of Dr. Zarkov; and, when one is planning a jewel robbery, what better way than to cut through the floor from below so that the whole well-guarded case of precious gems simply falls out of sight in front of its police guard?

Plot situations like this are cunningly developed at the rate of at least one per episode, but sometimes pure action-suspense scenes aren't handled as well. Elaine, bound and gagged in a drainpipe and slowly being drowned by the rising Hudson River, isn't as exciting as it should be merely because the editing in that sequence is commonplace. However, it picks up a good deal of steam as it progresses. Episode Six, *The Vampire* (more appropriately retitled *Blood for Blood* by the French distributors), is a lulu of a chapter; The Hand, far more concerned about his men's safety than most serial villains, has Elaine kidnapped (she has shot and nearly killed one of his henchmen) so her blood can be transferred to him, even though the operation will prove fatal to her. In Chapter 7, Kennedy is almost as medically inventive himself for, in order to get a captured heavy to talk, he threatens to inject him with leprosy bacteria! This same episode also has a beautifully done fight atop a tall church steeple.

THE MILLION DOLLAR MYSTERY (1914): One of the first major serials. Audiences were invited to pit their wits against the on-screen detectives and by reading the story in newspapers concurrently with the film's exhibition, to try to solve the mystery first!

Other highlights of the serial's fourteen chapters include an episode in the sewers; The Clutching Hand's marvelous escape through a rolltop desk; an imaginative bit in which Elaine is given a wrist watch for her birthday—the said watch having been doctored so that at three o'clock it will inject poison into her veins; a macabre scene in which Elaine is led to believe that she has killed a man and envisions her own death in the electric chair; The Hand's casual decision to escape by having himself turned into a suspended animation mummy; and Elaine's encounter with Chinese devil worshippers under the leadership of Wong Long Sin, who points out that their god demands "a bride who is blonde, beautiful, and not of our race"!

Just as Elaine becomes less of an observer and much more of an involved participant in the latter episodes, so, in a parallel manner, do Kennedy's inventions become more and more prophetic and up to date, even including a wiretapping tape recording device. Unlike many later serials, *The Exploits of Elaine* has a continuous variety of plot content and avoids repetition of incident and of actual footage. It is also quite enterprising in getting Kennedy and Elaine out of their various predicaments without any cheating. One of the best of the early serials, it also offers one of the most intelligent and showmanlike uses of the detective as a hero figure in that period.

The third and, happily, smallest category to use the detective in the silent film was the "B" picture—or, to be more accurate, the cheap independent six-reel quickie, since the double-bill market established itself only toward the end of the twenties and the phrase "B" picture was not in common usage. There was nothing quite as bad as a really cheap silent quickie. Because they were turned out on meager sets and in a minimum of time, they could not even boast the careful lighting and well-composed camerawork which was often a spectacular saving grace in otherwise mediocre silents. Moreover, these cheapies deliberately *over*used titles to pad footage and to save the expense of additional shooting. Off-screen events—that in more enterprising productions would have been handled as flashbacks or superimposed narratives, but in any event in some *visual* way—were related by a series of long titles. (One western, which spent several unexciting reels building up to Custer's Last Stand, had a rider gallop up and *tell* everyone about the massacre, not a frame of which was shown!)

Obviously, the detective film was a way to use lengthy subtitles with some legitimacy—but the matter-of-fact interrogations, the dull cutting back and forth between faces, and the frequent repetition of information made these time-wasters excruciating. There were bad and unimaginative talkie "B" detective stories too, but at least the dialogue provided for some kind of pacing and a modicum of wit. Fortunately, these appallingly bad silent detective quickies were not great in number or widely shown, and few have survived.

During the silent period, however, independent producers did occasionally manage to secure short-tenured berths at major studios—and the methods they used often stood out like the proverbial sore thumb when compared with films by the studio's regular producers and directors. A good case in point is a little mystery (based on a play) made for Fox in 1926 and entitled *Whispering Wires.* It was produced and directed by Albert Ray, who would always specialize in low-budget detective mysteries, and was doing the same kind of films as talkies in the early thirties (*The 13th Guest, A Shriek in the Night*). *Whispering Wires* uses the typical economy gimmick of "starring" a big name who had slipped (in this case, Anita Stewart) but actually using her for a minimum of footage which consisted mainly of screams, scared reactions to telephoned threats, and the occasional embrace.

The plot was an enjoyable enough variation on the "old house" thriller: an escaped convict and his semi-demented inventor-aide ensconce themselves in a hidden room in the mansion owned by the man who caused the convict's arrest and, with the aid of a series of mechanical gadgets, begin to kill off their accusers. The murders are quite ingenious, involving a bullet concealed in the receiver of a telephone and fired by remote control. The sets are interestingly atmospheric, though artificial-looking and below normal Fox standards; the camera-work, however, by John Ford's permanent cameraman at Fox, George Schneidermann, is stylish and generally first-rate, the one element of the film that doesn't smack of independent methods. The use of detectives, however, again illustrates how scenarists of cheap films would utilize them for purposes of padding.

The mystery is finally solved by a physical confrontation, not by deduction, and it is achieved by the film's hero, Edmund Burns. Three detectives are involved in the story without adding one iota to the development of the story *or* to the entertainment values: Scott Welch as a serious enough detective, who makes a great many inquiries and is finally kidnapped by the villains, and his dim-witted assistants, played by Mack Swain and Arthur Housman as a kind of bungling Laurel and Hardy team.

Since Swain and Housman physically resemble Laurel and Hardy a little, it is just barely possible that Laurel and Hardy saw the film and expanded on its ideas in their own *Do Dectectives Think? That* short came out in mid-1927 (the Fox film had been released in late 1926); it was the first short in which Laurel and Hardy really worked as a team and, coincidentally, their costuming and relationship, also both established in that film, were remarkably similar to that of Housman and Swain. It can probably never be proven whether they did see *Whispering Wires;* even if they did, their own building on the two uninspired models was so extensive that they deserve all the more credit for recognizing such potential in a subembryonic stage.

One would *like* to think that this was the case, for it gives some justification to *Whispering Wires,* and confirms that even the mediocrity can have some value in the overall filmic pattern. The detective "comedy" of Mack Swain and Arthur Housman is, in itself, extremely feeble, with much chasing in and out of rooms, pratfalls, and accidental handcuffings one to the other. Since Swain had proven such an excellent comedy foil to Chaplin and a good solo comedian of real warmth and pantomimic talents, it was doubly sad to see him in such unfunny material. The detectives in *Whispering Wires* must eat up at least two and one half of the film's six reels—and do nothing but slow it down and lessen its suspense value.

By far the most prolific group of silent detective films were those in which the detective was the secondary character, did little real sleuthing, but was an ever present potential nemesis to the hero (usually a wrongly convicted or suspected man trying to prove his innocence and having to work outside the law to do it, or a "gentleman crook" trying to go straight and threatened with capture for former misdeeds). John Barrymore's delightful and sprightly 1917 version of *Raffles* is a prime example of this latter category. His efforts to save a friend (Frank Morgan) from suicide and disgrace involve some unethical (but not dishonest) sleight of hand with stolen jewels at a weekend party—where one of the guests is a near fanatical Javert-like detective who has been on Raffles' trail for years and is now waiting for that fatal slip so that he can pounce.

In an even lighter vein is 1925's *Paths to Paradise,* with Raymond Griffith and Betty Compson as a pair of engaging confidence tricksters. The film, quite undeservedly forgotten, is one of the comedy classics of the twenties, a joyous welding of the dry wit of Keaton to the spectacular sight-gag chase slapstick of Lloyd, yet dominated by the elements of sophistication and surprise which were a hallmark of Raymond Griffith's work. Again, the bulk of the action takes place at a weekend party and, again, the detectives are on hand not for traditional sleuthing but as watchdogs waiting to pounce. Tom Santschi played the dedicated detective, with Fred Kelsey already well into his particular stereotype as the dumb sergeant who is forever falling asleep or unwittingly providing the thieves with easier access to loot or escape routes.

Isle of Lost Ships, made in 1929, is certainly not a detective film and is only nominally a silent (since it was made as a talkie and released also in silent form), but it does provide a useful example of a frequent alternate use of the detective. Jason Robards is a supposed criminal being taken back to justice by detective Robert Emmett O'Connor. O'Connor, slight of stature, unmistakably Irish, with a pugnacious nature humanized by a cherubic grin, was a useful stock detective figure in the twenties and thirties. Although his mannerisms never varied, he was equally adept at playing (as in *Isle of Lost Ships*) the honest but compassionate detective, the tough guy used to satirize police brutality (as in *Blessed Event*), or the crooked cop taking graft and bribes (*Gabriel Over the White House*). There is no detection at all involved in *Isle of Lost Ships*. While in his custody, however, Jason Robards performs heroically during a storm at sea, saves Virginia Valli from the lecherous advances of Noah Beery, defeats a shark, and repairs a submarine fouled in the seaweed below the Sargossa Sea—all understandably leading to a last reel wrapup in which detective O'Connor somehow undertakes to prove the hero's innocence.

Such purely "custodial" activity for the movie detective was also to expand, particularly in the sound era, to such love stories as *One Way Passage* (and its forties remake, *Till We Meet Again*) wherein the unusually sympathetic detective (Warren Hymer in the original, Pat O'Brien in the remake) is taking a convicted killer back to New York and the electric chair but on the interim ocean crossing allows him the freedom to fall in love, tragically, with a woman who likewise has but a short time to live.

The use (or *non*use) of the detective in silent films often provides useful insight into the methods of the film maker. D. W. Griffith, for example, in the hundreds of short films he directed for Biograph between 1908 and 1913, many chase, suspense, crime, or cops-and-robbers melodramas, seemed to have no use for a detective hero at all. Possibly, he felt that the mere process of detection might slow down films designed primarily to exploit speed, action, and the new methods of editing with which he was experimenting. Thus he settled for a policeman hero (as in *The Telephone Girl and the Lady,* a 1913 thriller) who could gallop to the heroine's rescue on horseback.

Even in his later films, Griffith used the detective only in a marginal way—to move the plot forward by his presence or by his actions but almost never by his deductions. In *The Doll House Mystery,* a detective provides the plot motivation by suspecting and hounding an innocent man because of his prior reputation; in *Intolerance,* Griffith's 1916 magnum opus, a detective ferrets out the information that will save the hero from the gallows, but only by working on instinct and the assumption that the guilty party always returns to the scene of the crime; in *One Exciting Night,* Griffith's 1922 forerunner of all the "old house" thrillers, the detectives are on hand as a required stage convention but contribute nothing to the solving of the mystery.

Griffith's principal competitor, Thomas H. Ince, made only slightly more enterprising use of the detective. *The Gangsters and the Girl* (1914) might possibly be the first use of that later standard plot twist of having the detective hero (Charles Ray) pose as a crook, join the gang, and obtain evidence from within. Producer Ince was evidently enthusiastic about this particular production since he played a bowler-hatted detective in it himself.

Conversely, a temporarily successful but much less enterprising competitor company like Edison made much greater use of the detective hero. The film-making branch of the Edison combine was as much of a factory as the departments making electric light bulbs or phonograph discs. The movie was a successful invention to be merchandised commercially, and that was all. Edison films had an assembly line look to them and it is significant that, apart from the early pioneer Edwin S. Porter, no directors, writers, or actors of note were developed by the company in its near-twenty-year span. Adoption of the detective story was a lazy device for them since it provided a logical excuse to tell a story by dialogue—and subtitles—rather than by action.

Typical is 1915's *The Secret of the Cellar,* directed by James Castle, with Frank Lyon as the detective. The jewel thieves who are the villains make things rather easy by *looking* like villains and by pantomiming their perfidy, with much eye rolling and suspicious sideways glances at every opportunity. Moreover, one of them is absentminded enough not to notice when, in a scuffle, a jeweler rips off his collar. When the unconscious jeweler is found later, the collar clutched in his hand, the telltale laundry mark puts the detective on the thieves' trail—and, as soon as he spots them, he conveniently recognizes them as notorious crooks. That is virtually the limit of the "deduction" within the film, but it provides the necessary peg on which to hang numerous inquiries and

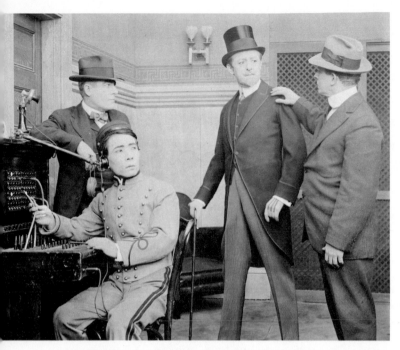

The caption on the back of the still—"I arrest you for the robbery of the Mordant Bank"—confirms the detective nature of this otherwise unidentified Edison film of circa 1915. The arrested criminal is. Marc McDermott, and the film has the stodgy and posed look of most Edison films of the period.

don a disguise, the director adds a few nonscript details to establish him in a Sherlock Holmesian light. For one thing he is obviously well-to-do. He is introduced in an expensive-looking apartment, attended by the traditional Oriental houseboy (a status symbol in the pre-nineteen-twenties, often an indication of depravity or at least hanky-panky thereafter) and wearing a dressing gown. When he later goes into the street, he is nattily attired in top hat, long black overcoat, and carries a cane—very much the uniform for the dilettante-detective. Apart from these added details, though, the director is pretty much at the mercy of a rather simpleminded script and sleuthing of the same order that characterized *The Secret of the Cellar*.

Again, everything is made very easy for the detective. The kidnapping was witnessed and the criminal was recognized—a man with a Vandyke beard. The initial description of the beard to the detective—and the detective's subsequent repetition of it in his investigations—allows for a great deal of pantomimed description of the beard. The detective's initial move (a fortuitous short cut) is to interrogate a row of cabdrivers (a rather charming and detailed shot that should be of great appeal to vintage auto enthusiasts). After the detective has repeated his Vandyke beard pantomime several times, he comes across a cabbie with instant recall who tells his story in flashback, convincing the detective that his passenger is the culprit. Donning a mustache to match the cabbie's, and borrowing his clothes, the detective goes to the house in question. His trouble seems hardly worthwhile since the wily kidnapper sees through his disguise right away. There is a reasonably lively fight, the kidnapper is vanquished, and his victim—the hero's fiancée—released.

It is an enjoyable little melodrama, but its use of a detective hero and alleged detective methods are somewhat of a cheat since they rely far more on pure luck than logical deductions and they also eliminate the visual and technical excitement that Griffith or Ince would have injected into such a story.

Even when not using a specific detective hero, Edison used this ultrasimple detective genre as the background for many other films. *The Old Reporter* (1912) had its hero being fired—and proving his worth (and gaining reinstatement) by getting the scoop on a gang of art museum thieves and bringing them to justice. Although the plot made great play of his discovering clues, the sleuthing boiled down to a barroom conversation that he happened to overhear by being in the right place at the right time.

Although this approach seems excessively naïve, it isn't that far removed from scripting practices still being employed as late as 1927, and by as big a production company as MGM, in a Lionel Barrymore vehicle called *The*

lengthy titles. At another rather unlikely juncture of the plot, a key character is trussed up and imprisoned in the cellar. In a happy collection of circumstances which wouldn't brighten the lot of too many real life detectives, there is a pipe leading from the cellar to the street above, the captive is conversant with Morse Code, and with superb timing he is able (with his feet) to rap out a message "Help! Help! The cellar!" at the precise moment the telegraphist is passing by, walking home from work!

Rather better was another Edison one-reeler, from earlier in 1915, entitled *An Unpaid Ransom*. Usually, Edison scripts were nothing more than three or four sheets of paper, listing the shots with the barest of information, and no supplementary suggestions as to mood, décor, manner of dress, or other data. Any good director would build on such a shot-list with ideas of his own; the fact that most Edison films were as lacking in atmosphere and excitement as the "scripts" they were made from merely confirms the mediocrity of most of their directors.

But *An Unpaid Ransom* (and, unhappily, neither the script nor the film itself credits a director) shows at least a little more care and thought than usual. The script does not even categorize the hero as a detective and is content to dismiss him merely as the heroine's fiancée. But since he is to perform detective work and even has a makeup kit handy for the time when he must

28

Thirteenth Hour. MGM made relatively few silent "B" pictures but when they did—as this film and the Tim McCoy western series attest—they gave them all their best production polish and gloss, even if the sets and plot did occasionally remind one more of Chesterfield Pictures than mighty Metro. Right away, *The Thirteenth Hour* gives evidence of real style, with elaborate camera angles, the use of zoom and slow motion effects, and above all the promise of a complex and bizarre mystery —all within the first reel. The title derives from the killer's consistent habit of committing his crimes at one in the morning.

At first, emphasis is laid on the fact that the killer has two fingers missing on one hand, that he uses white gloves to conceal this, and that once his disguising wig is removed he turns out to be the apparently kindly criminologist, Professor LeRoy (Barrymore). Opposing him (but, of course, with no idea of his identity) is one of the city's ace detectives, played by Charles Delaney, who enjoys the comic support of another traditionally dumb detective (Fred Kelsey) and the much more intelligent and physically energetic aid of a wonder dog, one of the best of many Rin Tin Tin competitors of the period, modestly named Napoleon Bonaparte.

With the promise of that opening reel, we seem in for a delightful essay in traditional mystery and detection. Then, suddenly, the heroine (Barrymore's secretary) accidentally discovers his dual identity. She is made captive by him, but not before she is able to get word to the police. Quickly, the detectives (including hero and wonder dog) arrive and surround the house—and what would normally have been the last reel climax to the film is expanded to a five-reel climax of nonstop action. It's wonderfully enjoyable serial-like stuff, with a never-ending parade of gimmicks: clutching hands, disappearing bodies, the heroine lecherously manhandled by the villain and stuffed into one secret panel after another, the overworked Napoleon Bonaparte falling through a trapdoor into an atmospheric Ben Carré–designed Paris sewer set borrowed from another picture. One of Barrymore's gimmicks is the utilization of a dummy replica of himself; once the police have satisfied themselves that it *is* a dummy, he takes its place, the better to listen in on their plans and brazening it out with superb self-control when the suspicious Napoleon begins to sniff at him and experimentally chew on his shoulder!

The film provides colorful action all the way, rather like a crossing of Buster Keaton's *The Haunted House* with one of the best silent serials. What marvelous fare this must have been for the youngsters—a gutsy change from westerns and jungle adventures, something to keep them alert the whole time, yet tongue-in-cheek enough not to be productive of nightmares.

Arnold Daly as Craig Kennedy in THE EXPLOITS OF ELAINE (1915), momentarily stymied by the advances of one of The Clutching Hand's vamp-minions.

Director Chester Franklin (a Griffith protégé and a specialist in animal films) keeps it on the move all the time, and Barrymore plays it all in grand style. Curiously, he has doubles in scenes calling for him to carry the heroine across the room, a feat either beneath his dignity or beyond his strength. Yet, for all its entertainment values, it's still somewhat of a cheat—a film that advertised itself as a detective mystery and turned out to be something quite different. Coincidentally, the story appeared in novel form shortly thereafter, adapted from the movie by British mystery writer Sidney Horler.

However, while *The Thirteenth Hour* is perhaps an extreme example of a film using a detective hero for a decidedly nondetective film, it remains fairly typical of Hollywood's general evasion of the detective story in the silent period. Josef von Sternberg's *Dragnet* (1928) has a detective hero in George Bancroft, but the plot revolves around his degeneration when he mistakenly believes that he has killed a friend and fellow detective in a gangland shootout. Only when he discovers that the killing was perpetrated by William Powell (and, again, he is *told* this by an informer, he does not deduce it) does he snap out of his despair and track down the real killer.

The Wakefield Case, produced in 1921 by the independent Lawrence Weber Photo Dramas Inc. and directed by George Irving, is another film related to *The Thirteenth Hour* in its shifting of emphasis from bona fide detecting to fast melodrama. It was well served, however, by the presence of Herbert Rawlinson as the detective hero. Rawlinson was a popular leading man of the silents who was slim and agile enough to handle physical action (as he often had to in serials) yet mature enough in

RAFFLES (1917): Detective Bedford, played by Frederick Perry, right, engages in a cat-and-mouse waiting game with his quarry, the cracksman Raffles (John Barrymore).

The movies' first Lone Wolf: Henry B. Walthall, left, with Lon Chaney, in FALSE FACES (1919).

appearance to portray a "thinking" hero. In addition, he looked good in a dressing gown, puffing at a pipe—obviously fulfilling all of the limited requirements for a silent era detective. (Coincidentally, one of his best talkie roles—though far from being one of his best *films*—was in the title role of a mid-thirties serial *Blake of Scotland Yard*.)

In spirit, if not in poetry or imagination, *The Wakefield Case* is somewhat akin to the earlier French serials. It is also possibly the silent screen's answer to *The Big Sleep*: few mysteries have ever been quite so full of inexplicable characters, red herrings, and plot complications. No little of the prevailing confusion can be traced to the fact that its scenario is written by a woman, based on an original story by a woman, so its total lack of logic must be accepted tolerantly. Characters are introduced too quickly and events happen too fast but, apart from the feminine hand beneath it all, its chaos is one of the lesser rules of the game and very much part of the fun. Even if one never knows quite what is going on, it's too intriguing ever to be boring and its old-fashioned plotting and masked villains hold constant interest.

Physically, the film comes to life in its closing reels and the climactic prowlings, chases, and fights have a lot of vigor to them. Filmed on the east coast, most of its exteriors are presumably in the Fort Lee environs. Not the least of its enjoyable sidelights are its lengthy and florid titles, although one of them seems, to say the least, redundant. The villain has just been shot in the eye by a detective and his faithful aide helpfully advises him: "Wakefield has put out your left eye" (a circumstance of which one would assume he was already quite aware!).

Columbia Pictures (in the late twenties a new and very small company) seemed to have a fondness for the detective format, expanded upon considerably in the sound period with their Jack Holt G-Man thrillers and the various series with The Lone Wolf, Boston Blackie, the Crime Doctor, and others. In the last years of the silents they made a brace of Lone Wolf mysteries with Bert Lytell, and also such films as *By Whose Hand?* with Ricardo Cortez coincidentally cast as Agent X-9 some years before Dashiell Hammett was to create Secret Agent X-9 officially, and also some years before Cortez would be cast as the movies' first Sam Spade. However, *By Whose Hand?* was another one of those weekend-party-in-high-society affairs and, once more, written very much in the "Raffles" tradition.

Although there wasn't a clear-cut "horror" tradition in the silent cinema, there was a certain amount of Grand Guignol and the ever present "old house" thriller, both species absorbing the detective either as comic relief or sometimes as a major figure. *The Bat, The Gorilla, The Terror* (all three remade at least twice apiece as talkies),

Herbert Rawlinson, popular hero of several silent detective features and serials.

and *The Monster* each found a solid place for the detective—*The Bat* with perhaps the most novelty since the apparent detective turned out in the final reel to be the mystery villain!

Lon Chaney's 1925 *The Phantom of the Opera* offered a good role to Arthur Edmund Carewe as an apparent suspect who turns out to be a French detective. Frequently, he pops out of the catacombs and shadows with news of the discoveries that he made but, true to form for the period, we are never shown how these deductions come about. Lon Chaney himself played a detective of apparently greater intuition than sleuthing ability in the famous *London After Midnight*. Convinced that he knows the culprit in an unsolved murder, he brings his additional talents for hypnotism into play and creates an elaborate vampire charade in order to force the killer to a confession. (The film was effectively remade, likewise by Tod Browning, as the talkie *Mark of the Vampire*, with Lionel Barrymore as the detective.)

Bert Lytell, foremost "Lone Wolf" of the silent screen.

DR. MABUSE (1922): Fritz Lang's classic early German thriller. The detective Wenck (Bernard Goetzke, left) is warned about Dr. Mabuse by his half-mad victim, Count Told (Alfred Abel).

In 1928's *While the City Sleeps,* Chaney was again a detective—but a rather Chaplinesque one. Tough yet inwardly sentimental, he shelters an underworld girl, falls in love with her, wants to marry her, but gives her up in favor of the boy she really loves—a small-time crook determined to go straight. To add to the confusion of titles, in between *London After Midnight* and *While the City Sleeps* came 1926's *While London Sleeps,* a Rin Tin Tin vehicle that was a combination of action and semihorror, with DeWitt Jennings, a reliable detective and police chief in so many talkies, cast as the Scotland Yard detective who wouldn't have solved the case without Rinty's spectacular help.

Lady detectives got a fair representation in the silent period too. Ruth Roland was probably the first with her "Girl Detective" series of shorts for Kalem in 1914–15. *The Great Jewel Robbery* and *Little Miss Hawkshaw* had Grace Darmond and Eileen Percy, respectively, as distaff investigators.

However, perhaps the most dedicated of all lady detectives appeared in *The Penalty* (1920), one of the very best of the Lon Chaney melodramas for Sam Goldwyn. It had the happy facility of allowing Chaney to play his role (as Blizzard, a legless and half-mad master criminal) completely straight and to maximum effect, while the rest of the decidedly wild-and-woolly

PATHS TO PARADISE (1925): Edgar Kennedy (center) is the dumb detective who lets confidence tricksters Betty Compson and Raymond Griffith slip through his fingers.

LONDON AFTER MIDNIGHT (1927): Detective inspector Lon Chaney's disguise as a vampire is understandably effective in helping him to crack a tough case.

melodrama was played tongue-in-cheek—with the subtitles confirming that this was in fact the intention, and not a case of mere rationalization some fifty years later. (Critics of the time were not used to Hollywood kidding its own genres, however, and often tended to take its flights of fancy with deadly seriousness, as they did in this case.)

The heroine is a government detective who is to infiltrate Chaney's vice headquarters. A predecessor who tried it wound up in the river; she is warned by her superior that discovery will almost certainly mean death or (an ominous pause)—worse! Flippantly she replies, "Oh well, it's all in the day's work!" She does in fact invade Chaney's hideout successfully, gets the goods on his operations, but also falls in love with him. Although she is discovered, her life is spared because she has become expert at pumping the pedals on Chaney's piano, he being a music lover and pianist handicapped by his lack of legs. Despite its apparent absurdity, it makes sense within its own bizarre framework—and for once the detective work does involve a modicum of investigating.

If, from all of the foregoing, it seems that the orthodox detective—Sherlock Holmes excepted—was generally slighted by the silent movie, that is a fair enough assumption to make. Bulldog Drummond, Sir Nayland Smith, Nick Carter, and others did make the occasional token appearances but the stress was much more on what one might almost, in modern vernacular, term the "antidetective"—performing the *function* of a detective, but from a position outside the law. Jewel thief The Lone Wolf, the cracksman Raffles, and ex-crook Boston Blackie got far more screen time in the silents than Bulldog Drummond or Charlie Chan.

A not inconsiderable contributing factor is that the great "Golden Age" of detective fiction (and, as a nonconnoisseur, I use that phrase not to describe quality but to indicate public interest and author productivity) didn't really begin until around 1926, reached its zenith in the thirties, and continued from the forties with a constant increase in quantity, if an understandable lessening of quality. Thus, the silent period was not able to draw upon the great bulk of detective fiction heroes—Philo Vance, Hercule Poirot, Sam Spade, Thatcher Colt, Nick Charles, Nero Wolfe, and so many others—because they just didn't exist until virtually the end of that silent period, and in many cases not until much later.

Film makers *were* clearly alert to public interest in the detective. Sherlock Holmes was brought to the screen just sixteen years after his creation while his American parallel, Craig Kennedy, was transferred from printed page to film only three years after his birth. The serial film, which brought Kennedy to the screen (and was to remain his permanent movie habitat), was in fact the most reliable (and suitable) outlet that the detective had in the silent period. The novels of Edgar Wallace provided the background for several silent serials. Others were actually or allegedly written by retired detectives, police chiefs, and secret service officials. After Kennedy's initial appearance in the Pearl White serial *The Exploits of Elaine* (1915), he returned in 1919's *The Carter Case* in the person of Herbert Rawlinson, in 1926's *The Radio Detective* (played by John Prince), and again in the sound era in a most enjoyable independent serial, *The Amazing Exploits of the Clutching Hand* in 1936. The multiplicity of characters, the verve and speed, the accumulation of gimmicks and gadgets, the colorful appearances of The Clutching Hand (accompanied by a unique little mysterioso musical theme), and the fact that everybody performed in this modestly budgeted independent opus as though it were a major studio production of genuine importance, all made it a thoroughly diverting chapter play.

Jack Mulhall was perhaps rather far removed from the original Holmesian concept of Kennedy as a science professor from Columbia University! Mulhall, a most engaging player, was always a shade *too* enthusiastic in his sound portrayals, less effective by far than in his silents. His rather smug deductions (often of totally unnecessary and extraneous matters) and his beaming smile of triumph as he reached the punch line of his somewhat unlikely reasoning made him a little difficult to take seriously. William Farnum, as an FBI official, usually played the Dr. Watson to these Holmesian flights of reasoning. Another major feat of Mulhall's Kennedy was his endless supply of handcuffs, remarkable even for a well-supplied city detective, but representing exceptional foresight for a private investigator. On occasion, dressed in a straightforward suit that showed no signs of being weighted down with hardware, he would give chase to groups of villains, subdue them all one after the other, and leave each one trussed up with a pair of handcuffs extracted from the same apparently bottomless pocket! *

The literary ancestry of *Blake of Scotland Yard,* if it exists at all, is somewhat dubious, but in any event Blake served as a kind of second-string Kennedy for a trio of movie serials. In 1927's *Blake of Scotland Yard,* he was played rather surprisingly by Hayden Stevenson—not an action star at all, but a good-natured character actor best known as the fight manager in the series of *Leather Pushers* two-reelers and as the coach in the *Collegians* series. Apparently, his debut as a serial hero-detective was not strikingly successful, since he didn't repeat the experience. A second Blake serial (*Ace of Scotland Yard*)

* Craig Kennedy later had a brief television fling in an unremarkable series starring Donald Woods.

THE THIRTEENTH HOUR (1927): Master criminal Lionel Barrymore (foreground) eavesdrops on detective Charles Delaney and secretary Jacqueline Gadson.

ROMANCE OF THE UNDERWORLD (1928): Robert Elliott, one of the screen's best detectives had one of his best and most sympathetic roles in this film, in which he champions the cause of Mary Astor.

DRAGNET (1928): Detective George Bancroft believes that he has killed his buddy, Leslie Fenton.

was made in 1929, with another character actor, Crauford Kent, in the lead. Blake, like Craig Kennedy, then retired and returned to the movies only once—in an independent serial of the mid-thirties, *Blake of Scotland Yard,* that was markedly inferior to the contemporary *The Clutching Hand.* Its rather illogical story line concerns a Death Ray perfected by one of the "good guys" and his attempts to (a) present it to the League of Nations in the interests of world peace, and (b) foil the efforts of master criminal "The Scorpion" to steal it. Destruction of the infernal machine—or, better still, its noninvention—would seem to have served the cause of peace rather

better. Herbert Rawlinson, however, was an excellent choice for the role of the now more mature Blake, while the bulk of the action was handled by the more youthful Ralph Byrd, soon to become the movies' official Dick Tracy. One of the greatest mysteries surrounding *Blake of Scotland Yard* was how children automatically seemed to know the secret identity of "The Scorpion," and in the weekly credits roundly booed the handsome, all-American-looking actor who was ostensibly one of the good guys, and who was revealed only in the final episode as the black-cloaked, lobster-clawed Scorpion!

ROMANCE OF THE UNDERWORLD: Not above bending the law to meet the ultimate ends of justice, detective Elliott contrives to have slimy blackmailer Ben Bard (right) bumped off by an underworld crony, whom he considerately allows to go free!

4 THREE CLASSICS

William Powell as Philo Vance   Alastair Sim as Inspector Cockrill.   Peter Lorre with Humphrey Bogart as Sam Spade.

Since a great deal of crime and detection is going to be discussed in this book, it might be as well to pause for a moment and consider the standards by which movie mysteries are judged. It would seem that there are three basic and not necessarily interrelated yardsticks: (1) How faithful is the movie to its source material? (2) How successful is it as a mystery, in successfully diverting the audience up the proverbial garden path without cheating in the denouement? (3) Can it possibly transcend the realm of mystery and detection to become a separate classic in its own right?

Question number three is admittedly a complex and controversial one. The notion that no kind of film designed primarily for light entertainment can produce a masterpiece is a widespread one, yet it is certainly refuted by the number of classic westerns and comedies that the screen has given us. The detective film has given us less, but I suggest that John Huston's *The Maltese Falcon,* the Japanese thriller by Kurosawa, *High and Low,* and some of the best works of Hitchcock and Fritz Lang quite certainly qualify.

Picking any kind of "Ten Best" list—whether yearly,

permanently, by genre, or by director—is inevitably somewhat futile. Quite apart from the often dubious qualifications of the selector, there is the impermanent nature of film itself: its values have a way of increasing (or diminishing) and constantly shifting through the years, and are influenced too by changing moral codes and audience flexibility in terms of interest and response. I am going to go out on a gigantic limb and select three films which seem to uphold the highest traditions of the movie detective film, particularly in relation to the three questions posed.

Taking them chronologically, to avoid the insurmountable problem of trying to place such diverse films in any kind of order of merit, we arrive first at *The Kennel Murder Case,* directed by Michael Curtiz for Warner Brothers in 1933, a year when the movie detective bonanza was at its height, and when Charlie Chan, Sherlock Holmes, Philo Vance, and Bulldog Drummond were still of considerable boxoffice importance in "A" features.

The Kennel Murder Case, the fifth film to be based on S. S. Van Dine's Philo Vance novels, is one of the very best films of its genre and William Powell, flawlessly cast as Vance, was by far the most satisfactory of the ten players who took on the role between 1929 and 1947. Not only was Powell facially and physically ideal and at the right age to play the debonair Vance but, also, since he had specialized in villain roles in silents, he was able to suggest without overstressing it the very faint hint of cruelty that existed in the character as written by Van Dine. In the novels Vance was always right, but somewhat long-winded and pompous as he expounded his theories on the psychology of crime.

In the movies, the essence of the character remained, but Powell's charm managed to translate the pomposity into a kind of amiable smugness. Robert McWade, a good character actor from Warner's stock company, made an ideal District Attorney Markham—peppery, a bit quick to jump to conclusions, but basically as intelligent as a man in that position should be. Eugene Pallette as Sergeant Heath was the inevitable dumb assistant, used mainly for (mild) comedy relief, but with the saving grace (rare in such a stereotyped role) of being hard working and dedicated to his job.

The Kennel Murder Case, with its classic "locked-room" murder puzzle, had a genuinely formidable gallery of suspects, headed by Mary Astor, Helen Vinson, Ralph Morgan, Frank Conroy, Jack LaRue, Arthur Hohl, and Paul Cavanagh, all of whom on other occasions had turned out to be the murderer in the final reel!

The beauty of the film is that it succeeds despite the limitations of its breed, and without really departing from a formula which was then very popular. Van Dine's novel is beautifully constructed and, unlike most movie adaptations, this one follows its parent novel to the letter.

Although the film is inevitably talkative, it manages to avoid the static, ponderous quality which had marred Powell's earlier Vance films at Paramount, *The Canary Murder Case* and *The Greene Murder Case* (both directorially dull and overlong), and which would likewise mar many later Vance essays. From its impressive opening titles of a flashlight beam on shuttered windows, *The Kennel Murder Case* has real zip and pace. Potentially slow scenes are broken up via camera movement, interesting lighting, and a stress on low-angle compositions which seem to put the audience into an eavesdropping position. There are some unusually good miniatures of the adjoining houses which figure so prominently in the action, and Curtiz frequently resorts to swish pans to keep the tempo lively. The foreground dialogue is suave, polished, and informative, as it should be in those mystery circles, while the background dialogue, all but thrown away, is both naturalistic and crackling.

The first reel, with its marvelous collection of suspects, works overtime in setting up motives for murder, since the victim-to-be (Robert Barrat) never seems to open his mouth unless it be to renege on a deal, issue a racial insult (the Chinese have quite a rough time of it in this picture!), or befoul the path of young love. If the identity of the murderer is obvious even before the killing has taken place, it is only because the suspect in question, quite apart from being the most cooperative and least likely suspect, has almost never failed to be revealed as the guilty party in the last reel of so many other examples of this kind of film.

However, in 1933 his perfidy was less well known, so this hardly constitutes a weakness of the picture, which not only has an unusually intriguing mystery (among the ramifications is a second murderer who shoots into an already dead body) but a logical and well-arrived-at solution too. All the clues are present on the screen although, admittedly, the pace of the film doesn't allow the audience time to put the puzzle together. Typical of the upper-crust mystery tales in which everybody lives in mansions but modestly calls them houses, *The Kennel Murder Case* should delight whodunit aficionados, but should also impress and entertain anybody who likes such exceptionally adroit movie making.

It's incredible that it took so long for *The Maltese Falcon* to achieve its wholly justifiable reputation. Granted, in 1941, the "private eye" cycle had not yet been launched; in fact, it was *The Maltese Falcon* that was to be partially responsible *for* that cycle. Audiences still regarded the detective melodrama in terms of fast action, or the polite frivolities of *The Thin Man.* The unorthodox nature of *The Maltese Falcon,* with its stress on characterization and psychology rather than clear-cut thrills, obviously baffled many audiences. Admittedly, too,

THE KENNEL MURDER CASE (1933): Helpful secretary Ralph Morgan, sinister butler Arthur Hohl, Philo Vance (William Powell), Sergeant Heath (Eugene Pallette) and Inspector Markham (Robert McWade) investigate murder of Robert Barrat (back to camera).

1941 was a tough year for a new director to win attention with his first film if that film was "merely" a thriller. Orson Welles and *Citizen Kane* were on hand that year to grab most of the limelight for dynamic new talent, while veteran traditionalist John Ford wrapped up most of the other honors (deservedly) with his Academy Award–winning *How Green Was My Valley*.

But, if its bypassing the Academy Awards was at least understandable (Warner's made no great effort to sell the film to the public, let alone to the Academy voters), its cold-shouldering by the critics is totally inexplicable. Reviews, while not ecstatic, were uniformly good. There was praise for Bogart in a new kind of role, recognition that Huston was a new director of promise, and acknowledgment that the film was probably the best thriller of the year—although, in view of the dearth of good thrillers in 1941, that was but faint praise. Moreover, it was released very late in the year, and thus should have remained fresh in the minds of critics busily assembling their "Ten Best" lists.

Yet it was roundly ignored by *The New York Times,* the New York Critics Circle, and most of the other "influential" listings. *Film Daily,* a trade paper, in its annual composite poll, culled from the combined lists of no less than 548 critics, showed it placing *twenty-first.* It achieved that rating with a grand total of 57 votes—as opposed to the 248 and 233 votes that respectively placed the very lackluster *Here Comes Mr. Jordan* and *Kitty Foyle* solidly in the "Ten Best" listing. None of which proves anything other than the absurdity of such listings, which have no permanent value as anything other than a barometer of popular taste.

The freshness and originality of *The Maltese Falcon* is all the more remarkable in that it was the third time that the Dashiell Hammett story had been filmed by Warner Brothers. The first version, made in 1931, was well received but quickly forgotten in the plethora of crime and detective films hitting the screen at that time, for it was a period of peak popularity for the gangster movie as well as the quieter detective story. Although it

THE KENNEL MURDER CASE: Vance uses a model of the town house to trace the murderer's footsteps.

GREEN FOR DANGER: Trevor Howard explains the functions of the oxygen tanks—a possible mode of murder—to detective Sim.

Alastair Sim as Inspector Cockrill in GREEN FOR DANGER (1946).

doesn't have the photographic style or casting advantages of the 1941 version, it was still a remarkably good film—and at times so similar to the later Bogart version that it seems inevitable that John Huston screened it at least once.

The changes to be made were already apparent in this first version, in which Sam Spade—a tough private detective, principled in his own fashion, but ruthless and not totally honest—was decidedly softened and given a modicum of charm in the hands of Ricardo Cortez. However, the mere casting of Cortez in such a role at that time indicated that considerable thought had been given to it, while the utilization of Bebe Daniels (then enjoying a new popularity in sprightly early sound comedies and musicals) as the femme fatale likewise showed intelligent reflection on the offbeat nature of the roles. Dudley Digges was an excellent Gutman, though inevitably his portrayal suffers from an unfair comparison with that of Sydney Greenstreet, who seemed born—and constructed—to play the role. Supporting roles were more traditionally typecast, but were nonetheless effective: Una Merkel as Spade's secretary, Walter Long as the partner who is murdered, Thelma Todd as the wife on the make for Spade, Robert Elliott as Dundy the detective, and Dwight Frye—inevitably, after his Renfield in *Dracula*—as Wilmer.

The ending remained as in the book, with Spade turning his lady in to the law, somewhat of a surprise in 1931 since the book, only written the year before, had not yet achieved the status whereby a deviation from it would have been deemed a compromise; moreover, the Production Code at that time was so loosely enforced that some kind of happy ending could have been arrived at without arousing censorial ire.

Although the film obviously owed a tremendous debt to its exceptional cast and to a good script from a fine original, the director—Roy del Ruth—can certainly share in the bows. He seemed to work well within the Warner Brothers machine, turning out punchy and fast-moving films—ranging from thrillers to satires and soap operas—during his brief Warner's sojourn. He also had a happy knack for handling actors well in these fast, brittle, often cynical frameworks, and several of the Warner stock company gave their best performances at Del Ruth's hands. By the mid-thirties, however, he had lost the spark; either that or he was a director who really needed the Warner factory behind him to boost what was probably not a major talent. In any event, his post-Warner films became increasingly conventional and dull.

Warner Brothers, more than any other studio, made a practice of constantly remaking their own properties, sometimes recognizably, sometimes totally distorted and reshaped. At times, the remakes (or composite remakes from several sources) even took on added qualities and vitality, and were a progression from the original. Such, unfortunately, was not the case with the remake of *The Maltese Falcon,* done in 1936 and retitled *Satan Met a Lady.* The reshuffling was nominal and quite ingenious: The Falcon statuette became a diamond-encrusted horn and the villainous Fat Man became an equally villainous and rather interesting Fat Lady in the person of Alison Skipworth. But all of the bite and cynicism of the original was gone, and the unifying theme of greed was sacrificed for a slick and straightforward crime story which obviously could never make up its mind whether it wanted to be a satire or not.

If it was so intended, it was far too heavy-handed to work, and yet enough of the original plot elements remained to resist turning the film into a comedy. As though aware of the inconsistencies of the script, nobody tried very hard. William Dieterle, the director, who had made some beautifully taut thrillers for Warner's, seemed to exercise no control over it at all. Warren William, who could employ effective bravura ham when the part called for it, and who had played both Philo Vance and Perry Mason with sober restraint, merely overacted foolishly as Spade (at least the character was rechristened) and was not helped by outlandish and conspicuous costuming. Bette Davis fared best, since her role was changed least

GREEN FOR DANGER: Suspects Leo Genn, Sally Gray, Megs Jenkins and Rosamund John are interrogated by Sim.

of all, but she was obviously not happy with the film's eccentricities, and stalked through it with grim determination rather than belief. The wacky comedy aspects of the film were stressed by the transformation of Spade's calmly efficient secretary into a dizzy blonde Marie Wilson! The only claim to style that the film had was in the always expert camerawork of Arthur Edeson who, coincidentally, was to photograph the later version as well.

When John Huston got his chance to write and direct *The Maltese Falcon* in 1941, production went smoothly. Huston himself downplays his own writing contribution, claiming that the original book was so exceptional that it could almost be filmed as written. However, he was doubtless also trying to "prove" himself with his first film, to show that he could come up with a film that was good and that he could make one quickly and efficiently, thus paving the way for more offers. Presumably, there had to be some last-minute rewriting too, since Sam Spade was originally intended for George Raft (who turned it down) and much of the dialogue seems specifically tailored to Bogart's staccato delivery which was vastly different from Raft's urbane and rather pallid style.

And, although Bogart's Spade is a far cry from the traditional movie detective hero of the period, at the same time, as subtly reshaped by Huston, it is a different and more admirable Spade than Hammett's: more honorable and less petty, and certainly with a greater sense of humor and an actor's ability to confuse and outguess his opponents. At one point in the book Spade gives way to an

These scenes from the 1931 THE MALTESE FALCON show how remarkably the more famous Humphrey Bogart version followed the original.

Ricardo Cortez as Sam Spade, Walter Long as Archer, his partner, and Bebe Daniels as Brigid.

Spade turns the tables on Wilmer just before meeting his boss, Gutman.

Spade is visited by Joel Cairo (Otto Matiesen).

Dudley Digges as Gutman.

Spade spots Wilmer (Dwight Frye) tailing him in a hotel lobby.

The three scoundrels await the Falcon.

The arrival of the Falcon.

Spade finds himself falling in love with Brigid.

The detectives, played by J. Farrell MacDonald (left) and Robert Elliott arrest Brigid on a charge of murder.

Spade is knocked out when he doesn't buy Gutman's offer.

Thelma Todd as the seductive widow of Miles Archer.

Una Merkel as Spade's secretary.

uncontrollable temper tantrum when things aren't going his way; in the movie Huston has Spade fake the tantrum to deceive Gutman's group, and afterward congratulate himself that the trick has worked. And, while in the movie Bogart has an implied (if inexplicit) affair with Brigid, it clearly means a great deal more to him emotionally than it did in the book, in which he resumes his affair with his dead partner's widow. On the whole, however, and reinforced by the splendid cast chosen to interpret the changes, Huston's reworkings are subtle and satisfying ones and, when they are done to satisfy the Production Code (as in the playing down of the homosexual interrelationships among Gutman's gang), Huston cunningly leaves a great deal unsaid, but is able to imply all that he wishes.

Photographically, too, Huston's methods are shrewdly but unobtrusively effective. While many of the setups and groupings of characters within a room *look* like duplications of the same scenes in the 1931 version, one vital factor has been added. Few scenes are handled in head-on closeups, or via direct cuts from one person to another. Huston uses the subjectivity of camerawork that was tried (as an unsuccessful trick) in *The Lady in the Lake,* where the audience saw the whole film through the eyes of Philip Marlowe, Marlowe himself never being seen except in an occasional mirror reflection.

Roy del Ruth, right, director, rehearses Ricardo Cortez and Bebe Daniels. Incidentally, doubtful of the name-value of the novel, Warners produced the film under the title of WOMAN OF THE WORLD, and changed it only just prior to release.

But the subjectivity in *The Maltese Falcon* isn't directed at Spade: the careful grouping of characters, the slightly off-balance angling, the frequent over-the-shoulder shots all combine to create a *consistent* subjective viewpoint throughout in which the *audience* is placed in the position of being an eavesdropper or even a silent participator in all the action.

It is this silent yet magnetic involvement of the audience in the film itself that is, I'm sure, responsible for its durability. *The Maltese Falcon* is overlong as mystery films go; it has little physical action and no specific highlights. Once the mystery is solved, its excitement should theoretically vanish—and yet it doesn't. If anything, the film gains with repeated viewings. So intense is audience involvement in the film that subliminally one admits the possibility that this time around, knowing so much more about the people and the intrigues, things may work themselves out a little differently. It would be absurd to offer that as a *conscious* rationalization for the film's continued appeal—but, as an unconscious factor, it seems perfectly valid. (Henry King's *The Gunfighter* exercised a similar emotional quality and likewise manipulated the audience to its own end.)

On a more superficial though no less important level, *The Maltese Falcon* succeeds superbly in its casting. Few films have been so flawlessly cast or their actors so well handled. Mary Astor's Brigid may be older than the equivalent character in the book but, in so being, it turns infatuation into genuine passion and heightens the poignancy of Spade's final decision to sacrifice her to the police. Well known (but always worth repeating) was Huston's method of keeping Miss Astor permanently out of breath so that she was forced to deliver her lines too quickly, without apparent thought, so that they would *seem* like the lies that they were. In writing Walter Huston's prospector role in *The Treasure of the Sierra Madre*, Huston deliberately had him annoyingly talkative, on the theory that while a garrulous man may not be a very intelligent one, he is automatically an honest one, since he has no time to think up deceptions. The reverse holds true for Sydney Greenstreet in *The Maltese Falcon*: his Gutman speaks slowly in rich, round tones and in exquisitely chosen expressions; obviously, he enjoys his own eloquence, but the theatrical manner of his speech suggests that either he has used those identical lines on other suitable occasions or that he is choosing his words carefully, constructing his sentences with a deliberate end in view. The end result: a man who is probably lying and who certainly cannot be trusted.

Greenstreet's rich delivery of his classic dialogue, the punctuation provided by his distinctive and hearty laugh, and the subtle use of expression and that enormous body itself—the traditional jolly fat man turning suddenly into

SATAN MET A LADY (1936): The second, misfire, version of THE MALTESE FALCON; Warren William and Bette Davis as renamed equivalents of Spade and Brigid.

SATAN MET A LADY: Alison Skipworth as a female Gutman, with Warren William.

a monster, Santa Claus becoming Satan via a fleeting change of expression or stance—all these things make his Gutman one of the most enjoyable and also one of the most memorable of all movie villains.

The rest of the cast is put together with equal intelligence, often notably against type. Ward Bond and Barton MacLane—so often cast as noisy, brash, stupid cops—here play well as uninspired but thoughtful and dedicated detectives, human enough to be humbled and embarrassed by their own mistakes. Peter Lorre's Joel Cairo and Elisha Cook Jr.'s Wilmer may seem like more conventional casting choices today, but it should be remembered that the success of that casting caused them to repeat the roles, with variations, in the ensuing decades.

Bogart's performance, of course, remains probably his best—and certainly the definitive "private eye" portrayal. Its uniqueness (rather more than the classic quality of the film itself, since that kind of stature has never dismayed imitators before) is probably the sole reason why the several planned remakes of *The Maltese Falcon* have never (as yet) materialized. Sam Spade *did* turn up as the hero of a television series, and star Howard Duff *did* project a boorishness which was a part (a *small* part) of Dashiell Hammett's original conception. But Duff was no Bogart. And it seems extremely unlikely that there can ever again be such a fortuitous convergence of directorial, writing, photographic, and acting talent under such ideal studio conditions to produce a fourth *Maltese Falcon* which could hope to compare with the quality of the 1941 classic.

Almost any film discussed after *The Maltese Falcon* would unavoidably suffer from an anticlimactic inferiority climax. But, fortunately, our third classic is a quiet, unspectacular film which makes comparisons unnecessary: its principal forte is not in being a dynamic piece of film making, but in being a thoroughly satisfying work that plays scrupulously fairly with its audience. The film is *Green for Danger,* a British thriller of 1947, and thus far the only film based on any of Christianna Brand's five "Inspector Cockrill" mysteries. Cockrill was an amiable and deceptively easygoing detective, much shrewder than he looked, who got his start in wartime England. Since his area was Kent (the gently rural countryside between London and the South Coast), he was spared the pressures for quick results that might have been visited on a Scotland Yard man and was able to work in a relaxed and often seemingly aimless manner. His initial cases were sometimes complicated by the war, but only tangentially involved with it. Alastair Sim was the perfect embodiment of him, especially since in 1947 Sim was as well known as a dramatic actor as he was a

THE MALTESE FALCON: Peter Lorre as Joel Cairo, with Bogart.

46

THE MALTESE FALCON (1941): Humphrey Bogart as Sam Spade.

THE MALTESE FALCON: Lee Patrick as Spade's secretary, with Bogart.

THE MALTESE FALCON: Sydney Greenstreet as Caspar Gutman, with Bogart.

THE MALTESE FALCON: Mary Astor as Brigid, with Bogart and Lorre.

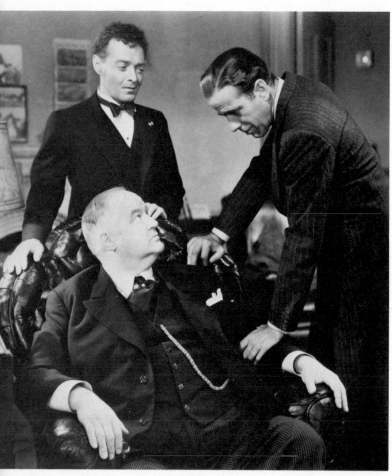

THE MALTESE FALCON: Greenstreet, Lorre, Bogart.

comedian, and had not then been typed (and wasted) in mass-produced comic-eccentric roles.

One of the J. Arthur Rank "prestige" films of the forties' *Green for Danger* was one of those few films that really seemed to have crashed the American market successfully. It opened with a big commercial splash at New York's large Winter Garden Theatre, and collected a spate of rave reviews with unanimous enthusiasm for Alastair Sim. A wide variety of alternate ads enabled the film to be sold as a "class" thriller, as a comedy, as a thick ear melodrama, and as a sex thriller. Yet it wasn't too long before its well-earned reputation had been largely forgotten and, retitled *The Mad Killer,* it was sent into the grindhouse market on a double bill with *Gang War,* which turned out to be Carol Reed's *Odd Man* Out!

Green for Danger is very much a classic of its kind, the perfect translation of a comfortable and civilized mystery novel into an equally civilized (though often far from comfortable) mystery movie. But, apart from the adroit mixture of comedy and thrill and the smoothness of all the playing, what really makes the film so unique in its species is its honesty and restraint. The plot is a good one: a mailman is injured in a bombing raid and taken to the nearby hospital for a simple operation. Just before the operation, the film takes the audience into its confidence and says that one person in the operating theater will murder two of the others. The operation then takes place, and the patient dies. Medically, there is no reason for his death nor an explanation; neither, assuming it is murder, is there any apparent motive. From that point on, the film plays scrupulously fair with the audience. There are no red herrings, no obviously unsympathetic characters, or any of the guileless, motiveless, and helpful charmers who in the average Hollywood mystery would automatically qualify for the number one suspect position! Too, the interplay among the characters —comic, romantic, dramatic, sad—is interesting and involving in itself, and not merely padding to sustain the mystery. The clues are all there on the screen—yet some of them elude the detective, too, so that even he is partially taken aback by the genuinely surprising ending, which is satisfying and logical as well as suspenseful.

The film was produced by the Frank Launder–Sidney Gilliat team, who had earlier, as a writing team, worked on Hitchcock's *The Lady Vanishes* and Carol Reed's *Night Train to Munich.* But it was directed and written by Gilliat, who can now be seen to have dominated the team much as Billy Wilder dominated the Wilder–Charles Brackett writer-producer-director team. As one would expect from Launder and Gilliat, *Green for Danger* is witty, lighthearted, and pleasingly unpredictable, the moments of terror and even visual horror all the more effective because of their lack of buildup. The swinging doors in the deserted dispensary at night, opening and shutting to reveal only fleetingly the silent appearance of the masked and gowned killer, provide a stunning moment of the macabre with a welding of sound and image that would have done credit to Val Lewton or James Whale.

With an uncharacteristic lack of generosity, Alfred Hitchcock has gone on record as saying that *Green for Danger* (and other Launder-Gilliat films, some of which were extremely good and not all of which were thrillers) doesn't work, and implies that the duo should have stuck to writing. He tends to overlook the fact that *The Lady Vanishes* was one of his very best films at least partially because of its superior script; and that while Hitchcock may have made better thrillers than *Green for Danger*, he never made a better detective mystery.

Alastair Sim completely wraps up the film with his off-beat detective, who also provides an occasional voice-over narration for the film, his matter-of-fact police-jargon comments often forming a complete counterpoint to the visuals that they accompany. Stumbling in a kind of ungraceful ballet to avoid Hitler's robot bombs that punctuate the film occasionally and remind us of its wartime locale, shrewd and addle-brained by turn, tossing off the witty asides with aplomb and perfect timing (at one point a doctor is soberly explaining the misconceptions about so-called laughing gas, explaining that "it is the impurities that cause the laughs" whereupon Sim comments, "Just like our music halls"), Sim created such a delightful character that critics both in England and the United States urged that he repeat the role. (There had been a like reaction to Ralph Richardson's similarly astute yet comical detective in 1938's *Q Planes*.)

Fortunately, the suggestions were never acted upon; just as a succession of Bogart Sam Spades would have cheapened *The Maltese Falcon*, so would a number of Inspector Cockrill sequels have lessened the subsequent impact of *Green for Danger*.

Sim d'd, however, play a number of memorably unique and individual detective roles in other films. In the popular Inspector Hornleigh mysteries of 1938–41, he played the comic sergeant to Gordon Harker's inspector, but with sufficient subtlety to lift the role out of the standard stooge rut. He was superb as the undercover detective in the wartime spy film, *Cottage to Let*, playing much of it for comedy, including a hilarious sequence in which he masqueraded as a German agent, complete with accent. But for the climax, a macabre composite of Hitchcock and Lang, wherein the enemy agent is unmasked and run to earth in a maze of distorting mirrors at a charity bazaar, Sim plays with deadly seriousness and reminds us again what a fine actor he can be. *Hue and Cry*, one of the earlier Ealing comedies and a film with echoes of the old German *Emil and the Detectives*, saw Sim in a purely comic role as a creator of blood-and-thunder comics for children, pulled unwittingly into the role of amateur detective to lead a gang of youngsters in tracking down ruthless crooks.

Hitchcock's *Stage Fright* gave Sim another good "amateur detective" role with scope for underplayed dramatics and comedy, and moments of genuine black comedy which might have been distasteful did not the camera focus on the drolleries of his facial pantomime. Far more serious, though certainly laced with wry humor, was Sim's performance in the title role of *An Inspector Calls*, in which his investigating detective causes a mildly intolerant household to examine themselves. After his departure, he turns out to be one of those heavenly messengers common to playwrights of both Britain and America, but especially beloved by such British authors as J. B. Priestley, who wrote *An Inspector Calls*.

But his Inspector Cockrill surpasses them all, just as *Green for Danger* towers over most of its ancestors and descendants in the long lineage of distinguished British detective movies.

THE MALTESE FALCON: Barton MacLane (left) and Ward Bond as the city detectives, with Bogart.

5 THE EARLY TALKIES

CURTAIN AT EIGHT (1934): Murder suspects are interrogated by dumb Sam Hardy (pointing) and more thoughtful C. Aubrey Smith (right).

Separately and together, the mystery and detective film enjoyed a tremendous boom when sound came in, and for a number of reasons which happily coincided in their appeal to the boxoffice. Initially, of course, it was enough that movies just talk, so it is not surprising that there was a great emphasis on the kind of movie in which the story *had* to be told by prolonged dialogue exchanges: the detective thriller and the "confession" and marital dramas. (These latter were especially prolific at RKO Radio, which seemed to exist on talkfests wherein Ann

Harding, Constance Bennett, and Lila Lee fought for, sacrificed, and regained their men—Herbert Marshall, Joel McCrea, and Conrad Nagel, usually.) Both the detective and confession stories had the advantage of being (for the most part) based on published novels or plays, so that the dialogue was already written and merely had to be condensed and rearranged.

This was no small matter since the talkie revolution caught Hollywood short in the critical area of writers. Silent-day scenarists were used to thinking in visual terms, constructing their stories so that essential information was conveyed by action or the pungent subtitle. Playwrights and novelists had little experience writing directly for the screen, and especially not for the new talkies, where every kind of scene had to be written with the limitations of the new techniques firmly in mind.

Too, the detective novel itself had attained new heights of popularity in recent years; since 1925 such sleuths as Hercule Poirot, Philo Vance, Sam Spade, The Saint, Mr. Reeder, Dr. Priestley, Charlie Chan, and Ellery Queen had made their publication debuts. For the first year of the talkies, at least, curiosity about the speaking voices of popular stars was naturally high.

A detective role was a logical way of introducing an actor to sound films, for it provided a perfectly legitimate excuse for him to do virtually nothing but talk. The only moderately successful silent careers of Ronald Colman and William Powell were immeasurably boosted by the poise and clear diction that they brought to their interpretations of Bulldog Drummond and Philo Vance, respectively. Of course, the reverse was true, too: that tremendously subtle silent comedian Raymond Griffith literally had a voice defect and could speak only in quiet and hoarse tones; to have cast him as Detective Trent in *Trent's Last Case* seems the height of folly, while Kenneth MacKenna's inadequacies (there was nothing specifically wrong with his voice, he was just a mediocre talkie actor) were likewise emphasized by his Bulldog Drummond role in *Temple Tower*.

The early sound period, as was to be expected, also produced a big cycle of musicals and many of these, in order to be topical, concentrated on subplots of Broadway gangsterism. Some, like *Broadway,* were based on hit plays and transported the stage stars to Hollywood to recreate their original roles. A logical offshoot of the detective film was the courtroom drama, which again allowed for a maximum of legitimate talk, and also permitted the use of flashbacks, many of which naturally overlapped into the area of the detective film. *The Trial of Mary Dugan, Through Different Eyes,* and *The Bellamy Trial* were three typical 1929 talkies that followed this route.

Most of the early talkie mysteries exploited dialogue and *noise* (the hubbub in a courtroom, police sirens, the din of printing presses) rather more than the nuances of sound, which were reserved for the occasional gimmick. This is at least partially due to the fact that many of the early sound films were also released in silent form, and subtlety was not always possible. The solution of *The Canary Murder Case* is partially brought out through the overhearing of a voice on a phonograph record behind a locked door. *Through Different Eyes* shows the same killing through the viewpoint of different and biased ob-

Willard Mack, star-writer-director of VOICE OF THE CITY (1929).

servers, a technique foreshadowing that of the Japanese *Rashomon,* before coming up with a surprise revelation about the real killer. One of the basic plot gimmicks was that the murder gun contained two bullets, the first of them a blank, and therefore it was imperative that the audience *hear* the shots since much of the action is staged off-screen. Conveying the idea of a heard but unshown noise seems to have defeated Fox's title writers, and the silent version is not only confusing on that score but also leaves unexplained a couple of apparently key characters who are just dropped—although, presumably, their loose ends were wrapped up by a line or two of dialogue in the sound edition.

However, dialogue had its pitfalls too. MGM's *The Unholy Night,* another 1929 detective mystery, and incidentally directed by Lionel Barrymore, had a most intriguing plot in which a Scotland Yard detective gathered together all the surviving members of a wartime regiment. The regiment is being decimated one by one in a series of apparently motiveless murders. They all meet at a typically gloomy mansion, where it soon becomes apparent that at least two opposing factions are involved in the mystery. A seance, and the actual or apparent materialization of the killer's prior victims, brings about his unmasking. There is a great deal to be explained:

The giant crane designed by director Paul Fejos to bring added mobility to BROADWAY (1929).

BROADWAY reconstructed on the Universal lot, with the California hills incongruously in the background.

the motivation for the killings and the mechanics behind the "ghosts," and, unfortunately, Ben Hecht's script concentrates all of these explanations in a lengthy climactic speech by the Hindu mystic played by Sojin. The rather harsh sound recording of the day, coupled with Sojin's fast, guttural, and totally incomprehensible Japanese accent, renders this critical piece of information just so much gibberish. One *sees* who the killer is, and learns that Boris Karloff is merely a red herring, but that is about all!

Admittedly, most of the early detective talkies did take the easy way out, relying on the popularity of the genre and the star, and on the novelty of sound itself. Cinematically, they were static and seemingly welcomed the plot contrivances that caused detective and suspects to sit around in offices or drawing rooms and just *talk*. There were many awkward problems involved in the early days of sound, and it *was* easier and quicker to render the camera completely immobile and just shoot what amounted to filmed theater. Innovative directors

like Rouben Mamoulian and King Vidor refused to accept the strictures of technicians that certain things "couldn't be done," and insisted on full camera mobility and a retention of the filmic grammar that had been at its peak when the silents ended. Unfortunately, Mamoulian and Vidor didn't make any detective films—although Mamoulian's *City Streets* was based on a Dashiell Hammett story and because of its stylization and fine pictorial inventiveness remains one of the most durable of the early gangster movies.

Not a few of the early talkie triangle or emotional dramas went out of their way to introduce a detective element into the story unexpectedly to provide a last-minute boosting of excitement. Or they may have been chosen for film treatment because in their prior form (a novel or play) they had that key ingredient.

A typical example is 1929's *Interference,* literally one of the talkiest and most static of all early sound films—although the plot itself was quite strong and with faster pacing and more relaxed acting it could have been quite

52

a powerful piece of work. As it was, it was a popular and critical success and its climax is still quite poignant. Its plot is a rather complicated affair of a ne'er-do-well (William Powell) presumed killed in the war, who comes back several years later to find his former wife now happily remarried to a successful public figure. His former mistress, Evelyn Brent (extremely busy in 1929, and unusually good in this film), spots him and threatens the wife with blackmail. Finding out he has only a short time to live, Powell kills her and turns himself in to the police. Prior to this, however, a complicated chain of events causes the husband (Clive Brook) and the wife (Doris Kenyon) to assume that the other has committed the crime.

Considerable time is spent showing how Clive Brook, at the scene of the crime, rearranges the evidence to suggest suicide, and how the detective (Brandon Hurst) shrewdly pieces it together again and proves murder. An interesting sidelight of this sequence (apart from the utilization of that same year's Philo Vance and Sherlock Holmes figures working *against* the law) was the appearance of a bored coroner, annoyed at the inconsideration of corpses who drag him away from his meals, a character obviously suggested by the testy and amusing Doctor Doremus of the Philo Vance stories.

Although only marginally a detective film, Universal's *Broadway* of 1929 was one of the most interesting of the early talkies. Directed by Paul Fejos (one of several European film makers who dominated the Universal lot at that time), it was based on the enormously successful play by Phillip Dunning and George Abbott, and was released in both sound and silent versions—the spectacular musical numbers, some in Technicolor, being the principal casualties of the shorter silent edition. Its key attention-grabber was a huge surrealistic nightmare of a nightclub set that was at least as high and nearly as wide as Grand Central, and seemed to use architectural motifs deriving from the nightclub in Fritz Lang's 1922 *Dr. Mabuse*. Universal neither knew nor cared that New York hadn't a single nightclub a fraction of the size of this one; all that mattered in 1929 was that it be the biggest in Hollywood.

As an adaptation of a play, *Broadway* has many of the flaws of the genre. Most of the physical action takes place offstage (gangster activity in the streets) and is merely talked about. Initially, the intention seems to have been otherwise. The script for the film (it was written as a nine-reel sound film, the silent version being edited from it and not in any way shot differently) is itself an unwieldy affair, full of stage directions to the actors, explanations of motivations, and suggestions to "Dr. Fejos" as to how certain photographic effects could be gained. Presumably, much of this proved impractical and

BROADWAY: Thomas Jackson, Paul Porcasi, Evelyn Brent.

was jettisoned. The original script called for far more physical action in the streets and for an opening montage which, as written, would have run for at least a reel in its "city symphony" survey of young love, factory hooters, traffic accidents, bootlegging, shootings, robberies, drug addiction, pawnshops opening for business, and so on.

There were also endlessly talkative scenes, however, such as an interrogation at headquarters. If the final film was much too "big" a production for its (now) fairly commonplace plot elements, it was at least a film that was determined to demonstrate *film* expertise, and not content itself with being just another filmed play.

Broadway is the film for which director Fejos and cameraman Hal Mohr designed the fantastic crane which more resembled an ancient scaling tower than a piece of photographic equipment. But the results achieved with it, even if its mobility does occasionally run riot, are both

53

BROADWAY: Thomas Jackson recreates his stage role as the detective.

The 1942 remake of BROADWAY saw Pat O'Brien in the old Thomas Jackson role, here unimpressed by an array of gangster talent.

impressive and creative. Rarely still, the camera charges in for closeups, sneaks around behind players, and zooms aloft like a suddenly liberated balloon so that the already bizarre nightclub décor becomes a jungle of diagonals and angles. Once in a while it even stands still long enough to catch a shot impressive for its composition rather than its movement, as in the scene of the detective viewed through the diffused violin bows! Universal continued to use this great camera crane through the years, often very effectively in mass action scenes, sometimes rather arbitrarily as when it swoops down on Deanna Durbin in *A Hundred Men and a Girl*.

Universal's film was by no means alone in the gangster/detective/musical field, nor was it even the first, since Warner's *Lights of New York* had really started the whole cycle a year earlier. But the commercial value of the play property made Universal understandably irked by such cheaper films as *Broadway Babes* (an Alice White vehicle directed by Mervyn LeRoy), made hurriedly to cash in on its fame and playing in direct competition. This prompted Universal to include the following line in the advertisements: "Use of the word Broadway in other film productions is unauthorized, and has no connection with this, the original play." The competition didn't hurt it, however: it opened on Broadway (naturally) at the Globe, following Universal's own *Show Boat*. Sold on a combination of sex and size, it used ads that were frankly erotic and contained such catchlines as: "Nothing but the biggest sets could be big enough for the biggest moments the stage has ever known—a million candle-power picture!" Reviews were good—and so was business.

For its size and importance, *Broadway* seems today to have a strangely unimpressive cast. Other than Evelyn Brent, perfectly cast in her old von Sternberg role as a gangster's mistress, the stars seem to be second-string. But at the time, in Hollywood and New York, if not in the rest of the country, they *were* considered top-liners. Glen Tryon is a decided liability as the bumptious vaude-ville-hoofer hero, but the gangster performances from Robert Ellis and Leslie Fenton were especially good. Thomas Jackson (the detective) and Paul Porcasi (the nervous nightclub operator) re-created the roles they had played in the stage version, and were to be typecast in those roles for the rest of their long Hollywood careers. Jackson's Dan McCorn was the prototype for all honest and incorruptible city detectives—courageous if colorless, working more by instinct than profound deductions, with an almost obsessive hatred for the big-time crook, yet with sympathy and pity for the "little" crook who might be redeemed and salvaged. The quiet underplaying of his role must have been doubly effective in 1929, when the screen detective was an outlet for bravura playing

BROADWAY: Pat O'Brien, Broderick Crawford, Ed Brophy, George Raft.

THRU DIFFERENT EYES (1929): Edmund Lowe, Mary Duncan.

—or writing—or both, and when the glamorous detective of fiction was stealing the limelight.

Thomas Jackson was and remained an extremely good actor, but often his movie detectives were too obviously written with his Dan McCorn in mind; the detective he played in *Little Caesar* in 1931 emerged almost as a parody, perhaps because he was the only essentially realistic figure in that rather grotesque collection of gangster stereotypes.

One of the more blatant imitations of Jackson's detective occurred early in 1929, before the film of *Broadway* was released, but well after attention had been focused on Jackson's stage performance. The film was MGM's *Voice of the City* in which writer-director-star Willard Mack patterned his hard-boiled but soft-spoken detective exactly after the Jackson characterization.

Of the many attempts to duplicate *Broadway,* one of the best was Universal's own now totally forgotten *Night World,* directed in 1932 by Hobart Henley. Like *Broadway,* it limited its action to a short period in the nightclub itself although, obviously influenced too by the recent *Grand Hotel,* it broadened its scope to include a number of personal stories that were solved (happily, or by death) during the course of the story's one-night duration. Boris Karloff was good (even though not totally convincing with his British accent) as the shady yet somehow honorable gangland operator of the club, Lew Ayres and Mae Clarke were the disillusioned couple who find each other—and a new life—and George Raft had an effective minor role as a lecherous gangster on the make. The dialogue was taut and often very amusing, and the nightclub set was smaller and decidedly more realistic than the one in *Broadway.* Busby Berkeley, who staged the film's musical numbers, designed some extremely effective and visually exciting numbers for the small chorus line that would have been appropriate for such a second-grade nightclub. There is no key detective figure involved, but the ubiquitous Robert Emmett O'Connor is on hand at the end to save the young lovers (who have just witnessed a double murder) from being executed themselves.

SCOTLAND YARD (1930): Donald Crisp, Edmund Lowe; one of the most complicated of all early-talkie mystery films.

THE BAT WHISPERS (1931): Gustav von Seyffertitz, and Chester Morris as Detective Anderson.

SCANDAL SHEET (1931): Fred Kelsey, the dumb detective prototype, with George Bancroft.

Universal remade *Broadway* in the early forties as a competent enough gangster film but one with little distinction. Pat O'Brien played the detective, Broderick Crawford the gangster heavy, and Anne Gwynne redid the Evelyn Brent role. George Raft played himself in a reshuffling of Glenn Tryon's hoofer. There were the expected nods to the newer and more stringent censorship. In the original, the murderess (Evelyn Brent) gets off scot free, the detective covering up her crime on "humane" grounds in that he found it quite justifiable. In the remake, events lead up to a similar solution, but George Raft (telling the tale in flashback) reveals that afterward she gave herself up anyway, and was let off with a light sentence! A most amusing (unintentionally) moment in the remake was when Raft, in the forties, goes to the stage door of the nightclub where he had been a hoofer in the twenties. Walking into the decidedly economical nightclub set, he remarks, "Funny, I remember it as being bigger than this!"

Relatively few early sound detective films carried the prestige and boxoffice importance of films like *Broadway,* and were usually assigned to rather stolid contract directors like Frank Tuttle, who had little filmic imagination, but who did turn their films out quickly and efficiently in those rather complicated times. However, the lack of thought that too many directors gave to these essentially all-dialogue films considerably lessened their potential. Players were still very much aware of the microphone, not only mentally but *physically,* since the microphones were concealed at vantage spots around the set (in a bowl of flowers or a suspiciously bulky telephone), and the actors had to be careful not to stray too far out of range.

Since their futures might well be at stake, they were concerned with how they would sound, and with remembering their lines perfectly so that fluffs and retakes wouldn't stamp them as unreliable. This concern, natural as it was, manifested itself in a total *unconcern* for the picture surrounding them. Groups of people, cut off in an old house and decimated by an unseen killer, seemed to accept the proliferation of corpses quite casually. When asked a question by the detective, they would launch into their answer immediately, allowing no time for thought, and by that pause encouraging the audience to formulate thoughts about their guilt or innocence.

One director who used sound intelligently in his crime films was Roland West although his ideas—intelligent and advanced then—were so quickly absorbed into the overall lexicon of film sound that these aspects of his films no longer impress. Fortunately, he was also an extremely visual director, most of whose work was done in the silent period, and whose trademark—like that of Maurice Tourneur—was a flair for striking, highly stylized, and often deliberately unrealistic pictorial composition. That aspect of his work has never been casually absorbed into a universal film technique, and thus his few talkies remain unique. *Alibi* (1929), his first sound film, was an adaptation of the play *Nightstick,* and was quite unique in killing off both its villain (Chester Morris, in a Cagneyish performance—well before Cagney) and its detective hero. Its dialogue was well spaced; people spoke only when they had something to say. In the police interrogation scenes, key phrases were repeated monotonously and aggressively. Dialogue exchanges overlapped in tense scenes, or were more measured in scenes where characters thought and reflected before speaking. Off-screen sound effects were scrupulously the real thing, and not mechanical approximations.

None of this can seem unique today, but in 1929 it showed an unusual regard for both realism and drama. When, for dramatic reasons, West wanted a total and even somewhat stylized silence, he merely turned off the recording apparatus since, even without dialogue or specific noise, recorded "silence" has a subliminal hum. Perhaps because it tried to do too much too early—a realistic and unglamourized portrayal of a killer, an honest and sometimes blatantly critical picture of police methods and occasional brutality, a mixture of theatrical drama and filmic stylization in its use of sound and picture—*Alibi* survives as a rather uneven and sometimes overly sentimental work. Regis Toomey's prolonged death scene as the detective is today more mawkish than moving. But, like so many trail-blazing films, its importance lies not in what it is now, but in what it *did* originally, and in its influence on other film makers.

West's second talkie, *The Bat Whispers,* was both better and more durable. Adapted from the barnstorming play that West had also made into a silent movie, it was a marvelously pictorial "old house" thriller, with the black-cloaked Bat—killer, thief, bankrobber, and all-around master criminal—oozing in and out of the shadows, presented in long silhouette shots or distorted shadows as a near supernatural phantom. Pictorially, the film is a stunner, with many deliberate echoes of Fritz Lang's most nightmarish shots from the twenties, and Ray June's superb camerawork was enhanced by the film being shot in the short-lived wide-screen 70-mm. process. (Even printed down, the film retains an added clarity of focus and richness of tone.)

West was a dilettante director who worked because he *liked* making films, and one of the peculiarities he indulged was a fondness for shooting only at night. His films were literally dark, nightmarish, shot at night as well as taking place at night. *The Bat Whispers* creaks a little in some of its theater-derived conventions and comic relief, but it never lets up in the variety of its pictorial

BEHIND THE MASK (1932): Jack Holt, Boris Karloff.

THE THIRTEENTH GUEST (1932): Policeman J. Farrell MacDonald, potential murder victim Ginger Rogers, detective Lyle Talbot.

THE THIRTEENTH GUEST: Dumb detective Paul Hurst and mystery killer.

57

ARSENE LUPIN (1932): A stylish thriller elegantly acted by John Barrymore (right) as the master jewel thief and Lionel Barrymore (left) as his detective nemesis.

SINISTER HANDS (1932): Dumb detective James Burtis, suspects Louis Natheaux, Crauford Kent, Gertrude Messinger, and detective Jack Mulhall.

MURDER IN TRINIDAD (1934): Nigel Bruce was one of the most off-beat of movie detectives in this interesting thriller, creating a novel characterisation of a slovenly yet astute investigator. The film was remade twice, first as MR. MOTO IN DANGER ISLAND, and later as THE CARIBBEAN MYSTERY. Shown in these scenes with Nigel Bruce are Heather Angel, Douglas Walton and Victory Jory.

effects for menace and thrill, and benefits from a deliberately (though controlled) overwrought performance from Chester Morris as the tough, sardonic, witty, and sadistic detective. When it is ultimately revealed that he is The Bat (having kidnapped and replaced the real detective), the neurotic quality of his performance seems perfectly justified and helps pave the way for acceptance of a no-holds-barred "mad scene" in which, even though manacled, he swears to come back—a particularly chilling fadeout, undistilled by any conventional romantic clinches.

Even though Morris is a bogus detective, the force of his performance until his final unmasking certainly entitles it to rank as one of the most interesting and offbeat of all detective characterizations. Morris also starred in West's third and last talkie, *Corsair* (1931), which had no detective element at all but was fascinating as a cynical gangster story in which all of the miscreants profited by their crimes (murder and bootlegging) and escaped scot-free at the end to enjoy their ill-gotten gains.

West's own career may or may not have paralleled this. He was implicated as a prime suspect in the death of his mistress, actress Thelma Todd. But since it was never determined whether her death was murder (as it seemed), suicide, or a freak accident, he was officially exonerated. It put an end to his directorial career, although his notoriety served to attract the morbidly curious to the restaurant which he established and which kept him comfortably solvent.

Observing the success of the "prestige" detective films, the programmers and the "B" films naturally began to emulate them. One of the more interesting of the early ones was Columbia's *The Donovan Affair,* which got off to a gimmicky start by stressing the surprise element in the killer's identity and asking audiences not to give the game away to their friends. It was built around one of the oldest ploys in the business: the much-hated host at a dinner party rather foolhardily creates his guest list of people who all have a perfect motive for wanting to kill him. Needless to say, the lights go out and he is killed. Detective Jack Holt arrives to investigate the case and starts off by reconstructing the scene of the crime. As the lights go off again, victim number two is dispatched. Embarrassed but undismayed, Detective Holt pursues the case until he runs down the one member of the assemblage who had no motive at all, and was therefore unavoidably the murderer.

The small independent companies embraced the genre too: not only did the talkative nature of the species enable them to play out their dramas in one or two small interior sets, but the changing status of stars at this

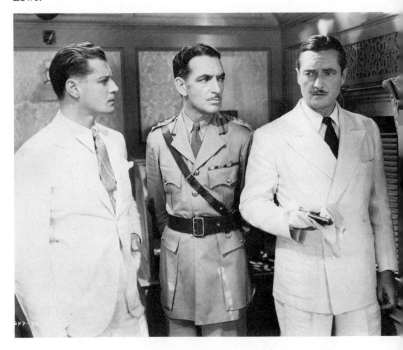

BOMBAY MAIL (1934): Ralph Forbes, Jameson Thomas, Edmund Lowe.

MURDER IN THE MUSEUM (1934): Henry B. Walthall (center) is flanked, at right, by detectives John Elliott and Joseph Girard.

59

transitional stage in the history of film meant that many secondary but still well-known names from the silent period were "at liberty" and could be employed for a pittance. The cast lists of some of these independent "B" mysteries would have done credit to major studio efforts just a few years earlier. However, the writing and directorial talent in these films often didn't match the histrionics.

The "B" detective film quickly became as standardized as the "B" western. Typical is *Sinister Hands,* an extremely economy-conscious Willis Kent production of 1932. Again, we have the murder of a man whose house guests have every conceivable motive for killing him. Dapper detective Jack Mulhall investigates the crime more by intuition than by sleuthing. Gathering all the suspects around him, Mulhall outlines their individual reasons for murder, based almost entirely on their physical or racial characteristics. Indian swami Mischa Auer faces a particularly rampant case of minority persecution when Mulhall tells him, "You're a Hindu, and have been trained to sneak stealthily through a darkened room."

The embarrassment to which the guests are thus subjected seems somewhat pointless when Mulhall comes to the final and most innocent-looking of all the suspects. Fortunately, Mulhall had played tennis with him the morning before and recognized in his overarm swing the kind of force that was employed in the murder. Fortunately, too, the exposed killer, not taking the time to think how flimsy such "evidence" would seem in court, or having the common sense to brazen it out, immediately admits his perfidy!

If, intentionally, I have neglected to do more than refer in passing to the *best* and most enjoyable detective mystery from this entire period—1929's *Bulldog Drummond* —it is because it is much too good and far-reaching a film to be given anything less than the major attention it can receive in a chapter devoted exclusively to the screen's numerous Drummonds.

ONE FRIGHTENED NIGHT (1935): An "old house" murder mystery, with Adrian Morris (right) questioning Regis Toomey, Charles Grapewin, Mary Carlisle and Lucien Littlefield.

6 BULLDOG DRUMMOND

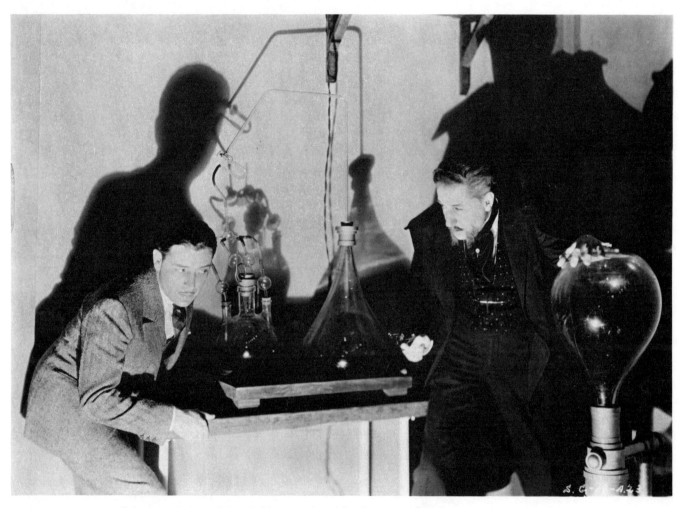

BULLDOG DRUMMOND: Colman and the evil Dr. Lakington, played by Lawrence Grant.

Captain Hugh "Bulldog" Drummond was created by H. C. McNeile and introduced to detective fiction fans in 1920. As his rank and the date suggest, he was a World War I veteran. He was also something of a Fascist and a thug, looking for an outlet for violence and finding it in a kind of moralistic crusade against crime. He was in his own way a forerunner of America's Mike Hammer, who was always so delighted when the criminals he dispatched or at least beat up unmercifully also turned out to be Communists.

Perhaps it was Drummond's attitude that prevented him from being either a major fictional success or of immediate interest to movie makers. Drummond was brought to the screen only twice in the silent period, both times by British companies. Carlyle Blackwell, who at least approximated Drummond's physical description, came first, followed by the dapper dancer and light comedian, Jack Buchanan, who certainly didn't.

Hollywood first got interested in Drummond in 1929, and its initial Drummond venture was an unqualified success that turned out to be not only the definitive Drummond film, but also one of the very best. Sam Goldwyn selected the subject (originally a play), signed playwright Sidney Howard to work on the scenario, and designed it as a vehicle for Ronald Colman.

In this latter respect it succeeded most spectacularly of all. Colman's flawless diction, his beautiful timing, and the sense of fun he brought to the role not only dominated the film, but influenced the tongue-in-cheek playing of the rest of the cast. This Drummond had nothing whatsoever in common with the surly Drummond of the books; it was a debonair and sophisticated interpretation, a Drummond who was really a twentieth-century D'Artagnan. In fact, there was a good deal of Fairbanksian flair in Colman's performance, and the character shared a great many of the qualities that had made up the Fairbanks "image" in his modern silent comedies—good society connections, an educated background, and an unstressed but apparently unlimited private income.

From 1929 on, Colman's Drummond became the yardstick by which all others were measured—and from which they copied. (There was a similar permanent metamorphosis in a book-to-screen transfer when Clarence E. Mulford's crotchety and hard-drinking Hopalong Cassidy became a gallant gentleman and embodiment of clean-living virtues in the hands of William Boyd.)

But, quite apart from Colman, who was instantly boosted to a much greater stardom, *Bulldog Drummond* was a first-rate movie in every way. It moved constantly; the sets and art direction of William Cameron Menzies and the camerawork of George Barnes and Gregg Toland retained the very best elements of the German-influenced photography of the late silent period, while never sacrificing simplicity to pretentious décor; and the only obvious concessions to the exploitation of sound for its own sake were the occasional interpolations of songs by Donald Novis. And even these were acceptable, since Novis did have a good voice and the songs were logically slotted in a saloon-bar locale. The very first scene stresses the film's far-reaching influences: a stuffy London club where Drummond cannot stand the boredom and the enforced silence.

Three years later, Rouben Mamoulian picked up the scene and expanded on it in his *Love Me Tonight,* while in 1935 Mark Sandrich returned the scene to its original locale and first-scene position and used it to get *Top Hat* under way with a bang—as the somnolent London club that Fred Astaire brings to life with a round of tap dancing.

Bored with life since the war, Drummond advertises in the *Times* for exciting adventure and from the deluge of letters picks the most promising one. The lady in distress turns out to be Joan Bennett whose uncle is being held prisoner in an insane asylum by bogus doctors who are

BULLDOG DRUMMOND (1922): The first and most faithful adaptation; Carlyle Blackwell, seen here disguised, played Drummond.

actually international crooks. There is little more plot to it than that, the development being a series of seesaw encounters with the villains, Drummond momentarily having the upper hand, only to lose it again. Lawrence Grant as Dr. Lakington was a deliciously slimy master villain, enjoying the opportunities for lechery and sadism as much as the monetary gains, and Montague Love (as Petersen) and the delightful Lilyan Tashman (as Irma) were his chief aides. In that era of relaxed censorship, Drummond was allowed to kill Dr. Lakington in comparatively cold blood (as punishment for the doctor's indiscreet fondling of the unconscious heroine) and to be a good enough sport to permit the basically sympathetic Petersen and Irma to escape the law.

It was all tongue-in-cheek, certainly, some of the exuberant action and villainy clearly played for laughs as much as excitement, and the whole mood dictated by the frequent shots of Drummond roaring through the night in his open roadster, grinning at the sheer joy of it all, his white scarf flapping in the wind, streaming out behind him like the white scarves of cavalier airmen in World War I movies.

BULLDOG DRUMMOND (1929): Ronald Colman was the first and best talkie Drummond.

If it wasn't quite as witty as it obviously thought it was, it can be forgiven for its smugness: in 1929 it was a real breakthrough. It recognized that the thriller was basically an entertainment, that it could be lighthearted to its advantage without sacrificing the effectiveness of its action and thrills. Certainly, this was too early for a satire of a genre that was hardly established, yet it worked on two levels: as a thriller and as a lighthearted spoof that *approached* satire. Among all the deadly serious detective films of the period and, in fact, amidst the leaden-paced films that were the norm, it was a breath of real fresh air.

BULLDOG DRUMMOND: Joan Bennett, Colman, Claude Allister.

Many critics pointed out that opponents of the sound film had only to look to *Bulldog Drummond* to realize what great possibilities the new medium had and, for once, critics and public were in agreement. While, in retrospect, Rouben Mamoulian's *Applause* (generally unappreciated at the time) can be seen to have been 1929's most significant movie, and academically its best, *Bulldog Drummond* is in many ways almost its equal. It made most of the "Ten Best" lists, although a kind of artistic snobbism pushed the very theatrical George Arliss vehicle *Disraeli* into first place, and the enormous popularity of the new Technicolor musicals was responsible for *Rio Rita* and *The Broadway Melody* garnering a few more votes. The director of *Bulldog Drummond* was F. Richard Jones, who had brought the same neat welding of seriousness and comedy to one of the last (and best) silent Fairbanks films, *The Gaucho*. He would appear to have made a totally successful changeover from silents to sound but, unfortunately, he died shortly after the Drummond film was completed.

Colman was rushed into an appropriate follow-up for Goldwyn, *Raffles,* and played it in the same vein. It was an enjoyable and tasteful romp but far less successful, due primarily to the fact that *Raffles* has a fairly uneventful story which is always repeated without change in each remake. Thus its principal value through the years has been as a showcase for personable and charming actors such as John Barrymore, Colman, and David Niven. When the star lacks their grace and magnetism—as House Peters did in a mid-twenties version—the property has nothing left to salvage it.

Fox's 1930 *Temple Tower* was a dull Drummond follow-up, now justifiably forgotten. Its creepy old house setting was ill used in a turgidly written and directed script and Kenneth MacKenna, projecting both a lack of self-confidence and an absence of virility (the very antithesis of Drummond), was probably the weakest player ever to tackle the role. None of Drummond's personal aides or Scotland Yard associates figured in the story, and only Henry B. Walthall's villain had any strength.

Drummond was temporarily abandoned for a few years and then revived by the new Twentieth Century company, releasing through United Artists, which was looking for blockbuster commercial subjects with which to establish itself. Its record was a good one for a while, but the momentum wasn't maintained and it finally merged with Fox to become Twentieth Century-Fox. The idea of another Drummond film, with Ronald Colman playing the lead again, was surefire and for once a mathematically designed film, aimed at the box-office pure and simple, paid off handsomely. Although the sequel, titled *Bulldog Drummond Strikes Back,* was less remarkable a film in the context of its year (1934) than the original had

BULLDOG DRUMMOND STRIKES BACK (1934): Ronald Colman vs. Warner Oland; in the background, Kathleen Burke, Mischa Auer, Georges Regas.

BULLDOG DRUMMOND STRIKES BACK: Halliwell Hobbes, Georges Regas, Ronald Colman.

been in 1929, by all other standards it was that rarity, a sequel superior to its original.

Detective purists sometimes denigrate the film because of its gaiety, and because there is no "mystery killer" to be tracked down and unmasked; but if there are any such rules governing the construction of detective novels or movies, *Bulldog Drummond Strikes Back* should more than justify the repudiation of them. Colman's dashing comedic flair was as much in evidence as before, but this time the lightheartedness was restricted to the "good guys," while the villains—Warner Oland, Georges Regas, Arthur Hohl, Mischa Auer, and Katherine DeMille, a formidable covey indeed—conducted their misdeeds without the slightest sign of a tongue in their swarthy cheeks.

The script delighted in dumping Drummond into the most inextricable of situations, have him admit the near impossibility of escape, and then proceed to effect that escape in a manner both absurd yet somehow logical. "Think of it, Algy!" he enthuses at one particularly dark

moment. "Alone, unarmed, surrounded by villains, locked in a cellar—from that, to complete mastery of the situation in ten minutes. If we can do that, we'll be magnificent!" At one point, too, Colman borrows a page from Oliver Hardy's comedy repertoire by looking directly at the audience, shrugging his shoulders in admitted defeat, and resigning himself to awaiting developments.

A secondary subplot and running gag involved the constant snatching of Algy (Charles Butterworth) from his bedroom on the night of his marriage to Una Merkel in order to rush off on derring-do, or to translate a code. The exploitation of this gag seems surprisingly risqué for a post–Production Code film and it has real bite yet, thanks to the innate charm of Butterworth and Merkel who worked extremely well together, it stays well within the bounds of good taste. The plot makes a point of kidding such clichés as the disappearing body, but by using them satirically it is able to use them *constantly* and so keep the plot in motion.

And the basic mystery plot is a good one: the sud-

BULLDOG JACK (1935): Atholl Fleming (left) as Drummond, with Jack Hulbert.

BULLDOG DRUMMOND AT BAY (1937): Hugh Miller and John Lodge (right) as Drummond.

BULLDOG DRUMMOND ESCAPES (1937): Ray Milland, Heather Angel.

denly changed room, the denial from all sides that the heroine ever had an uncle, the implication that she is imagining everything—all of this stemming originally from an actual happening at the Paris Exposition at the turn of the century when all traces of a person's existence had to be instantly wiped out since he had contacted the plague, news of which could have wiped out the fantastic investment in the Exposition. That actual story was filmed much later in a British film of 1950, *So Long at the Fair;* earlier, its basic premise had been used in a novel, *The Wheel Spins,* filmed by Alfred Hitchcock as *The Lady Vanishes.* In 1934 the plot—a good one by any standards—also had the advantage of being new to movie audiences.

While *Bulldog Drummond Strikes Back* perhaps scores most on its witty script and delightful playing (Loretta Young a most appealing lady-in-distress, C. Aubrey Smith a superbly irascible Colonel Nielsen of the Yard), it is also an extremely handsome film to look at, its sets beautifully designed, and superbly photographed by Peverell Marley. Roy del Ruth, the director of the first *Maltese Falcon,* kept it all moving with incredible verve. The two Drummond films with Colman remain models of their kind: no subsequent forays were as ambitiously planned or as successfully executed. In fact, with one late exception, Bulldog Drummond was rather surprisingly to be consigned to the "B" film field thereafter.

The British made their first Drummond talkie in the same year as Colman's *Bulldog Drummond Strikes Back.* The fact that it was similarly titled (*The Return of Bulldog Drummond*) and not as good consigned it to an early oblivion. However, it was faithful to the mood of the original stories and had a number of off-beat elements. Drummond, happily married and apparently retired, continues his crime-smashing while posing, Zorro-like, as a fop. (The film is too brisk to waste time on this masquerade, but establishes it quickly via dialogue.) His orthodox detection here is virtually nil; instead, as the mysterious leader of The Black Clan, he takes the law into his own hands in a crusade against warmongers and armaments profiteers.

Ralph Richardson played Drummond. It was only his third film, and though he was already a fine actor, he wasn't really the type for a dashing hero. Neurotic villainy (*The Ghoul, Things to Come*) were much more his forte. Moreover, he was too much the gentleman to look at home on a motorcycle as the black uniformed and goggled "Captain America" type who led The Black Clan on its avenging forays. He was fine at emulating the debonair polish of Colman, but less convincing as a man of action. Too, the character as written was not particularly attractive. When in command of the situation (and highhandedly undertaking kidnapping and assassination)

Drummond is suave and witty; but when he is outsmarted by his opponents, he loses both poise and temper. Nevertheless, it was a virile little film, good to look at, fast, and with top-notch sets and photography. The climax of the Clan rushing to Drummond's rescue via plane, car and motorcycle was really rousing.

Ann Todd, with little to do, was attractive as Mrs. Drummond, Claude Allister was Algy again, and Francis L. Sullivan made a superb Carl Peterson. Coincidentally, the following year Richardson played a wild and woolly Moriarty figure in the clever Drummond spoof, *Bulldog Jack.* Drummond was played by Atholl Fleming—rather too mature and stolid an actor for the role, but since he made only a couple of token appearances before turning the reins over to an impersonator (Jack Hulbert) it hardly mattered.

The year 1937 saw a total of four Drummond films, and three different actors in the role. The British *Bulldog Drummond at Bay* used American actors in the leads: John Lodge as the detective, Dorothy Mackaill as the girl, and Victor Jory as the villain. Claude Allister, who had been Algy in the first Colman film, repeated his dithering "silly ass" comedy in the same role. At the time, *Bulldog Drummond at Bay* seemed an exceptionally good thriller, and was certainly full of good melodramatic and serial-like incident. However, it does not survive the years well: much of the action is amateurishly staged, the miniature work (especially that involving the villain's escape and crash in a plane) too obvious, and the sets artificial. Nevertheless, it had a major asset in John Lodge who was, and is, one of the screen's best Drummonds. There was an aggressiveness in his speech and an arrogance in his bearing which would have made him ideal for the role had the novels' conception of Drummond been followed. Lodge was an extremely able actor in British and Hollywood movies of the thirties who was unfortunately lost to the screen when he moved into politics as the governor of Connecticut.

The first of the new Hollywood entries was *Bulldog Drummond Escapes.* Although based on a play by McNeile, it bore remarkable structural similarities to the first two Colman films, and Ray Milland was clearly basing his devil-may-care interpretation on the Colman performance. It was a slow but carefully made film, better and slightly longer than a "B" yet by no means an "A." The two following films showed, however, that Paramount had no illusions about making a "prestige" series and were quite content to turn out a "B" product with action and speed the dominant factors.

The first of the new series, *Bulldog Drummond Comes Back,* as is often the case, also turned out to be the best. Even if it did dash through the mystery like an express train, the plot—based on McNeile's *The Female of the*

Species—was a good one. An old enemy of Drummond's kidnaps his bride-to-be and leaves a series of clues, including complicated rhymes on phonograph records, the unraveling of which sends Drummond and his aides chasing all over England in pursuit of the next clue. A waterfront dive with a trapdoor into the Thames and an old mansion with a concealed time bomb are two of the venues for the good action scenes.

In this and in the remaining six films in the series, John Howard was Drummond, with E. E. Clive as the faithful butler Tenny and Reginald Denny as Algy. Again, Howard tried to emulate the Colman-Milland manner and acquired an unemphasized but adequate English accent. However, his American brusqueness and impatience were a departure from tradition, and may even have been a personal reaction against some of the foolish comedy interpolations. E. E. Clive, a consummate actor, made more than the most of his limited opportunities as the literate butler with a practical mind who frequently saves the situation. Reginald Denny, an extremely likable comedian, was badly wasted, however, with inane material. His tendency (in talkies) to overact was not curbed by a succession of relatively weak directors for the Drummond films. His bride, Gwen,

BULLDOG DRUMMOND ESCAPES: Ray Milland, Porter Hall, Heather Angel.

The new Drummond/Nielsen team: John Barrymore (left) and John Howard as Drummond.

wandered in and out of the films from time to time, but little was made of her.

The basic plus factor of *Bulldog Drummond Comes Back,* apart from its speed and the written-and-played-with-relish villainy of J. Carrol Naish, was the presence of John Barrymore as Inspector Nielsen. It was virtually an insult to place an actor of his caliber into a "B" action series, and giving him top billing was hardly a compensation. (Youngsters of the period, who had never heard of Barrymore, could never understand why his name was billed above that of Howard, who carried all the action, and they resented it.) Nevertheless, perhaps because the role seemed to have been tailored for him, Barrymore entered into the spirit of the film with gusto and gave a delightful performance. It seems unlikely that a Scotland Yard official would stoop to donning disguises (and, into the bargain, disguises so grotesque that they invited attention) but, that consideration apart, Barrymore had a grand time with the role and played effectively during the straight dramatic moments. Much of the pantomime and byplay seemed to be improvisational on his part. Removing a false nose and stretching the putty to an elongated point, he intones mournfully, "To think that I should ever descend to being an *actor!*"

Although it was most enjoyable, *Bulldog Drummond Comes Back* was undeniably cheap and set the pattern for the rest of the series. All of them were brisk, running just about an hour. Much of the action took place at night or was confined to the interior of houses so that standing sets could be used without additional art direction to convert street and building sets into some semblance of being British. The idea of the delayed wedding was parlayed into a running plot gimmick for the whole series, and soon became predictable, silly, and tiresome. Louise Campbell was the initial Phyllis Clavering, and then the role was taken over by the equally ladylike,

John Barrymore in disguise as Colonel Nielsen in BULLDOG DRUMMOND COMES BACK (1937).

charming, and thoroughly British Heather Angel. While the series *was* formularized, it was slick, and such limited standards as it set itself it maintained to the end. It also boasted an interesting array of guest villains, ranging from J. Carrol Naish and Porter Hall to George Zucco, Eduardo Cianelli, and Leo G. Carroll.

The second in the series, *Bulldog Drummond's Revenge,* was unquestionably the weakest. Nothing whatsoever happened in the film—certainly no kind of action that could remotely be constituted as "revenge"—and Frank Puglia was a mild and ineffective villain.

But the others—*Bulldog Drummond's Peril, Bulldog Drummond in Africa, Arrest Bulldog Drummond, Bulldog Drummond's Secret Police,* and *Bulldog Drummond's Bride*—all had their comments. If nothing else, there was the polished bravura villainy of George Zucco in *Arrest Bulldog Drummond,* about to drop a netful of Drummond's aides into a pit of slime ("Care to come and see the splash?") or J. Carrol Naish in *Bulldog Drummond in Africa,* tolerantly accepting the slurs on his honor from Colonel Nielsen and retaliating by binding him to a tree just out of the reach of a (loosely) chained lion.

Bulldog Drummond's Secret Police, based on *Temple Tower,* turned out to have quite surprising quality in its second half. Initially, one felt one was in for a real "economy" film since Drummond, in a state of prewed-

BULLDOG DRUMMOND COMES BACK (1937): Algy (Reginald Denny) captured by J. Carrol Naish.

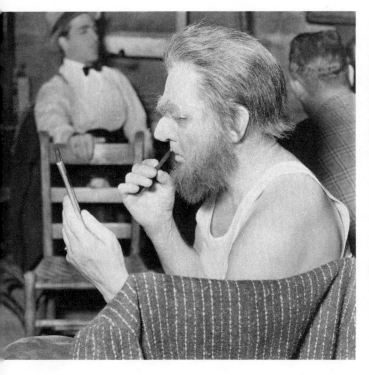

ding jitters, dreams of his past adventures and we are treated to a number of stock footage highlights from earlier films in the series. But the prolonged climactic prowlings in the tunnels of the castle—complete with hidden treasure, ancient torture instruments, and an underground torrent—are fine stuff. The elaborate set was constructed specifically for this film and was not a borrowed castoff from another, and the whole atmospheric sequence—with Leo G. Carroll as the mad killer —was superbly lit and photographed. Had more of the series had the quality of this one sequence, it might have been both more important and more successful.

Three actors played Colonel Nielsen in the Paramount Drummonds. Sir Guy Standing essayed the role in *Bulldog Drummond Escapes*. He was a fine actor of the old George Arliss school: essentially, always the same with a hesitant style of dialogue delivery that initially suggested spontaneity, but could soon be recognized as an acquired mannerism. But if he always gave the same performance, then the kind of roles he had—the stalwart British commander on the Indian frontier, the gentleman crook, the urbane detective—always fortuitously demanded that particular performance. He was an ideal Nielsen. Unfortunately, it was his last role; he died of a heart attack shortly after its completion.

John Barrymore took over as a much more colorful Nielsen in *Bulldog Drummond Comes Back*. But there were problems with the second and third films in the John Howard group. Either the novelty had worn off for Barrymore and he was proving hard to handle, so that

the scenarists literally wrote him out of the films except for token appearances, *or* his roles were initially so small that Barrymore resented it and showed it by his performances. Either way, his Nielsen became morose and bad tempered, shouting his lines, glowering, mugging, and showing no signs of wanting to give either a serious performance or a gaily lighthearted one.

That excellent actor H. B. Warner was brought in to replace him. Oddly enough, Warner (possibly in awe of Barrymore) based his *initial* Nielsen performance on Barrymore's last bad ones. Warner, too, became short tempered and overacted badly, qualities extremely uncharacteristic of Warner's subtle and usually underplayed acting style. However, either the word got to Warner or he recognized his own shortcomings in the role for by the next film he had reverted to his own natural, dignified style, and for the rest of the series was a tower of strength as Nielsen.

With Drummond finally married off to Phyllis at the end of *Bulldog Drummond's Bride*, the series came to an end in 1939. Critics had been unusually harsh toward it, irritated, no doubt, by its unnecessary comedy and that irksome delayed-wedding ritual and, when they had the opportunity to bid it farewell, they did so with enthusiasm!

Bulldog Drummond was absent from the screen during the war years, the generally unenthusiastic response to the idea of Sherlock Holmes pitting himself against the Nazis perhaps preventing Drummond from following the same route. His ultimate return was unheralded and

BULLDOG DRUMMOND COMES BACK: A simple set that, underlit, serves effectively as a hidden room with a trapdoor to the Thames.

ARREST BULLDOG DRUMMOND (1938): Jean Fenwick, George Zucco and Georges Regas with Death-Ray constructed from old projection equipment.

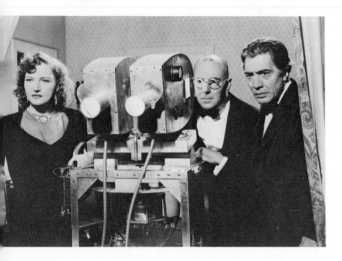

Richard Johnson, the Drummond of DEADLIER THAN THE MALE and SOME GIRLS DO.

BULLDOG DRUMMOND'S SECRET POLICE (1939): Reginald Denny, E. E. Clive, Heather Angel, John Howard and H. B. Warner threatened by Leo G. Carroll.

largely unnoticed. In 1947 Columbia made *Bulldog Drummond at Bay,* with Ron Randell in the lead. Some attempt was made to utilize British players in supporting roles—Terry Kilburn, for example—but on the whole it was just a routine "B." No better and somewhat slower were 1948's *The Challenge* and *Thirteen Lead Soldiers,* with Tom Conway playing Drummond with little differentiation between it and his better known role as The Falcon. Again, they were just "B"s.

In 1951 MGM made their first Drummond film, the best in many years, though its merits are only relative. Obviously, MGM had no great interest in resurrecting Drummond for a series, but it was a period when co-production between Hollywood and England was financially advantageous. British production was also a useful way of utilizing production and acting talent that would otherwise lie dormant in Hollywood while still drawing contractual salaries. *Calling Bulldog Drummond* had typical MGM production gloss, top photography (F. A. Young), and a good director in Victor Saville. A perhaps slightly-too-mature Walter Pidgeon was cast as Drummond, but rather effectively so, the plot explaining away his age by presenting him as an older Drummond called out of retirement by a Scotland Yard unable to cope with a current crime wave. David Tomlinson provided subdued comedy relief, Robert Beatty was a good villain, and Margaret Leighton, Bernard Lee, and James Hayter were other thoroughly reliable players in an above-average cast. It was the last of the traditional Drummond mysteries.

Cashing in on the James Bond phenomenon and the audience interest in crime-spy-detection films when laced with gimmicks, sex, and brutality—and increasingly elaborate physical action—*Deadlier Than the Male* was an aggressively up-to-date Drummond adventure. Nigel Green, whose face suggests too much integrity for him to be a really desirable villain, was nevertheless a good enough actor to overcome that "handicap" and make a really formidable Carl Peterson, employing sexy and deadly female assassins as part of his international operations. The killings were sadistic and ingenious, and Richard Johnson's fashionable boudoir activity helped compensate for the somewhat chaste lives led by previous Drummonds. It, and a similar 1971 sequel, *Some Girls Do,* also with Richard Johnson, rate a nod of approval for being at least the most spectacular and expensively mounted of all the Drummond films—and for allowing the detective hero to make his farewell (if, indeed, it is to be that) from the screen in a blaze of glory instead of in an ignominious "B." But with all their size and color, to say nothing of the delectable Elke Sommer and Sylvia Koscina in brief bikinis, they were unable to approach (let alone duplicate) the charm and flair of Ronald Colman's two definitive Drummond films more than three decades earlier.

H. B. Warner, the Nielsen of the later Drummonds.

CALLING BULLDOG DRUMMOND (1951): Walter Pidgeon, David Tomlinson.

7 THE ORIENTAL DETECTIVES

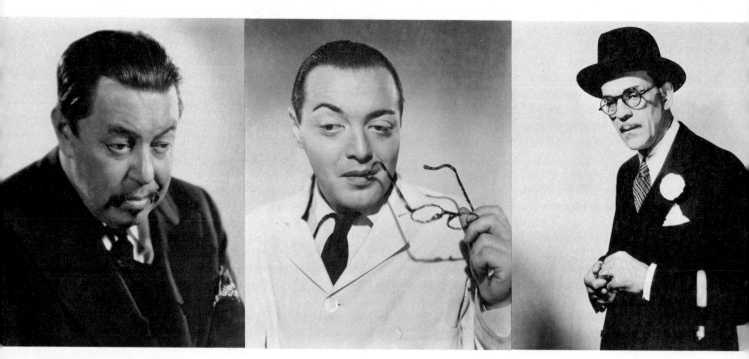

Warner Oland as Charlie Chan.　　　Peter Lorre as Mr. Moto.　　　Boris Karloff as Mr. Wong.

The Oriental sleuth was virtually ignored by the silent film, and the fact that the most famous fictional one of them all, Charlie Chan, was not created by Earl Derr Biggers until 1925 is only partially a contributing factor. During the teens and twenties, the height of "Yellow Peril" concern, the Oriental was almost invariably depicted on the screen as either a subhuman menial or as a cunning villain. The outstanding exceptions to this rule—the popular American films of Japanese star Sessue Hayakawa—were unique in that for the most part they did not have contemporary settings or connotations, and sought instead to be artistic and poetic picturizations of Japan's legends. For the rest, the Oriental was a standard villain in such films as *Old San Francisco* or the Fu Manchu films; or, if he *was* depicted sympathetically (as in Griffith's *Broken Blossoms* or the Lon Chaney vehicle *Shadows*), he compensated for that sympathy by dying very conveniently at the end.

From the beginning, though, film makers were convinced that there was something exotic—and commercial

—about the combination of the Oriental and a mystery plot, as witness the reproduced trade paper advertisement for Edison's 1915 *The Mission of Mr. Foo,* with its decidedly peculiar conceptions of Chinese characteristics. *The Mission of Mr. Foo* had no detective, but was otherwise a clear-cut forerunner of the Fu Manchu brand of detective adventure. One of H. C. McNeile's Bulldog Drummond stories was titled *Bulldog Drummond and the Oriental Mind,* and Sir Nayland Smith's condescension and outrageous racial slurs on the Chinese in the film of *The Mask of Fu Manchu* (1932) were undiplomatic, to say the least, for a representative of the British government. In *The Kennel Murder Case,* Eugene Pallette as Sergeant Heath is all ready to snap the handcuffs on the Chinese cook and accuse him of the murder merely because "The Chinese are full of those tricks"!

So it's not surprising that, even after the success of the first Charlie Chan books in the late twenties, producers were cautious in springing an Oriental "good guy" on audiences in large doses and introduced Charlie only casually.

A year after *The House Without a Key* was published, Pathe turned it into a ten-chapter serial for their popular team of Walter Miller and Allene Ray. The year was 1926 and Charlie, in a supporting role, was played by George Kuwa, a Japanese actor. No prints are known to exist.

Far more disturbing is the loss of *The Chinese Parrot* (1928), the next Chan film. Concentrated searches of the world's archives and company vaults have thus far failed to reveal a single print of this film, which is admittedly less important as a Charlie Chan vehicle than as the second American film of the notable German pictorialist director, Paul Leni. It was his follow-up to the highly successful *The Cat and the Canary,* and contemporary reviews show that it employed the same highly stylized and symbolic pictorial style. The same reviews indicate that Japanese actor Sojin (who had a decidedly villainous appearance but also a sense of fun) stole the show quite effortlessly with his Chan portrayal.

The third Chan film, and the first talkie one, 1929's *Behind That Curtain* still exists in the form of one good 35-mm. print secured in Fox's Beverly Hills vaults. It disappoints on two levels, however. First, it was reshaped as a vehicle for Warner Baxter and Lois Moran, who spend the bulk of the film fleeing across the desert from a murder charge wrongfully hanging over Baxter's head. Chan appears only briefly toward the end of the film in the not very prepossessing person of E. L. Park, a British actor. Significantly, Chan turns up out of nowhere with the vital evidence in the case, but his utilization is almost a lazy plot lever.

Considering the success of *The Chinese Parrot,* Fox's failure to exploit the character more fully is hard to understand. The film itself, while it goes out of its way to exploit different kinds of sound effects and a variety of languages, is dull and plodding. The desert locales do nothing but emphasize the space in which nothing happens and also limits the number of characters involved, so that the interchange of dialogue is lengthened into tedium by long delays and reactions. The whole film is much more pedestrian than its basically good story and cast (including Boris Karloff) would indicate.

The series proper, with Chan spotlighted and starred, got under way in 1931 with *Charlie Chan Carries On,* and the Swedish actor Warner Oland, heretofore primarily typed as a villain, proving a most engaging Chan. In fact, Oland provides the only real explanation for the continuing popularity of the series. He made sixteen Chans for Fox, and on his death Sidney Toler assumed the role to make another eleven before moving over to a much lesser continuation of the series at Monogram.

None of the twenty-seven Fox Chans could be considered truly outstanding though, oddly enough, the later ones with Sidney Toler (who was personally well below the Oland standard) tended to be slicker, better paced, and often more imaginative in their stories. The whole series was directed either by former important directors now slipping to oblivion by the "B" picture route, or by newcomers or promoted assistant directors gaining experience on the way up. They were essentially formula pictures but, happily, it was a formula that was liked and was held together by Oland's easygoing style and musical diction. There was never much mystery about any of the "hidden killers" in the Chan movies, nor much variety in their unmasking. Invariably, Chan would gather all the suspects in one room, detail each one's participation in the case, and finally turn on the guilty party with a complacent "You are murderer!" No matter how cunning the killer had been up until that point, he would invariably throw in the towel right away, or perhaps rasp "Very clever, Mr. Chan" and make a halfhearted attempt at escape. Since in many cases Chan was just bluffing, the piece of damning evidence he held in his hands merely a sheet of blank paper, a little more self-assurance and patience on the part of "murderer" would probably have enabled him to put Chan firmly in his place through lack of evidence.

Most of the Chans were slow, and here the "fringe benefits" of Warner Oland were used to advantage. He had a happy knack of getting the most out of (and even devising) the wise and witty Chinese aphorisms. Some, such as "Alibi, like dead fish, cannot stand test of time!", were genuinely amusing and related to the action at hand. Most, however, were merely inserted at regular intervals as a kind of punctuation, and would have lost their effect without Oland's winning way of reading them.

The *Cinema News* describes this as

"The Rarest Type of Cinema Play."

Here is a chance to show your patrons something different.

Get "The Mission of Mr. Foo."

Gorgeous Chinese settings.

Rare specimens of Chinese antiques and lacquer work which took six months to collect.

Real Chinese actors—this is the astounding part of the subject, on account of the fact that the Chinese won't face the camera.

And a plot dealing with subtle Chinese cunning, and political intriguing. Simply great! Get it.

That's why "The Mission of Mr. Foo" is called the rarest type of cinema play.

The Mission of Mr. Foo

Released Monday, June 7th.
Approx. 1,135 ft.

SIX-SHEET AND QUAD-CROWN POSTERS.

164, Wardour Street, London, W. Phone: Regent 668

THE MISSION OF MR. FOO (1915).

Chan's large and fluctuating family relieved the monotony, too, and the gradual increase of footage for the number one and number two sons was definitely to the films' advantage, since it broke up the action from a concentration on Chan's plodding sleuthing and permitted cutaways to subplots with an element of physical action.

But if Oland's Chan films as a group don't seem to deserve the success they have achieved, at least they offered some entertaining diversions. Their casts were often quite interesting, with players like Ray Milland and Rita Hayworth using them as schoolrooms on their way to stardom, while "guest stars" (though they were never billed as such) like Boris Karloff and Bela Lugosi made colorful red herring suspects.

One notable exception to the rather disappointing overall quality of the series was 1935's *Charlie Chan in Egypt,* Oland's eighth and easily the best. The location—Egyptian tombs—enabled the film to be developed as a thriller and even as a semihorror film, and not just as a detective mystery. Effective use of background music, good set design, and superb camerawork by Daniel Clark created some genuinely nightmarish sequences which are still chilling today. (Some of Fox's best cameramen were assigned to the series. Apart from Clark, Hal Mohr, Rudolph Maté, Ernest Palmer, George Schneiderman, and Lucien Andriot worked on various Chan films.) Stepin

THE HOUSE WITHOUT A KEY (1926): George Kuwa, the screen's first Charlie Chan.

THE CHINESE PARROT (1928): SoJin (Chan No. 2) with Edmund Burns.

THE HOUSE WITHOUT A KEY: Allene Ray, Walter Miller, George Kuwa.

BEHIND THAT CURTAIN: Warner Baxter, Lois Moran.

Fetchit's bizarre racist comedy as the Negro stereotype to end them all also dovetailed rather nicely with the unemphasized racial quality of Oland's performance, in which Oriental humility was constantly succeeding where white arrogance failed. But in terms of mystery, and despite a rich and fruity assortment of suspects, there was never for a moment any doubt about the identity of the killer in *Charlie Chan in Egypt*. Behavioral patterns and Fox's rigid adherence to formula right away knocked out everybody but Frank Conroy!

Even in some of the later Sidney Toler Chans, Fox's refusal to be innovational robbed the series of surprise elements. *Charlie Chan on Treasure Island* had one of the most ingenious plots of all, and one of the cleverest concealments of the villain; yet a typical plot contrivance knocked the supports out from under their carefully constructed box of tricks, and tipped off the "surprise" revelation of the killer's identity somewhat ahead of schedule.

Twentieth Century-Fox concluded their Chan series, still on a fairly high level of competence for such a long-running series, with *Castle in the Desert* in 1942. They were now clearly "B" pictures, but were not markedly different from the first films in the series which had rated "A" playing time mostly by virtue of their initial novelty and the Oland personality.

Even the earlier films had been commendably brief, however; 65–71 minutes was the average running time, and only *Charlie Chan in London* (1934), at 79 minutes, had really gone on too long for its own good. (Especially as the hidden killer was even more obvious than usual!) The last Warner Oland entry, *Charlie Chan at Monte Carlo* (1938), had been by far the weakest of his group, possibly due to his own ill health, but largely because of the excessive footage given to the overacted theatrical French policeman of Harold Huber, and perhaps too because the old team was getting a little bored. Certainly, the addition of Norman Foster to the panel of directors added much-needed vitality to the new Sidney Toler series.

Fox exercised considerable ingenuity in finding new locales for Chan's investigations and in keeping them topical where possible. The 1936 Olympics provided a useful excuse to take Charlie to Berlin for a collaboration with the German police. *Charlie Chan at the Olympics* was livelier than most in its period, and the interpolation of newsreel footage of the games with neat back projection and the use of some of Fox's standing sets created an effective illusion that the film might have been shot there.

Fox's scenarists were constantly coming up with new plot gimmicks for Charlie, and some of the unused stories *sound* a great deal better than ones that *were* selected. The old Andrew Soutar novel *The Devil's Triangle,* filmed in 1932 with Ralph Bellamy as *Almost Married,* was revamped in 1940 as a Chan property. Particularly intriguing is *Charlie Chan in Vaudeville,* written in 1937 by actor-director-writer Gregory Ratoff. Charlie is a guest star on a vaudeville bill though the synopsis, alas, gives no indication as to the nature of his act. Presumably, the project was shelved because the location was Paris and Charlie had already been there in 1935, immediately before his trips to Egypt and Shanghai. However, elements of the plot turned up in later Chans.

Charlie Chan at College might have been especially intriguing, since for once it seemed to be deliberately leading the audience up the garden path and might even have fooled them. Charlie is lecturing on criminology at college and during his talk a murder is committed. He stays on to solve the case and more murders follow, with the Oriental history professor a prime suspect. During the obligatory confrontation with suspects, Chan forces a confession from the least likely party—whereupon all of the murder victims walk in, very much alive. The whole charade was a hoax staged by Charlie to illustrate his thesis!

Equally tongue-in-cheek, even to its title, was *Charlie Chan Comes Clean* in which Charlie and son Lee work under cover but keep in touch by writing messages in Chinese to each other on linen. Charlie has set up a Chinese laundry as a blind so that the passage back and forth of so many messages in Chinese will pass unnoticed!

Undoubtedly, the most exciting prospect of all was a story written in 1942, possibly in an attempt to revitalize the Chan series, forgotten when the series was abandoned. Titled *The Four Star Murder Case,* it dealt with a jewel robbery and a series of bizarre murders in one of those "upstate New York mansions" which proliferate so conveniently for detective fiction writers. Philo Vance is on hand as a guest when the trouble starts—and when his investigations do not yield immediate results, Charlie Chan, Mr. Moto, and Fox's current private eye, Michael Shayne, are called in to lend a hand. The mystery itself does not seem worthy of their combined efforts, though it would have been worth the waste of their talents to

BEHIND THAT CURTAIN (1929): E. L. Park (right), Chan No. 3, with Gilbert Emery.

Warner Oland, fourth and best known of the Charlie Chans.

CHARLIE CHAN IN PARIS (1935): Warner Oland, John Miljan, Henry Kolker.

CHARLIE CHAN IN EGYPT (1935): Warner Oland flanked by obvious red herring Nigel de Brulier, heroine Pat Patterson, least suspicious suspect Frank Conroy and hero Thomas Beck.

CHARLIE CHAN IN LONDON (1934): Warner Oland, E. E. Clive, Ray Milland, Alan Mowbray.

see Charlie Chan and Mr. Moto politely exchanging Oriental pleasantries before (presumably) Mr. Moto was returned to his wartime internment camp.

Charlie Chan's move to Monogram in 1944, after a two-year hiatus, did not bode well. Although Monogram, a small company, had made good "B" films, they lacked the slickness of their competitor studio Republic and when it came to "series" films—whether westerns or comedies—they had a reputation for losing interest quickly and slashing already none-too-generous budgets. Since the very first entry, *Charlie Chan in the Secret Service,* was already a tedious and talkative film with a dreary musical score, there wasn't much cause for optimism. Too, Sidney Toler —who had never been as personable an actor as Warner Oland, but had at least approached his Fox Chans with a certain zest—was now beginning to show his age and ambled through his routine scripts with little enthusiasm.

In an attempt to expand the comedy values of the series, increasing footage was devoted to the sleuthing misadventures of the Chan offspring (usually Benson Fong, though later Keye Luke and Victor Sen Yung, individually or as a pair) and their traditionally scared Negro chauffeur, played by Mantan Moreland.

The films were produced by the independent team of Philip Krasne and James Burkett; the first five were directed by Phil Rosen, and after that by alternating directors who included Phil Karlson, Lesley Selander, Terry Morse, and William Beaudine.

Sidney Toler died in 1947 after eleven Chans and a then relatively unknown character actor, Roland Winters, was brought in for another six films, beginning with *The Chinese Ring* in 1947 and concluding with *Sky Dragon* in 1949. Certainly, there was no attempt to increase the budgets for this final group. Some of them even saved on scenario money by reusing old Monogram stories: *Docks of New Orleans* was a fairly exact remake of the first of Monogram's "Mr. Wong" series with Boris Karloff. And, when the stories called for more exotic locales (Mexico or a South American jungle), the limited resources of Monogram's rather tatty art direction, backed up by over-zealous use of the process screen, were taxed to their utmost.

But, in some ways, the six Winters films had more life to them than the Tolers, even if less production values. The casts seemed a little better: interesting veterans like Nils Asther, Evelyn Brent, Robert Livingston, Douglas Fowley, Erville Alderson, George Lewis, Lyle Talbot, and Iris Adrian added conviction and expertise to supporting roles. And Roland Winters himself was an amiable ham who seemed to delight in the role and play it to the hilt.

Recognizing this, writers seemed to construct their dialogue with *him* rather than Chan in mind and the result

CHARLIE CHAN IN LONDON: Supporting players Murray Kinnell and Drue Layton (left) with the film's director Eugene Forde and at right, assistant director Edward O'Fearna (brother of John Ford).

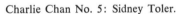

Charlie Chan No. 5: Sidney Toler.

Toler's assistants in his Monogram series: Victor Sen Yung as Number One Son, and Mantan Moreland as Birmingham, the chauffeur.

Roland Winters as Charlie Chan No. 6 in THE GOLDEN EYE (1948), with Tim Ryan and Bruce Kellog.

was a good deal of deliberately florid dialogue which genially kidded the old Chan delivery. Whereas Warner Oland had a distinctive way of wrapping up a scene by murmuring in clipped tones, "Thank you so much," Winters had a tendency to *dismiss* the scene with a flippant "Well, so much for—so much." And on one memorable occasion he instructed an aide to inform him whenever "any other incidents permit themselves the luxury of occurring."

Chan's movie demise was a casualty of the systematic disappearance of the "B" film, and especially of the glut of half-hour detective films made especially for television. Chan himself ventured into television via a series starring J. Carrol Naish, and plans afoot to produce a two-hour Chan color special for television may or may not have been affected by the disappointing reaction to Sherlock Holmes' pioneering foray into the same market with *The Hound of the Baskervilles.*

The Chan movies themselves, staples on television for years, in the early 1970s suddenly found themselves the center of a new cult, part of the general craze for nostalgia of the thirties and forties. As a result, they were repackaged, their television licensing fees skyrocketed, and, placed on the 16-mm. market, they commanded hefty rental rates commensurate with fees for major classics. (A few years earlier, smaller distributors had no interest or faith in them whatsoever, and they could be booked for as little as five dollars!)

Mr. Moto, the Japanese detective created by J. P. Marquand, joined Twentieth Century-Fox in 1937, just before the death of Warner Oland, and for a very brief period the two sleuths worked side by side. Moto operated rather differently from Chan, employing disguises, working under cover, watching and waiting, and then pouncing in the last reel. There was much more scope to the Moto adventures, and murder was often only an incidental. The films gave the impression of being produced on a much bigger scale than the Chan films, but this was largely an illusion. Moto got out of doors more than Chan, so that there was a greater use of exterior locations. Too, there was more physical action, resulting in well-staged chases through the elaborate Fox street sets, which in the Chans were often used only for quick establishing scenes. Moto was also a small lithe man, and an expert at jujitsu: with the help of a double, of course, Peter Lorre engaged in some extremely lively fight scenes which often brought the films to a much more rousing conclusion than the predictable confrontations of the Chans.

Lorre made eight Mr. Moto films between *Think Fast Mr. Moto* in 1937 and *Mr. Moto Takes a Vacation* in 1939. Although *Mr. Moto on Danger Island* was rather below the prevailing standards, perhaps because director

THANK YOU MR. MOTO (1937): Peter Lorre, John Carradine.

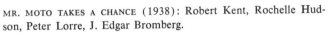

MR. MOTO TAKES A CHANCE (1938): Robert Kent, Rochelle Hudson, Peter Lorre, J. Edgar Bromberg.

RETURN OF MR. MOTO (1965): Henry Silva.

MR. MOTO IN DANGER ISLAND (1939): Robert Lowery, Jean Hersholt, Peter Lorre, Leon Ames, Richard Lane.

Herbert Leeds seemed unable to get any speed into it, and the story *was* fairly commonplace, even it was an entertaining little film. Six of the eight were directed by former actor Norman Foster, who became a really notable though infrequent director in the mid-forties. Even the last film in the series, *Mr. Moto Takes a Vacation,* was an expert blending of fun, mystery, and action, showing no slackening of enthusiasm.

It also had a particularly strong duo of villain suspects in Joseph Schildkraut and Lionel Atwill. Atwill, as the most obvious suspect, was sometimes handled so much for comedy ("Oh, what a zany I am!" he exclaims in mock chagrin as he drops a vase that is a key piece of evidence) that is seemed almost as though the scenarists (Philip MacDonald and Norman Foster) were outsmarting the audience for once, and that the number one suspect would indeed turn out to be the number one heavy!

The series was finally dropped partly because Lorre was going on to bigger roles, and because the war situation made acceptance of a Japanese hero dubious.

In 1939 Warner Brothers made an amusing satire of the Moto films in *Porky's Movie Mystery,* an oddball cartoon in which Porky Pig, as Moto, is called back from an island vacation to run down a phantom killer who is terrorizing Hollywood and who, when finally unmasked, is revealed to be Hugh Herbert! Mr. Moto made only one curtain call on the screen, also for Fox, in *The Return of Mr. Moto* (1965). It was a more ambitious film than the Lorre ones, though still relatively short. Henry Silva, however, made no attempt at a characterization that would distinguish Moto from any one of a dozen private eyes and secret agents in films at that time, and if there had been any thought of reactivating the series it was quickly quashed.

Cashing in on both Charlie Chan and Mr. Moto, Monogram Pictures ushered in their own Oriental detective in 1938 with Boris Karloff as *Mr. Wong, Detective.* Possibly his effective playing of a Chinese warlord the year before in *West of Shanghai* had suggested the casting. With horror films temporarily in the doldrums and his career needing a fresh tangent, Karloff jumped at the chance to play the gentlemanly and dignified sleuth of the Hugh Wiley stories.

It was an unexpectedly lucky break for Monogram, too; in 1939 horror films returned with a vengeance and Karloff, making expensive chillers for Universal and lesser ones for Columbia, was suddenly a much bigger name than Monogram could have afforded were he not already contracted. His Mr. Wong was a very methodical detective in the Holmes manner, deducing much from the smallest of clues, and conducting all of his interro-

gations with flawless good manners. His only concession to Oriental characteristics was a minimum of slant-eye makeup, blackened and greased-down hair, and, most of all, a calm imperturability in the face of all disasters. This demeanor was underlined by the contrasting of Captain Street, a brash, loud detective given to hasty conclusions and of value only in providing physical brawn to help Wong out of an occasional tight spot. Street was played by Grant Withers, and was a parallel to the equally loud and unthinking Lieutenant Steve McBride, being played by Barton MacLane over at Warner Brothers in the Torchy Blane thrillers.

The first Wong film was by far the best, and a credit to a small company like Monogram. Its script was good, the characters interesting, the mystery well developed with an extremely ingenious method of murder (if partially inspired by a device in *Charlie Chan in Egypt*) and for once the identity of the killer was a genuine surprise, yet a logical one.

No little credit for the success of *Mr. Wong, Detective* belongs to Scott R. Dunlap, an expert producer who obviously enjoyed making movies, and really tried for "plus" quality. Monogram used—or exploited—him by signing him to produce the initial ventures in several new series (The Cisco Kid, the Rough Riders) and gave him a decent budget so that the series could establish a reputation. Then, his job done, he was replaced by a lesser producer and a reduced budget and the series would coast for a while on its momentum before deteriorating into a more routine product.

The next two Wong films, *Mystery of Mr. Wong* and *Mr. Wong in Chinatown,* were again produced by Dunlap and retained his values. The fourth and fifth—*The Fatal Hour* and *Doomed to Die*—were done without him and showed it, although they still had good plots and the Karloff performance. Whereas the Dunlap films had been specials, their production and release staggered, the last two were both made within 1940 and, in fact, were joined by a third Wong film, *Phantom of Chinatown,* in which Key Luke experimentally tried the role. It was a rather good melodrama, somewhat above the standards of *Doomed to Die,* but without Karloff in the lead exhibitors lost interest in the series, and it was dropped.

Enjoyable and diverting as the mysteries of Messrs. Chan, Moto, and Wong were, they of course remain nothing more than formula entertainments. It is to the Japanese that we must turn for a classic film on the Oriental sleuth—although actually the film in question, *High and Low* (1963, directed by Akiro Kurosawa), is based on an American novel by Ed McBain and is not markedly Japanese in theme or action, other than for the value it places on personal honor and integrity.

MYSTERY OF MR. WONG (1938): Craig Reynolds, Boris Karloff, Ivan Lebedeff.

MR. WONG, DETECTIVE (1938): Boris Karloff.

Grant Withers played Captain Street in all of the Mr. Wong films with Karloff.

Keye Luke took over as Mr. Wong in PHANTOM OF CHINATOWN (1940).

DAUGHTER OF SHANGHAI (1937): Philip Ahn as a Chinese FBI man, with Anna May Wong.

Undoubtedly, it is the most complex detective film of all, although I use the word "complex" in reference to its structure and to the several levels (moralistic, symbolic, narrative) on which it operates. It is not "complex" in the way that the circuitous plot of a *Big Sleep* is complex; on the contrary, its story line is well ordered and its characters uncomplicated. Although the detectives who solve the case occupy a good deal of the second half of the film and they are presented very much as individuals, at the same time their work is depicted as a team effort and the concentration on individuals is limited to the villain (a kidnapper) and his victim, the father of a child. Only it subsequently turns out that the child is safe and that the kidnapped child is actually the son of one of his own employees. Does his responsibility, or the actions he has set in motion, lessen thereby?

The first half of the film is necessarily actionless, though far from static; the second half, concerned with the chase, has both physical action and steadily mounting tension. It is far too good and classically constructed a film to be dismissed as "merely" a detective thriller, although detective aficionados can find it only a model of its kind. It provides the same kind of thorough and increasingly rewarding satisfaction that one gets from repeated viewings of *Citizen Kane,* and it contains so many nuances of narrative, photographic technique, and act-

ing (Toshiro Mifune's ordinary, confused little businessman is a superbly realistic portrait, the bravura style of his samurai roles completely suppressed) that, like *Citizen Kane,* it demands seeing far more than once. Its use of the CinemaScope screen area alone is innovative and exciting; for once here is a film that really explores that once fashionable screen shape instead of being merely trapped by it.

By any and all standards, *High and Low* belongs in Chapter 4 of this book as an example of a great detective film, but it so transcends the genre (as *The Maltese Falcon* did too) that to have attached it, for discussion and comparison purposes, to those more orthodox films would have created an untenable inconsistency.

These few notes can hardly do it justice, but the detailed analysis of the film in Donald Richie's *The Films of Akiro Kurosawa* (University of California Press, 1965) is highly recommended reading, while the film itself— and hopefully it will always continue to remain in some kind of distribution—should be given the highest priority rating by any detective devotee whom the film has so far eluded, probably by virtue of its unpromising title (much subtler and more meaningful in the context of the film, and in its pretranslation stage) and its strangely unappetizing advertising.

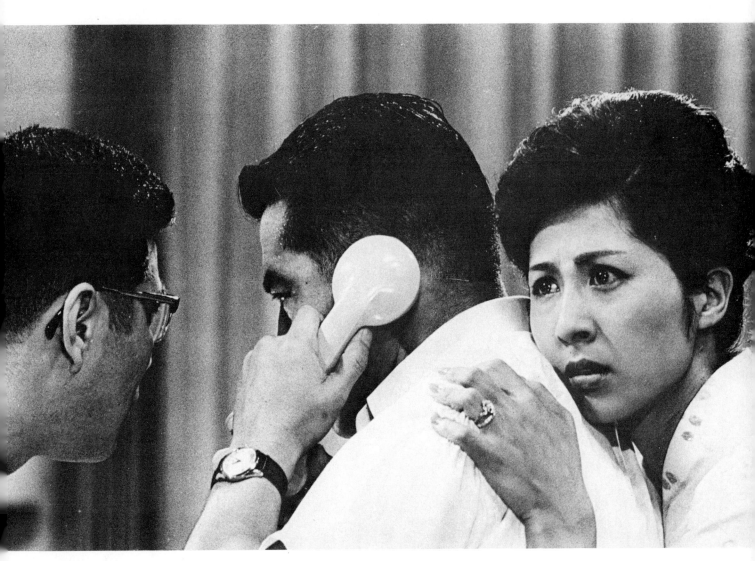

HIGH AND LOW: The detective, left, listens in while the husband
(Toshiro Mifune) talks to the kidnapper.

8 THE PRIVATE EYES:
1. The Gentlemen

PRIVATE DETECTIVE 62 (1933): William Powell, Margaret Lindsay.

If, in this computerized age, one were to mathematically isolate the various ingredients that go into the making of a successful detective (or mystery) movie, some amazing and revealing generalizations might appear. Even without a computer, one can take all of the titles of mystery movies (at least from 1929 on) and find a surprisingly consistent reliance on certain words.

For example, up to the mid-forties, the words "murder" and "mystery" recur most frequently in titles. After about 1947 there is a shift and, strangely enough, among the oft-used words now are "street" and "city" (as in *The Sleeping City, The Street with no Name, The Naked City*). Crime has somehow become urbanized: the emphasis is not on the individual murder, but on the layers of political graft and organized crime uncovered by the investigation of a single crime. Interestingly enough, one word that overlaps both periods is "night": titles like *The Longest Night, Night of Terror, Night of Mystery,* and *Under Cover of Night* in the pre-forties; *The Night and the City, The Night Walker, The Night Holds Terror, The*

Night Has a Thousand Eyes in the later years. This is perhaps not surprising since, indirectly, the word "night" connotes fear more than any other single word except possibly "death," usually considered by Hollywood too morbid and "uncommercial" a word to be used in a title except when absolutely necessary. "Murder," "mystery," and a related phrase "murder case" all predominate in the thirties, and they rightly suggest that the detective film *then,* a far cry from today's *Klute,* was essentially a polished light entertainment, usually based on a novel, or at least built around a detective who originated in a novel.

It was in fact the heyday of the debonair private detective, and no player essayed this role as well (or with so many variations) as William Powell. He wore elegant clothes with aplomb; he could don spats and carry a cane without losing one jot of his masculinity; he walked with a jaunty air of self-assurance; and his well-modulated voice—deadly serious when interrogating suspects and verbally reasoning out clues, half mocking when talking to the official police who are always two jumps behind him—was one of his major assets.

Powell was the screen's first Philo Vance in *The Canary Murder Case* (1929) in which he tracks down the killer of nightclub entertainer Louise Brooks. The film was originally made as a silent by Mal St. Clair who, though a director specializing in sophisticated comedy, was a master at making silent films with a minimum of subtitles that told essentially "dialogue" stories in totally visual terms. So, while the film is unfortunately no longer available for reappraisal, one can accept as authoritative statements that it was quite a remarkable film in its silent form. (Among its advocates is Louise Brooks, one of the few stars who really understood the art of film construction and direction, and whose shrewd comments on such of her films as do still exist are invariably pertinent, pithy—and right.)

All that *is* available of *The Canary Murder Case* is the revamped sound version, redirected stodgily by Frank Tuttle. Miss Brooks, who had been in Europe filming for G. W. Pabst, was unwilling to work on the sound edition, and her dialogue was dubbed in by Margaret Livingston, a good actress whose voice, however, was hard and brittle, just the opposite of the musical voice that one knew *had* to go with that exquisite Brooks face. The picture and sound editing that accompanied the salvaging of the Brooks footage was quite astonishing: voice-over dialogue, cutaways, insertion of new footage, in only a few scenes in which the camera carelessly got close enough to reveal Margaret Livingston's substitution. For 1929, when technical problems were not easily solved, the ingenuity was considerable. Unfortunately, after Miss Brooks was murdered, all the film had left

to sustain interest was the polish of the Powell performance. It was enough in 1929; it is not enough today. The film is awkwardly structured, overlong in its dialogue scenes, and lacking in excitement.

The Greene Murder Case, which followed that same year, had the same basically stodgy direction but the film was shorter and faster. It is giving away no secret to reveal that the "hidden killer" was quite obviously Jean Arthur from the very beginning, and the climactic scenes of her chase across snowy rooftops and her fall into the Hudson River contained some real excitement as well as interestingly designed sets.

Powell's third Philo Vance for Paramount was the shortest and the weakest of the trio: the 65-minute *The Benson Murder Case,* in which a killing (and the solving of it) all take place on a stormy night in an isolated hunting lodge full of guests with a good supply of motives and alibis.

Fortunately, Powell's farewell to Vance was made at Warner Brothers three years later in *The Kennel Murder Case,* best of all the Vance mysteries, and a genre classic that has been discussed thoroughly earlier in this book.

From 1930 on, Philo Vance proliferated, prospered, and *changed* from picture to picture with a rapidity that was confusing. Basil Rathbone was a rather stiff and haughty Vance in *The Bishop Murder Case* (MGM, 1930), too British to capture the relaxed, man-about-town air that Powell had done so well, although the picture itself was a good one, with an intriguing plot and surprising mobility of camerawork. The murders were photographed subjectively, through the killer's eyes, just as Philip Marlowe's investigations were (less successfully) given the subjective treatment much later in *Lady in the Lake.*

Warren William was a logical successor to William Powell in Warner Brothers' second Vance thriller, 1934's *The Dragon Murder Case.* It was a long way below the standards of *Kennel,* not least perhaps because the director, H. Bruce Humberstone, was not of the regular Warner "establishment," didn't move or organize films as well as Curtiz, and in fact through his career was always to be too relaxed when handed a murder mystery, even so heady a one as *I Wake Up Screaming.*

The Casino Murder Case (MGM, 1935) had the most unlikely Vance of all in Paul Lukas; a capable actor, but still new to the American screen, and certainly never able at any phase of his career to suggest anything but a strongly *European* intellectual. Purnell Pratt was a good Markham, but Ted Healey too much of a buffoon as Sergeant Heath after the more sensible casting of Eugene Pallette.

Nat Pendleton continued the "dumb" tradition as

Heath, with Grant Mitchell a satisfying Markham, in the next and last MGM Vance, *The Garden Murder Case*. Edmund Lowe was at least superficially a good Vance; wearing a mustache added a patina of sophistication to his otherwise rather rough exterior, but he was never *quite* able to overcome a Brooklyn accent. However, apart from his strong interpretation of Sergeant Quirt in *What Price Glory?*, Lowe never seemed to attempt an in-depth characterization. Whether he was playing Chandu the Magician or Philo Vance, he was always exactly the same: the veneer was polished but there was no subtlety or differentiation between roles beneath it. With a running time of only an hour, albeit with the MGM production gloss and cast (Virginia Bruce, Gene Lockhart, Benita Hume, Henry B. Walthall, Jessie Ralph) to compensate, *The Garden Murder Case* marked a turning point for Philo. Hereafter, he would never get out of the programmer category, and would in time wind up in "B" pictures. During the early thirties concentration on Vance in Hollywood, Paramount—to comply with the legal requirement to make a certain percentage of British films—had made of *The Scarab Murder Case* an ultra-economical British "B." Wilfrid Hyde-White, then a totally unknown British character player, and without the comedic polish that came to him in later years, played Vance.

Paramount's *Night of Mystery* (in 1937) was a fairly elaborate remake of *The Greene Murder Case*. The comedy values were increased: Roscoe Karnes, as Heath, was second in the cast, much higher than Purnell Pratt, repeating as Markham. Grant Richards as Vance was facially acceptable, but he somehow projected a kind of insincerity which made him much better fitted for weakling or villain roles. However, the direction by E. A. Dupont—a former German "master" who never quite made it in Hollywood and was trying to impress his bosses with a plethora of pictorial style—was lively and pictorially atmospheric. Paramount didn't follow through with another Vance film until 1939 with *The Gracie Allen Murder Case*. It was not based on any published S. S. Van Dine story; he wrote it directly for the screen.

Gracie Allen's dithering comedy and frenetic puns are

THE GREENE MURDER CASE (1929): E. H. Calvert as District Attorney Markham, Jean Arthur, William Powell as Philo Vance.

THE GREENE MURDER CASE: Eugene Pallette as Sergeant Heath, E. H. Calvert as Markham.

very much of an acquired taste and can vary considerably from picture to picture, depending on her writers. But she has her adherents. Luckily, Warren William (returning to the Vance role) was allowed to play it straight and to satisfy audience frustrations by frequently loosing a blast at Miss Allen, especially when she called him Fido Vance. The comedy apart, the story was a typically involved Van Dine mystery, with the audience shown some key clues in a rustic hayride party prologue. For the first time, Markham became a comic figure himself (via that admirable exponent of frustration and the slow burn, Donald MacBride) while William Demarest was Heath. The murderer was a cultured, charming, cooperative gentleman who retains his suavity until the bitter end, pulling a last-minute double-cross on his partner, and only then showing himself in his true colors. Without giving the game away, let it be recorded that Jerome Cowan and Horace MacMahon were among the suspects, and that dignified H. B. Warner was also in the film.

In 1940 Warner Brothers remade *The Kennel Murder Case* as *Calling Philo Vance,* neatly transposing the original murder into a yarn about foreign agents. The list of suspects was almost as formidable as in the original version (Ralph Forbes, Martin Kosleck, Don Douglas, Wedgwood Nowell). Henry O'Neill made a serious and business-like Markham. Vance was played by that excellent and extremely promising actor, James Stephenson. He was handsome, possessed of a beautiful speaking voice, and, though unmistakably British, he had acquired an American suavity that made him eminently suitable for the role. Strong parts in such important films as *The Letter* had brought him a great deal of attention: Warner's were in the process of building him up to star status and, had he not died in 1941, he might well have assumed the romantic mantle of a Ronald Colman or a Herbert Marshall.

Calling Philo Vance was the last good Vance film. In 1947 producer Howard Welsch made three Vance "B"s for Producers Releasing Corporation, the smallest

THE BISHOP MURDER CASE (1932): George Marion, Basil Rathbone as Philo Vance, Clarence Geldert as Markham.

THE DRAGON MURDER CASE (1934): Eugene Pallette as Heath, Warren William as Vance, Robert McWade as Markham.

Paul Lukas, the Philo Vance of THE CASINO MUR-
DER CASE (1935).

THE GARDEN MURDER CASE (1936): Edmund Lowe
as Vance, with Virginia Bruce.

CALLING PHILO VANCE (1940): James Stephenson assumes the Vance role.

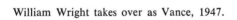

William Wright takes over as Vance, 1947.

PHILO VANCE'S SECRET MISSION (1947): Alan Curtis, the last Vance to date, with Sheila Ryan.

of the established independent companies. Welsch was a decided cut above the average level of their producers, and his directors and cameramen were likewise elevated —*slightly*. As PRC films, undoubtedly, they had a little extra polish. But they were still "B"s and their Philo Vance—William Wright in *Philo Vance Returns,* Alan Curtis in *Philo Vance's Gamble* and *Philo Vance's Secret Mission*—could just as well have been Sam Spade or Philip Marlowe.

William Powell was unquestionably the best of the Philo Vances, and indeed the epitome of the elegant dilettante-sleuth of the thirties. Commercially eclipsing his Vance success was his Nick Charles in 1934's *The Thin Man.* So successful was he personally, in tandem with Myrna Loy as wife Nora, that no other players ever attempted the roles on screen * and no company other than MGM ever made "Thin Man" films. Even MGM limited them to one every two or three

* Peter Lawford and Phyllis Kirk did repeat the roles for a television series.

years over a twelve-year period. Though the six films made declined somewhat in quality toward the end, they retained their popularity and boxoffice standing and thus far have been the only detective series (not counting James Bond and other currently new sleuths) never to descend to at least a programmer level.

Although *The Thin Man* was a surprise hit at the time, bringing to the detective film the same kind of warm comedy that the same year's *It Happened One Night* had brought to the love story, its success is not hard to understand. Quite apart from the fact that it's a fast, efficient, well-knit, and thrilling film, put together with all the style that one would expect from a crew including Albert Hackett and Frances Goodrich (writers), James Wong Howe (camera), and W. S. Van Dyke (director), the teamwork of the stars was immensely appealing. As tippling and occasionally battling husband and wife, Powell and Loy were clearly no paragons. But their devotion to each other was obvious, and they had *fun.* They also satisfied a kind of wish fulfillment from audiences in those rather grim days in that they solved the depression by completely ignoring it rather than by offering patronizing platitudes or artificial solutions. The Charleses were obviously wealthy people unaffected by the depression; audiences might envy their way of life, but they didn't *resent* it because Nick and Nora never stressed their wealth and certainly never *squandered* it (unlike Robert Young and Constance Cummings as the married-battling-tippling-detecting couple in *Remember Last Night?,* a 1935 mystery obviously based on the formula of *The Thin Man* and its leading protagonists).

The first "Thin Man" was the only *unique* one, and also the only one in which the title character appeared. But the follow-ups, some of them written by Dashiell Hammett, and all but the last two directed by W. S. Van Dyke (who died in 1944), retained its charm and plot characteristics, even if these elements began to be rather too mechanically written and applied after the first three films.

The second film, *After the Thin Man,* was more than half an hour longer than the first but, initially, it seemed as though it was going to surpass it. The first third of the film is frenetically paced, full of throwaway wisecracks and endearing characters. Then the plot—and murder—rear their inevitable heads and the film takes off down standardized and predictable, though still enjoyable, pathways. Critics at the time seemed upset by the "surprise" revelation of James Stewart (MGM's fast-rising romantic rival to Gable and Taylor) as the killer at the film's end, yet this seemed almost too patly predetermined from the very beginning.

Given *any* mystery film in which the boy loves the girl but something about his personality prevents her loving *him,* and given, too, Hollywood's fondness (then especially) for the happy ending, there is obviously no justifiable reason for a boy-girl team to exist with unrequited love involved, unless one of them turns out to be the killer at the end. (Universal's *Secret of the Blue Room* is another perfect illustration of this.) With one's suspicions about Mr. Stewart aroused from the start, his every noble and selfless act can be seen to have a sinister purpose behind it, and in this case the audience should he well ahead of Mr. Charles with their own deductions.

The only real surprise is why Stewart—having maintained his humble, self-effacing "Mr. Deeds" mien, the stumbling "sincerity" of his speech, and the wistful pain in his eyes so convincingly for close to two hours—should suddenly turn into a raging, snarling, low-key-lit maniac at the moment of his denunciation by Mr. Charles. These amiable "murder in the family" mysteries, of which the aforementioned *Remember Last Night?* is another classic example, also rather neatly sidestep the moral question of how one feels about proving a lifelong

THE CASE OF THE CURIOUS BRIDE (1935): Allen Jenkins, Warren Hymer, Warren William as Perry Mason, Olin Howland.

THE CASE OF THE VELVET CLAWS (1936): Claire Dodd (as Della Street), Warren William as Mason, Eddie Acuff, Wini Shaw. (Della finally married Mason in this one!)

THE CASE OF THE BLACK CAT (1936): with Ricardo Cortez as Mason and June Lang as Della Street.

THE CASE OF THE STUTTERING BISHOP (1936): Joseph Crehan, Edward Mc-Wade, Linda Perry, Donald Woods as Mason.

THE THIN MAN (1934): Nat Pendleton, Myrna Loy, William Powell.

friend guilty of murder and sending him to the electric chair?

Another Thin Man (the title a definite misnomer, since it refers to the Charleses' newborn baby, thus indicating that Powell is the *original* Thin Man, which he wasn't), *Shadow of the Thin Man, The Thin Man Goes Home,* and *Song of the Thin Man* rounded out the series, while Powell and Loy interspersed them with occasional lunatic comedies that cashed in on the series' popularity.

Powell made a number of expert detective mysteries (and near related spy films) in the thirties which drew their inspiration from his Vance and especially his Nick Charles roles. *Private Detective 62* was a neat and enjoyable Warner mystery, while two neglected comedy-mysteries of the mid-thirties all but equal the first two Thin Man films: *Star of Midnight* (opposite Ginger Rogers) and *The Ex-Mrs. Bradford* (with Jean Arthur). Coincidentally, stalking through several of these Powell films (and as many others as he could find time for) was the urbane and smiling Ralph Morgan, the self-effacing Uriah Heep of Hollywood whodunits. Detective buffs who were only interested in *who*dunit and not why or how could safely get home early when his name appeared in the cast, confident that he and the Hollywood type-casting system would not let them down.

Warren William and Adolphe Menjou were actors who came closest to duplicating William Powell's urbane detection, though Warren William was frequently cast in the Barrymoresque attorney roles wherein detection was a sober adjunct of a no-nonsense career. Both Barrymore and William tended to indulge in somewhat unlikely theatrics once they had their clients (or victims) in the courtroom. Both actors played variations on "The Great Mouthpiece," the celebrated lawyer Bill Fallon.

It was probably William's success in such films as *The Mouthpiece* that suggested to Warner Brothers that he would make a good Perry Mason in the mysteries adapted from the Erle Stanley Gardner novels. A far cry from the popular Perry Mason TV films of the sixties, with Raymond Burr as a technically precise Mason and protracted courtroom encounters as the "action" highlights, the four Warren William Masons between 1934 and 1936 were slick but traditional mysteries, reasonably faithful to their source novels, but with the emphasis away from the courtroom. Mason's restrained romance with secretary Della Street did culminate in marriage in the final film of the quartet. Claire Dodd played Della.

As an upright and strictly honest (if occasionally unethical) lawyer, Mason offered a striking comparison with the shady shyster lawyers of Claude Rains, John and Lionel Barrymore, and William Powell (and Warren William too!) that had been rather overdone since

1931, and were now going out of fashion. Too, in handling crime as strictly as business—Mason had a big, efficiently run organization—he made a more convincing and logical crusader than those amateur sleuths like Vance who did it all just for the fun of it. Mason's slick operations and plush offices also make interesting comparison with the dingy little rooms later used as offices by Philip Marlowe!

The six movies all represented exercises in neat mystery writing, in intelligent legal discussion, in gimmicks, and in plot surprises. There was never much menace, little or no physical action, few thrills. The excitement came from the surprises in the stories themselves, and perhaps in a way they didn't altogether play fair with the audience since the solutions invariably evolved from information known only to Mason.

The first in the series, *The Case of the Howling Dog,* one of the last good films directed by Alan Crosland, was perhaps the most satisfying to mystery addicts because of its atmospheric trappings and the interesting ambiguity in the role of the heroine. Played by Mary Astor, she *did* turn out to be a good girl, but for a while the role seemed to be a forerunner of her cool murderess in *The Maltese Falcon,* a deception fostered by the relatively little footage that she was given, usually a reliable tipoff to homicidal talents where a big name star is concerned. Even though the film is literally all talk, Crosland keeps his cameras mobile and his pace fast. Surprisingly, there is no background music at all, except on one occasion when the radio is turned on and we are treated to a spirited rendition of "Dames"! Dorothy Tree is a charming and resourceful Della Street, and it is pleasing to find Allen Jenkins playing the fly-in-the-ointment cop as a competent but rather unpleasant type, instead of aiming at the usual dumb detective so-called comedy. *The Case of the Curious Bride* (directed by Michael Curtiz) and *The Case of the Lucky Legs* (directed by Archie Mayo) were enjoyable and well-written sequels. Thereafter, Warner's seemed to lose interest, transforming them from eight-reel "A" features to six-reel "B"s, with a corresponding substitution of unimportant directors like William McGann. *The Case of the Velvet Claws* was a slow and talkative mystery with—if memory serves correctly—no script reference to or explanation of the intriguing title. (In the original novel, it was a piece of literally catty antifeminist propaganda!) Ricardo Cortez effectively took over the Mason role in *The Case of the Black Cat,* in which Della Street (played by the very pretty June Travis) curiously returned to her maiden (or, at least, unmarried) status. The wrap-up of Warner's series was provided by *The Case of the Stuttering Bishop* (1937), the weakest of the group, though with a fascinatingly complicated plot line. Unfortunately,

AFTER THE THIN MAN (1936): Asta, William Powell, Myrna Loy.

SONG OF THE THIN MAN (1947): William Bishop, William Powell.

THE EX-MRS. BRADFORD (1936): William Powell, Jean Arthur, James Gleason, Charles Richman.

THE EX-MRS. BRADFORD: William Powell and Jean Arthur, a new variant on the "Nick and Nora Charles" team.

STAR OF MIDNIGHT: Private detective Powell surrounded by official detectives Robert Emmett O'Connor and J. Farrell MacDonald.

STAR OF MIDNIGHT (1935): Ginger Rogers, Ralph Morgan, William Powell.

Donald Woods was too youthful and too much of an eager beaver to suggest Mason's courtroom experience.

Thatcher Colt, the creation of Anthony Abbott (Fulton Oursler) was an interesting combination of Perry Mason and Philo Vance. Crime was both a career for him (as the New York Commissioner of Police) and a hobby (the really interesting cases he'd investigate himself, working independently). Since the novels describe him as the best-dressed bachelor in town, it was perhaps a foregone conclusion that Adolphe Menjou would be assigned to the role. Columbia announced three Colt mysteries but only two were made: *Night Club Lady* (1932) and *The Circus Queen Murder* (1933), the latter directed by Roy William Neill, who, if not an innovative director, certainly managed to inject both speed and atmosphere into his mysteries. *The Ninth Guest,* also for Columbia, was a particularly enjoyable exercise in gambits that was among his better earlier thrillers, while in the forties he produced and directed all but the first of Universal's twelve Sherlock Holmes films.

Unfortunately, Columbia's programmers had a way of displaying their economy in both the paucity of sets and in the soft and grainy photographic style that was a company trademark.

The films, though quite well liked, did not in any way match the elegance of Menjou's performance. He continued to dabble, though none too seriously, in detective roles through the years, via such films as *Mr. District Attorney* and *The Sniper*. In the latter, shorn of his mustache in a move to deglamourize his detective and present him in a semi-documentary light, he delivered one line superbly illustrative of the jump-in-and-start-swimming school of detection. Faced with a probable sex killer, he instructs his men: "Bring in all the rapists and perverts and find out what they've been doing lately."

Menjou's sojourn as Thatcher Colt was so brief, and the films so lost in the supersleuth shuffle at that time, that many detective fanciers do not realize that Thatcher Colt was ever brought to the screen. Actually, he made a third appearance in 1942 in an unusually intelligent and well-made "B" for PRC, *The Panther's Claw.* Sidney Blackmer's well-tailored Colt fitted his literary description to a T and Herbert Rawlinson (the former Blake of Scotland Yard) was equally well cast as his assistant. One of the novelties of the film was its heaping suspicion on a familiar red herring player who never had enough backbone to turn out to be the villain—but here he *does.*

There's a dash of Bulldog Drummond's romanticism (the *Colman* Drummond, that is) in Leslie Charteris' character "The Saint"—although the overlapping is accidental since he made his first appearance on the

THE LONE WOLF RETURNS (1935): Melvyn Douglas, Tala Birell.

THE LONE WOLF IN PARIS (1938): Walter Kingsford, Francis Lederer, Frances Drake.

COUNTER ESPIONAGE (1942): Warren William as The Lone Wolf, with Eric Blore.

printed page several years before the first Colman film was made. Detective fanciers have little respect for the Charteris novels, diverting time killers at best. The Robin Hood–like aspects of The Saint spill over into other lesser detective figures and, basically, he is a derivative of The Lone Wolf.

The Saint films were rarely more than program fodder, growing less and less interesting as time went on and production values went down, while the charm and sophistication of the stars playing the role diminished with their age. *The Saint in New York,* made in 1938, was probably the best of the series because it was the first and the freshest, though even from the beginning there appears to have been little studio enthusiasm for the series, and RKO Radio was strangely reluctant to provide a good director or anything but a strictly "B" picture cast. Louis Hayward, never a very likable hero and somehow much better at playing weaklings and semi-villains was nevertheless then at the peak of his short-lived boyish charm period, and the insincerity of his playing was appropriate since The Saint *was* a thief as well as an amateur detective. George Sanders, however, was a distinct improvement in the second in the series, which seemed to concentrate·more on finding fresh venues (London, Palm Springs) than original plots. The jaunt to London was revitalizing, since it was shot there and benefited from the fresh beauty of its leading lady (Sally Gray) and the sprightly direction of John Paddy Carstairs.

The Saint's Double Trouble had some mild novelty value in a dual role performance for Sanders, as hero and villain, and in the unexploited supporting villainy of Bela Lugosi. Two more London-made films in the early forties were brisk and benefited from the change of pace and a new and less sardonic Saint in Hugh Sinclair. Then the series lay dormant for eleven years, winding up with another British-made episode, *The Saint's Girl Friday,* the dullest of the lot though coming full circle in that Louis Hayward replayed the lead.

In 1941 RKO Radio supplemented Hollywood's growing list of standardized "B" sleuths with Michael Arlen's The Falcon. All that was really retained of the original stories was The Falcon's fondness for the ladies and the smoothness with which he moved in high society. Arlen's creation was also quite hard boiled. With George Sanders starring, the movie series really did little more than change his name from The Saint to The Falcon. The format remained identical, with the same tourist urgency to set stories in Mexico, San Francisco, Hollywood, and other locations easily established with a process screen. Stressing the similarity to The Saint films was the reuse of Wendy Barrie, Sanders' feminine sparring partner in three of the Saint episodes, in his first two Falcons.

THE LONE WOLF IN LONDON (1947): Gerald Mohr, Eric Blore.

THE CLUTCHING HAND (1936): Jack Mulhall (right) as Craig Kennedy, with Rex Lease as his assistant Jamieson.

FATHER BROWN, DETECTIVE (1935): Gertrude Michael, Paul Lukas, Walter Connolly as Father Brown.

TROUBLE FOR TWO (1936): Despite its misleadingly modern title, this was an excellent adaptation of Robert Louis Stevenson's "The Suicide Club". Robert Montgomery as a European prince turned detective was inevitably the most gentlemanly of *all* sleuths; with Louis Hayward and, in a Dr. Watson-ish role, Frank Morgan.

FATHER BROWN, DETECTIVE (1954): A British remake, with Alec Guinness.

NICK CARTER, MASTER DETECTIVE (1939): Henry Hull, Walter Pidgeon as Nick Carter, player, and Addison Richards.

In retrospect, only two of The Falcon films have more than passing interest. *The Falcon Takes Over* (1942) has a much more involving and genuinely interesting mystery plot, plus a colorful set of characters, since it was based on Raymond Chandler's story "Murder My Sweet." The essentials, if not the subtleties, of the original story were followed well and, because it was such a complicated story, it *had* to keep moving—fast—to cram everything into its six-reel running time. The cast showed a little more than routine contract player shuffling, too, with Helen Gilbert, Lyn Bari, Ward Bond, Ann Revere, Turhan Bey, and Hans Conried intelligently selected to interpret Chandler's offbeat roles. Some of Philip Marlowe's integrity even seemed to rub off on the superficial Falcon. Two years later the film would be remade with the care and scope it deserved, introducing Marlowe officially to the movies.

The second Falcon film, in 1942, *The Falcon's Brother,* also had a little more than the average talent behind the cameras. The script was by two experienced mystery writers, Craig Rice and Stuart Palmer; the above-standard photography was the work of Russell Metty and the film's tightness can partially be attributed to the editing by Mark Robson, who would soon branch out as a director himself, specializing in thrillers. Its principal claim to attention was its novelty casting of actual brothers George Sanders and Tom Conway as on-screen brothers, the ruse allowing George Sanders to be killed off and remove himself from the series, while enabling Tom Conway and the series to carry on without perceptible change.

The film had perhaps too much plot and a corresponding lessening in comedy values, although this was not necessarily a disadvantage. However, Sanders' "demise" indicating a lower budgetary allocation for the rest of the series, James Gleason (as The Falcon's detective friend and nemesis) and Allen Jenkins (as The Falcon's aide) were permanently removed as well. They were missed in *The Falcon's Brother,* and *sorely* missed in the following entries. Removing two such capable and enjoyable character players and replacing them with only Cliff Clark as an irascible detective is *not* a fair swap by any standards! Despite the infrequent use of such interesting directors as Edward Dmytryk and Joseph H. Lewis, the remaining nine Falcon adventures with Tom Conway were cut to a pretty standardized pattern. The at least smoothly efficient caliber of that pattern became apparent only *after* RKO Radio concluded the series in 1946, and the rough-hewn and unsophisticated John Calvert tried ineffectually to carry on with three independent cheapies—*The Devil's Cargo, Appointment with Murder,* and *Search for Danger,* produced in 1948–49.

To date, there has been no reason to let The Falcon fly back to the big theater screen. Television welcomed him with open arms, and for once exercised a little imagination. TV's Falcon was played by Charles McGraw, certainly a closer approximation to Arlen's character than any of his movie impersonators had been.

Michael Lanyard, alias The Lone Wolf, who probably inspired The Saint, has had one of the longest and most entertaining careers of all the "gentleman" detectives. One *can* call him that since, although he was created by Louis Joseph Vance as a thief with a French background, the movies, gradually settling him in America, have invariably presented him as a *reformed* thief, using his underworld connections and knolwedge of the criminal mind to prevent or solve crime. During the war years he was also put to work as a counterspy.

Bert Lytell was the most popular of the silent-screen Lone Wolves; he was the first (in 1917) and also the last (in 1929). Lytell was a handsome man, but not particularly dashing. Like Thomas Meighan, Milton Sills, and many other silent stars, he projected reliability and integrity rather than derring-do, qualities appreciated by the more mature ladies who comprised a much greater percentage of movie audiences than they do today. In fact, even Jack Holt, certainly a virile action star, was a little restrained in the "dash" department, while Henry B. Walthall, who also played the role, was short of stature and a gentle, dignified antithesis of the standard "Lone Wolf" image.

Walthall's one film in the group, *False Faces** was perhaps the best of the silent period, being faithful to the French locale and the spirit of the original stories. By the end of the twenties, the series had transplanted The Lone Wolf to America and the usual weekend-party-in-high-society plots, with the reformed cracksman apparently blackmailed into one more job and managing to turn the tables on the real crooks.

Bert Lytell was also the movies' first talkie Lone Wolf, although the film (*Last of the Lone Wolf,* released in 1930) was the final entry in Lytell's trio for Columbia. It was pure Ruritanian hoke, with no detective work involved, but would be especially interesting to see again because it was directed by the curious and always unpredictable Richard Boleslawsky.

Columbia reactivated the series in the mid-thirties with a brace of "A" minus (or "B" plus) efforts that were quite enjoyable. The first, 1935's *The Lone Wolf Returns,* offered Melvyn Douglas in the lead. Douglas was possibly the most overworked actor of stature of the thirties: he turned up everywhere, at every studio from

---

* This title has caused some confusion, since Paramount reused it in the late twenties for one of several versions of *Heliotrope Harry.* Harry was also a master cracksman, but the mood of the story was sentimental, dealing not with detection but with the reformed crook's great sacrifices for the daughter who is unaware that he is her father.

MGM to Majestic, romancing Garbo and Fay Wray, battling Karloff and Atwill in horror films, playing detectives, lovers, authors, fathers—seemingly whatever he was offered. Since one could hardly go to a movie theater without bumping into him, it was obviously impossible for him to identify with any one role, and there were no follow-ups to his Lone Wolf characterization.

Three years later, Francis Lederer had a try at the part in *The Lone Wolf in Paris*. Although Lederer was a good continental actor who had made his debut in Pabst's silent *Lulu* as Jack and Ripper, apparently he never accepted (until the nineteen-forties) that he was infinitely more suited to villain roles. In the mid-thirties, he tried hard to fill the shoes—and the void—left by Maurice Chevalier, but his gaiety was just too mechanical and desperate to have the spontaneous charm that The Lone Wolf needed. His was an enjoyable little film, but no more.

However, finally Columbia hit just the right note in 1939 by abandoning hopes for "A" playing time, concentrating on a quality "B" product instead and settling for Warren William as the star. The former Philo Vance and Perry Mason knew all the tricks of the trade, and the more free-wheeling Lone Wolf character gave him the chance to indulge in his real talent for comic and bizarre disguises. The first film in the series, *The Lone Wolf's Spy Hunt,* provided him with a bonus in leading ladies (Ida Lupino and Rita Hayworth), that intelligent (if ill-used) actor Don Beddoe as the detective inspector, and Tom Dugan as the inevitable dumb sergeant. There was even the ubiquitous Ralph Morgan.

William's eight Lone Wolf films (winding up in 1943 with *Passport to Suez*) gradually surrendered to cheaper budgets but remained solidly entertaining, held together by the William personality and some interesting directors still on the way up to much better things: Andre de Toth, Edward Dmytryk, Michael Gordon. (One of the stories was written by Dalton Trumbo.) The casts were a veritable showcase for Columbia contractees, many of whom were eventually promoted to better things. Eric Blore's comedy as The Lone Wolf's gentleman's gentleman, even if a repetition of his more inspired work in *Top Hat,* was consistently amusing.

There was a short-lived attempt to revive the series in 1946 but Gerald Mohr, who made three films, had none of William's natural charm or acting ability and, in addition, had been so typed as a villain that it was difficult to accept him as a hero.

The last of the series, 1949's *The Lone Wolf and His Lady,* starred Ron Randell, an unsuccessful Bulldog Drummond, equally unsuccessfully. As always, television seemed to hammer the nails into a somewhat tarnished coffin with the aid of Louis Hayward in 1954.

PHANTOM RAIDERS (1940): Florence Rice, Walter Pidgeon as Nick Carter, Joseph Schildkraut.

THE PANTHER'S CLAW (1942): Sidney Blackmer (left) as Thatcher Colt, with Herbert Rawlinson.

One of the most enjoyable (and most forgotten) series of polished light detective films—if one can call a trio of films a series—was built around the husband-and-wife team of Joel and Garda Sloane, created by Harry Kurnitz. MGM started the movies, exactly in the "Thin Man" image, in 1938—presumably as a means of exploiting the genre without running their original meal ticket into the ground by making it overfamiliar through too frequent repetition. Yet private detective mysteries and light thrillers were so proliferating in the late thirties that MGM followed through with two more films in the Sloane series in 1939, the same year that they released their third Thin Man film. Obviously trying to create films that could stand on their own and not be shunted into a "series" category, MGM changed the husband-and-wife combinations from picture to picture.

The first duo in *Fast Company* was Melvyn Douglas and Florence Rice. Apart from being debonair sleuths and happily married madcaps in the tradition of the Nick Charleses (and why did we seem to get only "madcap" heiresses and families in the thirties?), they were also authorities on rare books, and their first adventure dealt with the theft of valuable manuscripts. The rare book racket also provided the basis for the mystery in the second, best and most expensive of the series, *Fast and Loose,* starring Robert Montgomery and Rosalind Russell, with old friend Ralph Morgan.

Montgomery, an expert light comedian, has been almost forgotten today by critics who extol the comedic performances of Cary Grant in the thirties but forget that Montgomery had been doing it—as a star—since 1930. His breezy detectives were few but always memorable (as witness also his Lord Peter Wimsey in *Haunted Honeymoon*) and make an interesting comparison with his later much more serious work as star and director in the Philip Marlowe mystery *Lady in the Lake*. MGM concluded the Sloanes' adventures with *Fast and Furious* (1939), in which the rare book angle was dropped in favor of more straightforward criminal endeavor. Franchot Tone and Ann Sothern inherited the lead roles this time. It was still a glossy and enjoyable mystery, the weakest of the trio but not so much so that it spelled a major disappointment. However, it *did* show signs of becoming formularized. Busby Berkeley directed.

As an example of the multiplicity of detective films in this period, one has to cite only the energetic activities of Melvyn Douglas. His seven 1938 films included, apart from *Fast Company*, the vastly enjoyable *Arsene Lupin Returns*. Taking over the old John Barrymore role, he played the master French thief (now in happy retirement) who joins with American detective Warren William in tracking down contemporary jewel thieves. That old maestro of the tongue-in-cheek adventure, George

Fitzmaurice, directed with all the panache that he had devoted to Valentino in the silent era. The film also provides an unimportant footnote to detective movie history in presenting a former and future Lone Wolf working side by side as a team. Douglas' 1939 schedule, which ended with *Ninotchka,* began more modestly but perhaps more excitingly with a beautiful minor detective classic titled *Tell No Tales*. Perhaps it isn't technically a detective movie, since Douglas plays a newspaper editor who follows up and solves a kidnapping case, but the plotting and construction is pure Philip Marlowe.

Logic is perhaps not a major asset of the production, but style and unexpected flashes of realism are. The film marked the directorial debut of actor Leslie Fenton, and it was a beautiful job. The investigator's blundering into alien worlds in his search include a moving and somehow disturbing involvement at a Negro wake, a sequence which somehow (by its stark contrast, if for nothing else) recalls the Chinese theater sequence in Orson Welles' *The Lady from Shanghai*.

The list of "gentleman" detectives of the thirties and very early forties seems endless. Even if most of us were living in a fool's paradise, turning our backs on the wars

THE SAINT'S DOUBLE TROUBLE (1940),
with George Sanders.

THE FALCON'S BROTHER (1942), with Tom Conway, George Sanders, Jane Randolph.

THE FALCON IN HOLLYWOOD (1944),
with Tom Conway.

107

and threats of wars that were piling up in Europe, it was still the last genuinely civilized era, a period when courtliness and good manners, taste, kindness, and consideration still meant something and were not merely discounted as quaint, time-consuming, and nonproductive. Small wonder that the gentleman detective prospered on the screen.

Clayton Rawson's magician Merlini the Great was, in *Death from a Top Hat,* a good example of the hero to whom applied politeness was an integral part of his profession. Merlini was renamed, and the plot somewhat changed, when Tod Browning used it as the basis for his last film *Miracles for Sale* in 1939—but Robert Young, in an approximation of the role, retained his smoothness and charm.

The vintage sleuth Nick Carter, who had never been presented on the screen in his original late eighteen-eighties period (although a current television series is doing just that), was brought to the screen for the first time (except for some silent shorts) in 1939 by MGM, whose studios were then overrun with amateur and professional sleuths. The role, as rewritten, was perfectly suited to the cool nonchalance of Walter Pidgeon. In the first film, *Nick Carter Master Detective,* Pidgeon goes to great pains to debunk his own reputation, and in a lengthy speech to Addison Richards enumerates all of the meticulous deductions from small clues that he is *not* capable of! It was a sober, not too exciting, but solidly satisfying little mystery.

The two follow-ups, *Phantom Raiders* and *Sky Murder,* though ultramodern in their locales (a luxury liner, a passenger clipper), reverted to the rather lurid melodramatics and action gimmicks of the original stories, the Pidgeon intelligence and personality being the steadying influence that prevented them from seeming absurd.

Another major advantage of the Carter films was one of the most delightful characters ever created as a detective's aide—Bartholomew, the Bee Man. Bartholomew, mild, gentle, wrapped up in his own little world of bee raising, provided an excellent opportunity for Donald Meek, as a kind of offbeat Dr. Watson, to inject both comedy and humanity and still keep the plots rolling along.

The first two films were directed by newcomer Jacques Tourneur (who would really establish himself as a major director of quality thrillers with his first two Val Lewton horror thrillers a couple of years hence) and the third by George B. Seitz, a silent serial and action specialist.

Footsteps in the Dark (1941) was intended as the first in a series of Warner thrillers that would launch Errol Flynn and Brenda Marshall as Burbank's own Nick and Nora, with William Frawley as the official police detective. The film was bright and amusing, Flynn obviously enjoying his sprightly dialogue and the modern change of pace from swashbucklers and westerns. But as a mystery it fell somewhat flat.

The omnipresence of Ralph Bellamy in a small part as a dentist gave the game away. Since he was neither his traditional loser in the battle of the sexes nor a detective himself (as he had been for Columbia in the early thirties' Inspector Trent series, and was currently for the same studio as Ellery Queen), there was only one role left for him to play. Unfortunately, his sporadic appearances in detective mysteries where he was *not* the detective always had audiences not just jumping but leaping to the correct conclusion.

In any event, *Footsteps in the Dark* did not create enough of a stir to warrant its continuation as a series. And that same year another Warner Brothers film, *The Maltese Falcon,* put the writing on the wall in ineradicable letters as it introduced the tough private eye to whom charm and consideration were not marketable commodities, or even usable ones if he wanted to survive.

If their exclusion from this chapter suggests that such detectives as Michael Shayne, Nero Wolfe, and Boston Blackie were *not* gentlemen, the slur was unintended. If anything, they veered more to the traditional older detectives, using politeness whenever possible, than to the newer and more aggressive style practiced by Philip Marlowe. But being a "gentleman" was never an essential part of their stock in trade, or a cultivated asset. I have totally excluded the incredibly prolific British detectives from this chapter for the simple reason that the British, by inclination, by temperament, and usually by birth, are automatically gentlemen and thus require a chapter (and, hopefully, one day, an entire book) all to themselves.

9 THE FBI AND THE LAW

C. Henry Gordon, usually typed as a villain but here playing a detective, organizes the final assault against the gangster's hideout: SCARFACE.

The detective film—in the context of a direct conflict between law, officialdom, and the underworld—has a long history and can roughly be broken down into seven periods and trends.

The genre really began in 1912 with such films as D. W. Griffith's *The Musketeers of Pig Alley* and Thomas Ince's *The Gangsters and the Girl*. There was really no big-time gangsterism in those days, since it took the catalyst of Prohibition to move the rackets into big-scale, well-organized crime empires. Nevertheless, from the very beginning, producers sensed the showmanship in the word "gangsters" and used it as much as possible, even though their plots dealt with little more than seedy small-time crime.

Nevertheless, these early one-reelers did establish in an embryonic form the plot lines of later gangster films. Selig's *The Making of Crooks* (1914) investigated the corruption of youth (with the poolhall already established as the center of the criminal's social life) in a way that predated the famous *The Public Enemy*. The

109

detective was not a dominant figure in these subjects, except in the action films of Thomas Ince where he became a big-city parallel to the cowboy hero. He was on hand as a figure of nemesis, or perhaps as a more human individual, trying to persuade the juvenile delinquent to turn his back on crime, but the direct confrontation between detective and criminal was infrequent.

In 1927 Josef von Sternberg's *Underworld* launched the gangster cycle proper during the heyday of Prohibition. As yet, the public knew only the superficial details of gangland, as represented in newspaper headlines. There was little understanding of the underworld's hold on politics, its tremendous profits, its involvement in white slavery, drugs, and other vices. Thus, while the movies didn't exactly glamourize criminals, there was no public opinion to rebel against their ennobling them. Most of the crime films in this period were inevitably affected by Hollywood's current style: slow, self-indulgent, romantic essays, showcases for directorial and photographic rather than narrative techniques. The gangster films of this period evoked underworld atmosphere and for the most part avoided physical action. They were sentimental in theme, the self-sacrificing gang leader in such films as Von Sternberg's *Underworld* and *Thunderbolt* or Frank Capra's *The Way of the Strong* being modern versions of the "Good Badman" of the early westerns. Such physical action as the films contained was usually concerned with the rivalry between gangs. It was implied that the gangster, while a social evil, really did no harm except to his own kind. There were "good" gangsters (George Bancroft) and "bad" ones (Fred Kohler); they lived in their own world of speakeasies and silken mistresses (Evelyn Brent, Louise Brooks) and the detective was a shadowy outside figure who might sometimes have the last laugh, but never the limelight.

In 1929–30 the picture changed radically with the coming of sound. Initially, as in films like *The Racketeer*, the emphasis remained on both talk (for its own sake) and on a sentimentalized picture of the gangster himself.

But as soon as writers and directors learned how much sound could benefit the gangster film and give it pace and excitement: the sheer noise of machine gun bullets and explosions; screeching tires and police sirens; the menace —and wit—of underworld repartee; the films took on a vivid, staccato style of their own.

Actors new to Hollywood, imported from the Broadway stage—James Cagney, Paul Muni, Lee Tracy, Clark Gable, Edward G. Robinson—brought new life and freshness to the gangster film, which also encompassed the tangential cycles of the prison movie (*The Big House, The Criminal Code*), the newspaper melodrama (*The Finger Points, Five Star Final*), and that oddly fascistic

series of violently antigangster movies (*Star Witness, This Day and Age, Gabriel Over the White House, The President Vanishes*) which proposed that the end justified the means, and advocated all-out war on the underworld, including summary executions without trial! (These films took the view that storm trooper tactics were not only advisable but necessary and that, even if the methods weren't in accord with the best traditions of Americanism, it didn't really matter because none of the gangsters were Americans anyway!) Inevitably, these crime films had certain social comments to make, and the detective became a useful spokesman for them.

Dramatizing the importance (but not the total responsibility) of environment in shaping the criminal's career, the films often used the theatrical structure of taking two friends or brothers from the same neighborhood and following them into adulthood when one becomes a gangster and the other a cop, a detective, or a crime-fighting priest. Most of all, of course, the conflict between law and lawlessness could be dramatized via the head-on conflict between gangster and detective, as in the snarling bravado of Edward G. Robinson versus the quiet self-confidence of Thomas Jackson in *Little Caesar*.

Considering the unemotional nature of many of these detectives, more officials than sleuths, their dedication to the abstract ideals of justice was often a little hard to accept and had to be strengthened by dialogue exchanges. The gangster always tried to buy off the opposition with a bribe that amounted to at least a year's salary for the detective. It didn't work in *Little Caesar* any more than it worked in 1955 when Richard Conte tried to buy off Cornel Wilde (*The Big Combo*). A further (and important) use of the detective was as a compromise for minority groups. There were frequent complaints that movie gangsters seemed to be almost exclusively Italian. If *Scarface,* in creating the story of Al Capone, stressed Italian gangsters, it also stressed that the honest and incorruptible detectives fighting them were Italians too. (Edwin Maxwell and C. Henry Gordon, usually the slimiest of villains, made a powerfully effective break from typecasting in these roles.)

With the crime film such big boxoffice in the early thirties, less important but more standardized detective films began to supplement them on all sides. In *Behind the Mask* (1932) Jack Holt was a somewhat excessively stoical G-Man (at one point, in order to establish an alibi, he shoots himself in the arm without batting an eyelid) assigned to break up a drug ring run by Boris Karloff and Edward Van Sloan for an unknown "higher-up." The writers were apparently unable to forget that Karloff and Van Sloan were more familiarly associated with the horror film and incorporated some bizarre electrical machinery and graveyard scenes into their narrative. The climax saw Holt at the mercy of Van Sloan, about to perform a dangerous (and unnecessary) operation on his captive, without benefit of anaesthetic and with a predictably fatal result. Edward Van Sloan milked this scene to the utmost, relishing every line that would normally have gone to Bela Lugosi.

Although not an outstanding film in itself, Warner's *Bureau of Missing Persons* (1933) was ahead of its time in trying to create a composite picture of detective methods, with a number of unrelated cases developed in parallel narrative. Directed by Roy del Ruth, it had the same crackling pace as his earlier *Blessed Event* and later *Bulldog Drummond Strikes Back*. Potentially grisly material was made genuinely funny by tasteful handling and an underplayed cold-blooded delivery. It was surprising how funny discussions about stitched-together corpses, or a murdered body having been ground up for fertilizer, could be—as delivered by experts like Allen Jenkins, and punctuated by that inevitable pre-Code question: "Have you been smoking hop?" Fast-talking Pat O'Brien (as the detective who prefers strongarm methods) and dignified Lewis Stone (as his more orthodox-thinking superior) made an excellent team, and the fast-paced story was further speeded up by such devices as the iris-out, the swish pan, and the habit of starting scenes *without* establishing shots, cutting right into an opening door, so that the film was in constant motion. While the cases it covered (taken from a book by a retired police chief) had the look of authenticity, one hopes that the detecting methods employed used a certain amount of dramatic license. Stumped because kidnappers have a secure hideout and can only be comunicated with via a carrier pigeon that they will send to their victim's associates, a detective is reassured: "Just have a fast plane standing by, and when that pigeon takes off, you follow it. . . ."

While the crime/gangster/detective cycle continued to grow in size, it also began to run out of steam a little. Films like *Doorway to Hell, The Public Enemy,* and *Scarface* had really said all there was to say on gangsterism. MGM's *The Wet Parade* (which included the spectacle of Jimmy Durante as a dedicated FBI man gunned down by the gangsters) was an ambitious attempt to weigh the pros and cons of Prohibition. Its rather old-fashioned earlier portions made no bones about condemning alcoholism per se, but it hedged on the legal issues of Prohibition, balancing the scales rather evenly and finally taking no stand at all. In *Little Giant,* Edward G. Robinson amiably spoofed the whole "Little Caesar" genre in a Damon Runyonesque takeoff. The Production Code cleanup of late 1933 did draw the teeth of many of the crime films, which seemed to be loaded down with violence, sex, amorality, and general corruption. Certainly, it had these ingredients in generous quantities, but their utilization was usually tasteful, often merely suggested, never as explicit as it was to become in the nineteen-seventies. The objection was not to the presentation of these elements but to their proliferation, out of fear that the warped standards they expressed might come to be accepted as the norm.

The fourth phase of the gangster cycle came into effect in 1935, when the Production Code's laundering of Hollywood had resulted in a total about-face for the crime film.

They continued unabated, but the emphasis now had been shifted from the criminal to the police. The change-over was doubly stressed by the switching of such former gangster stereotypes as James Cagney and Edward G. Robinson to the right side of the law as FBI or other official enforcers. (The gangland thrones they left vacant were soon filled by newer players: Humphrey Bogart, Cesar Romero, Bruce Cabot.)

Edwin Maxwell, a stand-in for a featured player, C. Henry Gordon, Paul Muni and George Raft in SCARFACE (1932).

Fortunately, too, the FBI's well-publicized record of success—Dillinger had been killed in a police ambush, Capone's power had been broken, the repeal of Prohibition had in any event lessened the public's sympathy for the gangster and the "social service" he had performed—so conditioned the public that they were ready and eager for a glamourization of the FBI. The basic action content of the gangster film was unchanged; indeed, it was increased, to become a kind of metropolitan western. Casual sex was absent, true, since the FBI man of the movies (and probably in actuality, too, for J. Edgar Hoover's rigid moral requirements were well known) was clean-living, moral, idealistic, with no time for sex unless he was a family man. And the detective with a wife and child was usually doomed in the movies, just as the flier in World War I films signed his own death warrant as soon as his unmarried girlfriend became pregnant. The death of an FBI agent with a family soon became a cliché, slowing down the pace of the film for an inspirational ceremony, and possibly a later scene when the sorrowing widow bravely holds back her tears as she reads a personal note from Mr. Hoover!

G-Men (1935), the best of the new gangster movies, embodied all of the clichés while they were still fresh. The key detectives—Cagney, Lloyd Nolan, Robert Armstrong—were all players who had heretofore specialized in gangster roles. The film moved too fast to take time out to establish the happy home life of married agents—but Regis Toomey, as Cagney's buddy, fulfills the same function by being shot in the back while about to make an arrest, his death prompting unsuccessful lawyer Cagney to join the department. The detectives were all young, clean-cut, handsome, idealistic, possessed of a sense of humor, and backed by the scientific and laboratory resources of the FBI.

By 1935 standards, the coverage of the agents' training and the explanation of scientific methods of deduction had at least the suggestion of documentary. In any event, the combination of such a fine body of men with such scientific aids to crime detection seemed to make the contest rather uneven. The Code-prompted deglamourization of the gangster had left them without the magnetic leadership of men like Muni, Cagney, and Robinson. Instead, they were an uncaptained collection of swarthy hoodlums—Barton MacLane, William and Edward Pawley, Ward Bond, Bruce Cabot, Mathew Betz—intellectually incapable of planning an intelligent caper and helpless without their sawed-off shotguns and high-powered cars. Their only redeeming feature was a kind of intergang comradeship and loyalty.

Even this, a hangover from such realistic earlier gangster films as *Quick Millions,* where crime was treated as a matter-of-fact business like any other, was a trait

that was on the way out. Soon the hoods would quarrel among themselves rather more, and double-cross each other without compunction, making it all the more surprising that the FBI didn't mop them up much more rapidly than they did.

G-Men was to the gangster film what *The Spoilers* is to the western. A grand outsized "show," the action is slammed over in blistering style—machine gun battles, car chases and crashes, fisticuffs, the poor old First National Bank being held up yet again. The dialogue crackles with bantering wisecracks, chorus girls and song numbers take up the rare slack between gunsmoke, and the hoods (all oily, black-suited, and still predominantly Italian) are headed by Barton MacLane who never lowers his voice to anything quieter than a bellow.

Its success spurred similar major gangster action films from most of the major companies, the most blatant imitation being Edward Small's *Let 'Em Have It.* It overlapped *G-Men* in many areas, including the death of the kid brother—fledgling agent, and the shootout at a woodland cabin hideout. However, it lacked the crackling pace of the Warner film; it was longer; too loaded down with plot, characters, and romantic complications; and Sam Wood, a "prestige" director, minimized the excitement of its limited action. Too, its stress on the efficiency of the FBI's lab work got a little out of hand, with the smallest of clues turning up dossiers of information.

Nevertheless, *Let 'Em Have It* was one of the best of the normally economy-conscious Edward Small productions, and its title was typical of a new trend that suggested violence was quite condonable if directed at the criminal, even though by law he was still presumed innocent until proven otherwise. Such films as *Muss 'Em Up, Don't Turn 'Em Loose,* and *Show Them No Mercy* usually had scenes in which the law, or innocent victims, finally had an opportunity to explode into all-out violence. In *Show Them No Mercy,* kidnap victim Rochelle Hudson grabs a tommy gun at the end and fires a row of bullets into Bruce Cabot's chest, a scene of explicit violence quite rare on the screen then.

MGM, which had made some of the most elaborate gangster films in the pre-Code period (*The Secret Six, Beast of the City*), put some of their best stars and directors into the genre but, mindful of the family audience that MGM was always conscious of, steered clear of excessive violence. They concentrated instead on the crime film in which *story* dominated (*Manhattan Melodrama* where boyhood chums grow up on opposite sides of the fence, District Attorney William Powell sending gangster Clark Gable to the chair) or the pure actioner like *Public Hero Number 1* with Chester Morris as an undercover FBI man tracking down a gangster in hiding.

Lloyd Nolan

Thomas Jackson

Robert Homans

Grant Withers

Cliff Clark

Paul Hurst

Frank Jenks

Warren Hymer

116

Neil Hamilton

Robert Young (extreme left) and Wallace Ford (standing, center) as FBI men fighting the illicit booze racket in THE WET PARADE (1932).

After *G-Men,* Warner's made few other gangster epics as elaborate, but turned instead to solid little programmers like *Public Enemy's Wife* with Pat O'Brien and Robert Armstrong as G-Men on the trail of escaped convict Cesar Romero. The emphasis was wholly on speed and physical action. The few attempts at illustrating detective methods—as when O'Brien and Armstrong pose as drunken fishermen—were neither very convincing nor reassuring. However, the expert action in little films like this was a saving grace and later proved to be an economical boon too when, in the forties, Warner's remade these films as tight little "B"s, using all the originals' big action scenes to lend a production value beyond the scope of "B" budgets. (*Public Enemy's Wife* was remade by William K. Howard as *Bullet Scars.*)

Cagney's career was somewhat botched in the midthirties. He was put in no big crime films to follow up the success of *G-Men,* and the overzealous attempt to diversify his roles and make him romantic tough, comedian, and adventure hero robbed his career of drive at a time when he needed it most, causing him to break—temporarily—with Warner's.

Edward G. Robinson stayed firmly on the side of the law or when he broke it—as in *The Amazing Dr. Clitterhouse*—it was in an offbeat, sympathetic, and semipathological manner. While he played for comedy, too, his base of operations remained the criminal world, and his principal role a detective or variation thereof. (Although renowned as a gangster specialist, Robinson did only a handful of gangster roles, some of those—like *Little Giant* and *The Whole Town's Talking*—satires, while his work as a detective was much more prolific.) In *Bullets or Ballots* he played a tough and unconventional detective, based on the real life Johnny Broderick, and one of its highlights was a well-staged fistic battle with Humphrey Bogart.

In *I Am the Law* (1938), Robinson plays a smalltown college professor on sabbatical talked into accepting a crime-busting commission by the secret head of the crime syndicate, who is convinced that he can control Robinson. Needless to say, after a false start Robinson comes through true blue, employing as a mass detective agency all of the law students from his college. One of the scenes in the film must have delighted film buffs, who had

Detective Victor McLaglen interrogates Adrienne Ames in GUILTY AS HELL (1932).

Warren Hymer as the sympathetic detective taking William Powell back to the electric chair: ONE WAY PASSAGE (1932).

MISS PINKERTON (1932), with Joan Blondell.

CRIME OF THE CENTURY (1933): Gordon Westcott, Wynne Gibson and familiar detective figure Robert Elliott.

MURDER ON THE BLACKBOARD (1934): Edna May Oliver, James Gleason.

Paul Kelly as the FBI man in THE PRESIDENT VANISHES (1934), with Harry Woods.

BUREAU OF MISSING PERSONS: Bette Davis, Pat O'Brien.

Lewis Stone, dignified detective of several thirties melodramas, including BUREAU OF MISSING PERSONS (1934).

suffered through years of typecasting of character actor Byron Foulger as the sneaking double-dealer, informer, and petty crook. Without any positive proof, Robinson rightly surmises—just from his looks—that he is the informer in his office and fires him. But not before chastising him verbally: "I don't like your face. Never have. You've got shifty eyes and a weak chin. Get out!"

Most companies, small and large, maintained an increasing schedule of "B" detective films in the thirties. Monogram put Milburn Stone into *Federal Bullets,* and Republic, William Boyd into *Federal Agent.* Universal had any number of "B" detective films, with a stress on physical action and glossy production values. Warner's maintained a fast and furious pace, with a predilection for gangster films about the intimidation of witnesses. There was little difference between an "A" like *Racket Busters,* with Walter Abel as the Dewey-like investigating attorney, and *Missing Witnesses* with Dick Purcell and John Litel doing the same work on a smaller budget.

Undoubtedly, Paramount made some of the best detective thrillers of all. William K. Howard's *Mary Burns, Fugitive* is perhaps a crime and suspense film *before* it is a detective film. The film's key detective, Wallace Ford, uses the wrongly imprisoned Sylvia Sidney (whom he firmly believes guilty) to track down her killer husband. He's one of the few honest yet unsympathetic detectives in movies of the thirties; but one can't really blame him for using the hapless Miss Sidney, since her total ineptitude at her trial and her behavioral stupidity thereafter are such that she deserves all she gets. Pictorially, the film has the same strong Germanic style as Howard's earlier *Sherlock Holmes.* Its limited violence is sharp and vicious, the FBI giving their quarry virtually no chance to surrender before mowing them down. Alan Baxter's subtle performance as the semipsycho killer was quite one of the best things he did prior to his Nazi spy in Hitchcock's *Saboteur.* Melvyn Douglas, doubtless exhausted from rushing back and forth between every movie lot in Hollywood, was rewarded with a role ideally suited to his physical condition. In one of the most nontaxing roles in movie history—especially for an actor given star billing—he appears only in the second half of the film, and spends most of it flat on his back as a hospital patient. He does get to his feet for the final scenes, not to save the heroine, but to be saved *by* her!

Much earlier in the thirties, Paramount had made *Guilty as Hell* (discreetly renamed *Guilty as Charged* in England), unique in that the audience knew right away that kindly old Henry Stephenson was the killer, while police detective Victor McLaglen and reporter Edmund Lowe (striving to maintain their Flagg and Quirt relationship in a detective framework) did not. In the mid-thirties they remade it as *Night Club Scandal,* with John

SPECIAL AGENT (1935): Bette Davis, George Brent.

Barrymore as the murderer and Charles Bickford and Lynne Overman in the detective-reporter positions.

Overman, an excellent light comedian with a caustic delivery, too often wasted as the comic foil with material stretched to breaking point in the Dorothy Lamour jungle epics, proved an excellent and unconventional detective and Paramount used him in such a role several times. One of his best was *Death of a Champion* (the title referred to a dog but the film quickly proceeded to non-canine killings) in which, partnered by a diminutive Donald O'Connor, he played a memory expert turned detective. His personal success in the role was such that one half expected it to be turned into a series. Overman also kept busy in Paramount's loosely termed J. Edgar Hoover series. After the success of *Persons in Hiding*, based on part of the Hoover book of that title, Paramount turned out a number of unusually expert "B" thrillers, allegedly also drawn from that book. Paramount had a reputation for making bad and boring "A's", but "B"s of real quality.

Interspersed with the authentic Hoover films (*Queen of the Mob, Parole Fixer*), which overlapped into the early forties, were a number of other thrillers and detective mysteries which had no official contact with the Hoover sourcebook, but which were so alike in production "look" and in cast that it is difficult to separate them. Typical is *Daughter of Shanghai*, dealing with the smuggling of aliens, which had the novelty value of Philip Ahn as a Chinese FBI man and Anna May Wong as an amateur detective investigating the murder of her father. Ahn was actually the nominal hero, but rather churlishly got billing at the bottom of the cast below such bigger names as J. Carrol Naish, Evelyn Brent, Buster Crabbe, and Fred Kohler, many of whom had virtually only a scene or two.

King of Alcatraz (its title is misleading for most of the action takes place aboard ship, and the villain—J. Carrol Naish—has escaped from Alcatraz *before* the picture starts) is not a detective film but is worthy of mentioning in passing since it is perhaps the best of this entire group and illustrates just what style, production value,

G-MEN (1935): Federal agent James Cagney unimpressed by the combined menace of Russell Hopton, William Pawley and Barton MacLane.

and movement can be packed into a 58-minute picture by a director (in this case, Robert Florey) who really knows what he is doing. Beautifully photographed, edited with precision, it takes over elaborate standing sets where feasible, uses cunning lighting to create illusions of height or size where none exists, and apart from its notable cast of Paramount regulars (Lloyd Nolan, Harry Carey, Gail Patrick, Robert Preston) uses as many trainee apprentices on the way up (Dennis Morgan, Richard Denning) and veterans reduced to "bit" status (Gustav von Seyffertitz, Tom Tyler) as seemed to be in the studio at the time, creating a cast that by today's standards is most impressive. And, moreover, every face, every acting talent, was *used*. Only in its two men—one girl romantic rivalry, and its attendant trite dialogue, did it ever slide down to normal "B" picture levels.

While *King of Alcatraz* is outstanding, all of the films in the series have the same efficiency. Some, like *Hunted Men,* a reformation story, stay principally with the underworld; others, like *Illegal Traffic* and *Tip Off Girls* switch their emphasis from time to time, first concentrating on the gangsters (Anthony Quinn, Buster Crabbe, Lloyd Nolan), then on the G-Men (Robert Preston, Ralph Bellamy, Lynne Overman). This constantly shifting emphasis enabled the series to acquire a kind of underplayed objectivity, quite remarkable in the face of the decidedly melodramatic content and the often deliberate playing down of any potential documentary values.

Lloyd Nolan, who appeared in so many of these Paramount "B"s, was one of the very few players who was able to switch back and forth effortlessly between detective and heavy roles without one suffering at the expense of the other. Perhaps this was partially possible because he was an actor rather than a star, without the following of a Cagney (or, later, an Alan Ladd), whose fans might be disappointed at the constant changing of image.

And, basically, Nolan did not change. The qualities he projected—nonchalance, professionalism, courage, a sense of humor—were appropriate to either role. Even when playing as coldblooded a killer as he did in *She Couldn't Take It* or *Johnny Apollo,* he somehow retained the respect of audiences. Probably, his villain roles remain more vividly in the memory because of this. After all, one *expects* to respect the hero. And, again, in detective roles he often made the greater impression when *not* the star. He was likable enough as Michael Shayne, Private Detective, but outstanding in the quite small role of the city detective in *Somewhere in the Night.* Walking into a restaurant, almost subliminally snapping his fingers in a half-suppressed salute to a recognized off-screen acquaintance, he is *both* the assured detective who knows his job and the assured *actor* who makes the most of a scene by immersing himself in it, but doing so casually, with no obvious demonstration of

technique. It is a pity that Nolan's long and varied association with the detective film (including his interestingly played *crooked* detective in *The Lady in the Lake*) has never given him the chance to *star* in a major film as a Marlowe or a Sam Spade.

From the "B"s of the thirties, the moviegoing public received a thorough education in the modus operandi of every conceivable kind of racket, while MGM's admirable little series of shorts bearing the overall title of "Crime Does Not Pay" covered even some of the more obscure rackets that didn't have enough mileage in them for features. One of the criminal activities receiving an inordinate amount of attention was the smuggling of aliens—primarily Chinese—into ,the country. Invariably, such films had a sequence in the first reel of the airborne gangsters, spotted by Border Patrol planes, pulling an all-purpose lever in the cockpit which caused the whole bottom of the passenger section to drop out, thus jettisoning the human cargo. Such callousness seemed acceptable because the victims were merely Chinese, and therefore no more human than the faceless redskins that bit the dust in westerns. This particular branch of gangster film usually required an airborne detective, so that the climactic sequence could be a dogfight rather than the traditional car chase and shootout.

The quality of these endless "B"s varied from company to company. There was an enormous difference between the skill of the Paramounts and the rather tangled and skimpy look of the Columbias, wherein young G-Man Robert Paige found himself up against racketeer brother Don Terry (*The G-Men Step In*) or American Legionnaire Don Terry turned detective himself to solve a murder in the particularly turgid and talkative *Squadron of Honor.* One enterprising little "B" series at Warner Brothers seemed out to devote one film to each major racket, systematically working its way through alien smuggling, counterfeiting, and other crimes, to be stopped only when star Ronald Reagan was promoted to better things. Nevertheless, in 1939–40, *Secret Service of the Air, Code of the Secret Service, Smashing the Money Ring,* and *Murder in the Air* managed to cover a lot of territory in the usual high-powered Warner Brothers manner, with stories (and fights and chases) that moved along too fast and too professionally for anyone to notice any holes in logic. Ronald Reagan was a breezy detective, Eddie Foy, Jr. his more-sensible-than-usual comedy relief, and John Litel their Washington superior.

In 1938 the whole gangster cycle was suddenly revitalized by the unexpected success of *Angels with Dirty Faces.* In the films that followed (*The Roaring Twenties, Each Dawn I Die, High Sierra*) the pattern of the earlier gangster talkies was repeated. Once more, the stress was almost exclusively on the gangster himself, and the de-

Scenes illustrative of the semi-documentary content of the film LET 'EM HAVE IT (1935).

G-MEN: Cagney tangles with William Pawley.

G-men Harvey Stevens and Richard Arlen: LET 'EM HAVE IT.

Richard Arlen and Bruce Cabot: LET 'EM HAVE IT.

BULLETS OR BALLOTS (1936): Charles Wilson, Barton MacLane, Edward G. Robinson.

PUBLIC ENEMY'S WIFE (1936): Margaret Lindsay, Cesar Romero, Pat O'Brien.

SECRET AGENT X-9 (1937): A popular comic strip turned into a movie serial: villain Henry Brandon (on top) battles hero Scott Kolk.

MARKED WOMAN (1937): Bette Davis and Humphrey Bogart.

THIS IS MY AFFAIR (1937): One of the most elaborate detective melodramas of the thirties, set at the turn of the century; with Robert Taylor as the government under-cover man, and Victor McLaglen as one of the heavies.

127

Glenda Farrell and Barton MacLane, stars of the "Torchy Blane" series.

A later "Torchy" entry: TROUBLE IN PANAMA, with Lola Lane and Paul Kelly.

tective took a back seat. Rather quickly this cycle was affected by the war years, and the gangster (Humphrey Bogart, Alan Ladd) was affected by a suddenly discovered patriotism, himself assuming the role of detective, and, freed of red tape, moving into action against Nazi and Japanese spies. The immediate postwar period saw a very tentative attention paid to the plight of the returning ex-soldier, unable to readjust to civilian life, and drifting into crime. Robert Florey's *The Crooked Way* was a good example of this school, although the British *They Made Me a Fugitive,* a grimly pessimistic film directed by Alberto Cavalcanti and starring Trevor Howard, was by far the best. Again, the detective had little to do in these films. However, the facts of life did not really support such a thesis—conditions were vastly different from those following World War I—and this cycle quickly petered out. The war did, however, bring a lucrative new pastime to movie detectives: the tracking down of Nazi war criminals who had gone into hiding (usually in small midwest college towns) to establish respectable reputations and await the day when the Nazis would rise again. Edward G. Robinson, who had been the first to track down Nazis before war was officially declared (in *Confessions of a Nazi Spy*), was first on the trail again in peacetime, pursuing, breaking down, and finally confronting Orson Welles in *The Stranger*—and driving him to a bizarre Wellesian end, impaled on the sword of a moving figure on a clock tower!

The mid-forties saw a tentative stab at resurrecting the old-time gangster film via Monogram's *Dillinger* and Fox's much-censored *Roger Touhy, Last of the Gangsters,* but while they were profitable they were too routine to warrant much attention or duplicating. The G-Man, the T-Man, and other specialized governmental detectives came to the fore again in the newly-in-vogue semidocumentary approaches to crime instigated by March of Time producer Louis de Rochemont. Extensive use of location shooting, careful reenactments of actual cases, and detailed depiction of the newest in scientific techniques, backed by the official if rather pompous tones of narrator Reed Hadley, made these films seem fresh and exciting for a while. Some of them certainly *were* novel; others, like *The Street with No Name* (directed by William Keighley of *G-Men,* and with the same straightforward style), were really basically familiar plots and characters decked out with documentary trappings.

The best film of this cycle was undoubtedly *Boomerang,* directed by Elia Kazan, with Dana Andrews, Jane Wyatt, and a group of then unfamiliar character players. It was the least sensational in terms of plot content (a murder mystery, but one that led to bigger questions of personal integrity within local government) and the one that

Another comic strip to serial transfer: RED BARRY (1938), starring Buster Crabbe with Frances Robinson.

THE PREVUE MURDER MYSTERY (1936): One of the best of several mysteries set against a film studio background. Thomas Jackson, still in harness, investigates a murder with the help of studio publicity man Reginald Denny.

Robert Florey, director of PREVUE MURDER MYSTERY, and some of the best of Paramount's fast and slick detective thrillers of the thirties; seen here with Anna May Wong, whom he directed in DAUGHTER OF SHANGHAI.

ILLEGAL TRAFFIC (1938): J. Carrol Naish has the drop on G-Man Robert Preston.

ILLEGAL TRAFFIC: Detective Monte Blue gives road-block instructions to police chief Joseph Crehan.

least emphasized its documentary format. Most of the ponderous pronouncements as to its authenticity were disposed of in the opening credits, and then the film settled down to being relaxed and thorough; the kind of spontaneous and realistic film that Elia Kazan had always wanted to make and would return to as often as he could in the future.

After *Call Northside 777* and one or two other high-caliber films, a documentary veneer became merely fashionable, used to no specific purpose. Anthony Mann's *T-Men* was a strong, tautly written film, photographed in low key as was Mann's style, very much of a studio-created film despite the presumed authenticity of its case history. It would probably have worked even better than it did (it was both a critical and a commercial success) if it had not had the documentary framework thrust upon it. It was enough that a deserted street was just that; it was not necessary to provide the actual address or the time and place of the incident. A long sequence in Hollywood's Farmer's Market is presumably made "authentic" by a couple of long-shot establishing scenes filmed there; but the intrusion of a line telling us that it is the Farmer's Market is both extraneous and also somewhat of a cheat, since the balance of the scene is shot in front of studio process screens. It's perhaps a gesture toward realism when one of the most likable T-Men in the case is murdered in cold blood; but it is also a reuse of an old cliché since he is that familiar old friend, the happily married agent. (True, dedicated married agents undoubtedly do lay down their lives in the course of their duty; but so, doubtless, do bachelors and widowers—except in the movies.)

The sheer novelty of the realist approach soon wore off, but not before it had been absorbed by the "B" pictures as well, becoming as much of a cliché as the melodramatic action content that it was displacing. Little films like *Special Agent* may have gained in superficial realism, and players like William Eythe and George Reeves would bring a certain freshness to their detectives because they were new to the game, but what these "B"s gained in conviction they usually sacrificed in excitement.

The postwar attention to the neurotic criminals and the fad for psychiatric themes led to interesting mergings of the psychology of crime and the documentary approach to produce films like *The Killers*. Admirably and creatively expanded from Ernest Hemingway's classic short story, it starred Burt Lancaster as the gangland assassination victim, and Edmond O'Brien as the unromanticized insurance detective who uncovers the facts in the case.

The investigation reveals several layers of multiple double-dealing involved in an armored-car robbery and, after a climax of mass slaughter in which the hoodlums who have not been wiped out by each other are gunned down by the police, the detective is rewarded with the knowledge that, thanks to the success of his work and the recovery of much of the loot, insurance rates for the following season may drop a cent or two!

In the mid-forties, director Robert Siodmak seemed to be the nearest rival to Alfred Hitchcock and Fritz Lang as a master of the suspense film. *The Killers* was one of his best, though strangely it does not survive too well, and such less technique-conscious films as *Criss Cross* (considered a disappointing Siodmak at the time) hold up rather better. It debt to *Citizen Kane* can now be recognized much more clearly, and its complex construction of a series of flashback interviews by which the detective pieces the puzzle together now seems somewhat pretentious, and by virtue of its stress on artfully lit closeups even seems to smack of television technique. Moreover, its occasional use of documentary style sits uneasily with its obvious studio sets, its glossy camerawork and lighting, and its once powerful but now cliché musical score by Miklos Rosza. Nevertheless, it was one of the better detective films of the forties and established Edmond O'Brien as the methodical, unglamorous modern sleuth, a role he played well in many subsequent films.

The gangster film made little headway on the screen in the late forties, having been rendered unfashionable by the cycle of private eye films.

However, James Cagney, who twice before had been a catalyst in launching cycles of gangster films, did it again in 1950 with *White Heat*—a tough, sadistic, fast, and violent return to the old style (but with new trimmings) by director Raoul Walsh. Although its basic plot was of the old tradition, it was modern enough to have a psychopathic killer as its villain. While the emphasis was on this colorful figure (Cagney) and on the action content of his crime wave, the construction of the plot gave almost equal time to the FBI, with Edmond O'Brien again the key detective. Documentary coverage of police methods was less exaggerated than in such earlier films as *Let 'Em Have It,* less prosaic than in the de Rochemont films, and aimed at keeping the film excitingly on the move. The film worked surprisingly well, and in time came to be regarded as a minor classic for both Walsh and Cagney.

Several lesser gangster films (including Cagney's *Kiss Tomorrow Goodbye*) followed, but it wasn't until Allied Artists' *Al Capone* in 1959, a fantastic boxoffice success, that a whole new series of "traditional" gangster films took hold. Production Code requirements had now relaxed, and the emphasis was more and more on brutality and sex. Cashing in on the growing fad for nostalgia, the gangster films tried vainly to emulate such past hits as *Scarface* via reconstructions of the twenties—*The Purple Gang, Pretty Boy Floyd, The Rise and Fall of*

PAROLE FIXER (1939): Jack Carson, William Henry and Lyle Talbot in training as FBI agents.

Legs Diamond. The detective was largely bypassed in these films. *Pay or Die,* an exception, was a realistic account of the Italian detective (played by Ernest Borgnine) who had first exposed the workings of the Mafia. *Hell on Frisco Bay* was an enjoyably simple old-time confrontation between detective Alan Ladd and crime czar Edward G. Robinson.

By now, Cagney had virtually retired; Raft played the cop more frequently than the hood but without much feeling or excitement; Bogart died. No new players with their dynamism came to take their place, and it was the writer-director who became the guiding force of the occasional worthwhile gangster film (*Bonnie and Clyde*). With the traditional gangster film all but dead and the FBI somewhat discredited through its involvement in wiretapping, harassment of civil rights leaders, and other activities bad for the public relations image, the FBI hero was all but dead too—except possibly on television. Director Mervyn LeRoy tried, via a large-scale Technicolor tribute *The F.B.I. Story,* to restore some of

PAROLE FIXER: Scenes establishing Jack Carson as a happily married (to Fay Helm) family man automatically assure him an early demise.

their sagging glory. But James Stewart, as the folksy, all-purpose, Frank Capra-ish agent inspired neither belief nor confidence, and the attempt to present a composite picture of FBI cases and methods didn't work nearly as well as the much less ambitious *Bureau of Missing Persons* back in 1933.

The local city detective, as opposed to the more publicized Washington-based FBI operator or T-Man, received but scant attention from Hollywood until the late forties. During the thirties, whenever a local detective was featured in a series of any duration, it was inevitably as a second-stringer to a private sleuth (the Inspector Markham—Philo Vance relationship) or, more embarrassing still, as the foil for a much brighter *female* amateur.

This latter pattern was probably set by Warner's *Miss Pinkerton* (1932), a lively adaptation of the Mary Roberts Rinehart story which managed to pack a surprising amount of traditional "old house" chills (including a black-cloaked killer, clutching hands, and the inevitable storm) into a more up-to-date mystery about the murder

that everybody (except the heroine) wants to dismiss as suicide. Running only just over an hour, it was one of several typical Warner Brothers comedy-thrillers of the period that offered "A" entertainment on a "B" running time. Joan Blondell as the private nurse–amateur detective and George Brent as the official detective on the case made a good team, Brent's suppressed frustration making for a better contrast than when her cohort was James Cagney, whose pepper and wisecracks matched her own. Although no world beater at the boxoffice, *Miss Pinkerton* had the stuff for a sustaining series, and presumably only the monetary obstacle of paying for the story and character rights prevented this.

Much later in the year, however, the most successful of the similar teamings got under way with *The Penguin Pool Murder,* the first in the series of RKO Radio's adaptations of Stuart Palmer's Hildegarde Withers mysteries. The redoubtable Miss Withers was an opinionated schoolteacher with a talent for sleuthing; her counterpart, a bachelor of the same somewhat over-forty age, Inspec-

NANCY DREW, TROUBLE SHOOTER (1939): Bonita Granville and Frankie Thomas cornered by killer Erville Alderson.

QUEEN OF THE MOB (1940): FBI men Jack Carson and Ralph Bellamy with Hedda Hopper.

THE NIGHT OF JANUARY 16TH (1941): Robert Preston, Ellen Drew, Nils Asther.

tor Piper, an intelligent detective but one not prone to dig too much in those proverbially "open and shut cases." The roles could have been written for craggy Edna May Oliver and sour and dubious James Gleason. Despite Hildegarde's constant one-upsmanship in proving him wrong, a genuine affection exists between the two that is never allowed to develop into anything sticky.

The series owed a tremendous amount to their characterizations and teamwork but, while the mysteries often got off to an extremely promising start, they never remained mysterious for long, and RKO's "B" product of the period was singularly lacking in snap and sparkle. The films tended to plod, telling more of their stories than was necessary in dialogue, and the photographic work was often listless. *The Penguin Pool Murder* offered the most potential in its opening—the discovery of a body in the zoo's penguin pool while Miss Withers has a class there on an outing. Both it and the second in the series, *Murder on the Blackboard,* were lacking in suspense and effective mystery. The third, *Murder on a Honeymoon*

I WAKE UP SCREAMING (1941), with Laird Cregar as the psychopathic cop who terrorizes Betty Grable and Carole Landis, and tries to shift the blame for his murder of Carole Landis on to Victor Mature.

(1935), was a distinct step up, however. It was set on Catalina Island and, while most of the backgrounds were provided by back projection, a unit did do some shooting there and the feeling of an at least partial escape from the studio into the fresh air was beneficial. Catalina's Casino was pressed into effective service as the background for some nocturnal prowlings and, while the identity of the killer was guessable, at least there was a little more doubt than usual. One advantage of the series was that thus far they had been well spaced—only one film per year—so that the plots and the characters were not stereotyped through overfrequent usage. Edna May Oliver left the series after *Murder on a Honeymoon,* but James Gleason stayed on as Inspector Piper for three more films in 1936–37. Helen Broderick took over in *Murder on a*

A young Alan Ladd as the detective and secondary hero of PAPER BULLETS (1941), just a year before he achieved stardom.

Robert Preston as the detective hero of THIS GUN FOR HIRE (1942), with Veronica Lake and Emmet Vogan.

THE MYSTERY OF THE 13TH GUEST (1943), another remake. Dumb detectives Frank Faylen, Tim Ryan, and a smarter one, Dick Purcell.

One of the most virile and no-nonsense of all serial detectives was Jack Holt. From HOLT OF THE SECRET SERVICE (1942), with Tristram Coffin.

BACKGROUND TO DANGER (1943): Intermingling of the detective thriller with the spy melodrama: Peter Lorre, Brenda Marshal, George Raft.

THE PHANTOM KILLER (1943), a neat remake of Lionel Atwill's old THE SPHINX. With Dick Purcell, Warren Hymer, John Hamilton.

Bridle Path, making Hildegarde more caustic and something of a shrew. ZaSu Pitts' transforming of the role into her customary dithering zany (in *The Plot Thickens* and *Forty Naughty Girls*) didn't help either, and the series died.

Coincident with its demise, however, a much brisker series was under way over at Warner Brothers. Torchy Blane was a wisecracking, fast-talking blonde, a newspaper reporter bundle of energy, and in her quest for scoops was constantly getting in the way of boyfriend Lieutenant Steve McBride. Torchy was played by Glenda Farrell, a delightful comedienne and character actress when playing in support of such Warner stars as Warren William or James Cagney, but a shade too overbearing when given the solo lead. (It may have been a delayed outcome of her role in *The Mystery of the Wax Museum* where she took over from the nominal heroine, Fay Wray, put the nonhero in his place, and solved the titular mystery herself.) Boyfriend Barton MacLane, in a welcome change from gangster roles, nevertheless played his detective rather like a thug; quick to use his fists, quick to jump to the wrong conclusions, slow to think, and constantly arriving on the scene to find Torchy already there and the story phoned in. As a concession to his masculine pride, most of the films usually had a climactic situation wherein Torchy had outsmarted herself and had to rely on his brawn for rescue. Like the Bulldog Drummond films of the same period, their delayed marriage was used as a plot gimmick, but fortunately the idea was not

THE BERMUDA MYSTERY (1944): Preston Foster, Anne Rutherford.

J. Edgar Bromberg and Charles Dingle question Barbara Stanwyck in LADY OF BURLESQUE (1943), based on Gypsy Rose Lee's THE G-STRING MURDERS. The killer is well in evidence in the still, obvious to moviegoers if not to the detectives on the case.

135

stressed and they were such an ill-matched couple that audiences were hardly holding their breath awaiting the union. Barton MacLane's main concession to his playing of the cop was that he shouted a shade less belligerently than when playing the hoodlum.

As his aide was the inevitable sergeant, both dumber and stronger, played by Tom Kennedy. Like all Warner "B"s, the Torchy Blane films had a certain speed and zip, crisp editing, good musical scores, and efficient casts. The best was *Torchy Blane in Chinatown,* but here for once was a series not particularly helped by its stars. Tentative switches in casting toward the end of the series resulted in Lola Lane and Paul Kelly—more subdued and more qualified than MacLane, one felt, for the rank of Lieutenant—in *Trouble in Panama.* The last of the series, *Torchy Plays With Dynamite,* offered a pert Jane Wyman as Torchy, playing the role on a less hard-boiled level, and rather like a slightly grown-up Deanna Durbin. Allen Jenkins' assumption of the role of Steve McBride was not particularly helpful, since he played more for comedy and the gap between him and the still retained Tom Kennedy was too narrow.

Perhaps the most striking generation and sex gap in the "B" detective mysteries of the thirties took place in Warner's Nancy Drew series. Drew senior, played by John Litel, was a lawyer rather than a detective, but was frequently drawn somewhat unwillingly into an investigative role because of close friends with murder raps hanging over them. Teenage daughter Nancy (eighteen in the books but played as closer to fifteen in the movies by a bouncy and effervescent Bonita Granville) follows the Philo Vance route by never accepting official parental or police verdicts—and, of course, is ultimately proven correct. Her harrowing escapades—including the unearthing of a body in a field, being pursued by a killer through a secret passageway, and being set adrift in a pilotless plane—seem to leave her with no traumas whatsoever. The four Nancy Drew mysteries were all directed by William Clemens and scripted by Kenneth Gamet, based with reasonable accuracy on a quartet from the endless supply of books by Carolyn Keene.

For films designed mainly for juvenile audiences, they were astonishingly noncondescending. The thrills were all genuine, even if punctuated with a certain amount of comedy relief, and the plots and villains were quite strong enough to stand up to adult scrutiny. Solid if not outstanding in production values (the small-town setting was not too demanding in that respect), the films were also surprisingly long for "B" pictures, some even running as much as eight reels, so that the plots did have time to develop neatly and not be rushed into a five-reel comic-strip format. Expert little films in their way and quite unappreciated in the thirties (when juvenile audiences had an

Fritz Lang's THE WOMAN IN THE WINDOW (1944): Detectives Raymond Massey and Thomas Jackson, unaware that their friend Edward G. Robinson is also the killer they seek.

One of the best detective mysteries of the forties: LAURA (1944),
with Dana Andrews, Clifton Webb, Gene Tierney.

abundance of riches at the movies), they could help to fill part of the gaping void in contemporary films for youngsters were they to be reissued. *Nancy Drew, Trouble Shooter* (the one in which the body is dug up in the cabbage field!) was probably the best of this enjoyable series.

Apart from Hildegarde, Torchy, and Nancy, lady detectives with their own series were not in abundance in the thirties, but on an individual basis they cropped up in film after film. Karen Morley had the title role in *The Girl from Scotland Yard,* a strange little movie with a whale of an opening reel (illustrating the ingenious uses to which Eduardo Cianelli put his Death Ray) and an equally exciting if not too believable climax of an aerial dogfight over Buckingham Palace. In between lay four reels of total tedium and the most moronic of detective

THE STRANGER (1945): Orson Welles' eerie chiller about a Nazi war criminal (Welles) brought to justice by mild-mannered (until the last reel) detective Edward G. Robinson.

THE KILLERS (1946): Insurance investigator Edmond O'Brien corners one of the robbery suspects, Jack Lambert.

THE KILLERS: The showdown. Albert Dekker lies dying, victim of double-cross by Ava Gardner. Detectives Edmond O'Brien and Sam Levene (left) look on.

MURDER IN THE MUSIC HALL (1946): Examination of corpse (Nils Asther) is witnessed by detectives Paul Hurst and William Gargan.

SOMEWHERE IN THE NIGHT (1946): one of the finest thrillers of the forties. John Hodiak, Nancy Guild, Lloyd Nolan and Richard Conte.

T-MEN (1949): Alfred Ryder, his T-man identity discovered, is killed by Charles McGraw while fellow agent Dennis O'Keefe is powerless to intervene.

T-MEN: Dennis O'Keefe gets a going-over from Charles McGraw and Jack Overman.

work. In the forties, Monogram put Jean Parker to work as "Detective Kitty O'Day" (with Peter Cookson as the downtrodden male in the case). Monogram also brought ZaSu Pitts back to the detective fold with a little item titled *So's Your Aunt Emma,* but the material was weak and Pitts badly wasted. *Mary Ryan Detective* (1949, with Marsha Hunt) was another of the infrequent and unfollowed-up distaff sleuths.

From the mid-forties on, there was a subtle change in the character of many of the screen's "official" detectives. In the thirties they tended to fall into two categories. There were the Inspector Markhams and Pipers, detectives doing a job well if rather colorlessly, without particular zeal or crusading convictions. Their opposite numbers were men like James Cagney, Chester Morris, and Richard Arlen—less concerned with the end than with the means, and like Errol Flynn's privateer in *The Sea Hawk,* in the game as much for the excitement as for any abstract ideals of justice.

The mid-forties, however, saw a new kind of detective hero emerging: the idealist, the romantic, typified best perhaps by Dana Andrews in Otto Preminger's still first-rate *Laura.* As the detective who finds himself falling in love with the picture and memory of the girl (Gene Tierney) whose murder he is investigating, only to have her turn up alive (and provoke a further murder attempt), Andrews (quite one of the best of the newer actors of the forties) created an original and far more human detective than we were used to. Mark Stevens was another who continued in this tradition.

The role became more hardboiled in the fifties and, if romance was included, it was often a soiled, secondhand romance. Glenn Ford (in *The Big Heat* and *Undercover Man*), Cornell Wilde (in *The Big Combo*), and Gary Merrill (in *The Human Jungle*) were fighting a new, computerized kind of crime, where illegal profits were hidden by legal books and tax loopholes. Anger and frustration, with the occasional added spur of personal revenge (for the killing of a wife or the loss of a position), were the incentives that kept these detectives on the job. *The Big Heat* was one of the best of these films; directed by Fritz Lang, it seemed almost like a modernization of one of his nightmarish German silent thrillers, with Glenn Ford trying to get the goods on a virtual untouchable, who not only controlled the outflung empire of a Dr. Mabuse, but wielded the additional weapon of being cultured, charming, and a family man with reputation beyond reproach.

Even in the littler, less ambitious thrillers dealing with the individual crime rather than the crime empire, the detective's image changed. With the gradual decline and disappearance of the "B" series pictures, the stereo-typed dumb cop and his dumber sergeant vanished too. In their place came sensible and well-scripted little pictures designed to use their detective hero once and once only, films like *Sudden Danger,* and *Bobby Ware Is Missing* (both good Allied Artists "B"s of the fifties, with Bill Elliott and Neville Brand as their respective detective heroes.

RKO Radio's *Strange Bargain* (1948) had a particularly cunning little plot about a bankrupt businessman who plans to commit suicide, but asks his accountant, a man badly in need of money (well played by Jeffrey Lynn), to change the evidence afterward to suggest murder so that his widow will still be able to collect the insurance money which would be invalidated on a suicide death. The accountant refuses but then, out of loyalty to his boss, goes through with the arrangement when he is too late to prevent his death. His guilt feelings are increased when another man is implicated and murder is proven. Real detective buffs should have no trouble spotting the identity of the real murderer from the usual least likely corner, but in this instance the solution is of less importance than the gradual and logical building of a case for murder and the interesting character study.

The detective in charge is a sardonic, slightly bitter World War II veteran with a limp and a cane; Henry Morgan uses these "props" and a world-weary style of speech to build the role into a much more interesting one than it probably was in script form. And for once it *is* the detective who solves the case, not the innocently involved heroes).

One of the most individual of all movie detectives (though he strove to be an underplayed composite) was Jack Webb's Sergeant Friday of *Dragnet.* TV so thoroughly drained the novelty of the documentary treatment of the thriller, so formularized it for a dozen minor series like "I Am the Law" and "Racket Squad," that it became almost a liability for the movie thriller. It returned only for the occasional film like *The Phenix City Story,* which, being based on then recent scandalous exposures and magazine articles about the corruption and crime czars in that Alabama town, *had* to be filmed on the actual locations and name names in the incredible recital of vice and murder, or it wouldn't have been believed. But, otherwise, the documentary detective film had become almost the sole property of television, and Jack Webb's "Dragnet" series its chief spokesman. Perhaps it overdid its hard-sell insistence on naming times, dates, places, and other details of its investigations, and the dead-panned unemotionalism of Jack Webb's Friday. Its musical theme and its catch phrases soon became standard jokes for lampooners and TV comics. But Webb had real talent as a director and was a good actor

MR. DISTRICT ATTORNEY (1947): Adolphe Menjou, Michael O'Shea.

KISS OF DEATH (1947): Brian Donlevy, Richard Widmark, Victor Mature.

THE BRIBE (1928): Charles Laughton as the weak link in the crime chain is pumped by detective Robert Taylor.

STAGE STRUCK (1948): One of several neat mystery films made by Monogram in the late forties; FBI hero Conrad Nagel, and Audrey Long.

INCIDENT (1948): Another good Monogram "B"; Warren Douglas, Jane Frazee.

HE WALKED BY NIGHT (1948): One of the best and least recognized of the semi-documentary crime cycle; James Cardwell, Jack Webb, Scott Brady.

HE WALKED BY NIGHT

to boot; when he turned "Dragnet" into a big-screen color movie for Warner's in 1954, he succeeded in riding roughshod over all the clichés and turning out a detective movie in the realist style that was sharp, vicious, and totally engrossing. Having proved that he could do it, he also had the wit not to follow through with more of the same. His next film as director-star, though similar in style, was totally different in content. *Pete Kelly's Blues* was a powerful and rather sad melodrama about a jazz musician in the twenties. The period detail was flawlessly evoked, and it was a much better film than *Dragnet,* though less well received. His later films, offbeat though they were, failed to restore the momentum of *Dragnet,* and his directorial career petered out: one of the most laudable failures of the fifties.

Between 1942 and the early 1950s, MGM turned out one of the most enjoyable and unpretentious groups of detective films—though they were unrelated by star, producer, or budget. In fact, they started out as high-caliber "B" films, designed at least partially as training grounds for new stars and directors, and they wound up as equally high-caliber programmers, good enough to rate

"A" playing time, short enough to qualify as co-features. One of their basic uses to the studio in this latter phase was as a way to keep contract players like Van Johnson and Ricardo Montalban busy in commercially reliable pictures after their particular boxoffice appeal had waned, but while their names still carried enough prestige to indicate a quality product.

Made in 1942, *Kid Glove Killer* was designed both to try out director Fred Zinneman, recently promoted from short subjects, in a "safe" feature, and to help build the studio's rather offbeat new star, Van Heflin. In comparison with all of the standardized "B" mysteries flooding the market at that time, *Kid Glove Killer* was a neat and crisp little film, concentrating on the laboratory methods of deduction (with Van Heflin as a police scientist), yet with enough concessions to traditional detective fare (including an exciting last-reel unmasking of the killer) not to alienate fans who didn't want too highbrow an approach to their favorite fodder.

Kid Glove Killer received deservedly good reviews and widespread exhibition. Recognition for Zinneman's talents were so immediate that after one more thriller—

144

CALL NORTHSIDE 777 (1948): Another of the documentary cycle; James Stewart as a newspaper reporter assumes the detective role in order to prove the innocence of Richard Conte.

the equally interesting *Eyes in the Night,* in which Edward Arnold played a blind detective—he was promoted to prestige production, and more than fulfilled everyone's expectations with his direction of Spencer Tracy's *The Seventh Cross.* Though an anti-Nazi propaganda piece (and a more balanced and sober one than most films of that period), it was also a suspense thriller and a logical extension of Zinneman's two earlier films.

Van Heflin made one more detective "B" himself (*Grand Central Murder*) which retained the MGM slickness, but otherwise was a film much inferior to *Kid Glove Killer,* much more stereotyped in its plotting. By the end of the forties, MGM had established an interesting formula for individual detective films that combined the costumary studio gloss with a nod to the fashionable documentary techniques and good, sober, basically realistic scripts. Films like *Scene of the Crime* (with Van Johnson) and *Mystery Street* (with Ricardo Montalban) were typical, most impressive of all perhaps being 1949's *Border Incident* dealing with the smuggling of aliens into the

U.S.A. from Mexico to be exploited as cheap farm labor. George Murphy and Ricardo Montalban were the Immigration Department investigators who found themselves up against a gang that was a monumental tribute to the Hollywood typecasting system: Howard da Silva, Charles McGraw, Arnold Moss, Rudolf Acosta, and Alfonso Bedoya! The location shooting along the Mexico-California border added to the film's realism and helped compensate for the rather ordinary story line of the investigators worming their way into the gang's confidence and working from the inside. The lack of any romantic or comedy relief and director Anthony Mann's always rather heavy direction and stark, low-key lighting tended to make it perhaps a little *too* serious. The killing of one of the detectives by having him run over by the revolving knives of a furrow-ploughing tractor—an unexpected shock scene at a time when co-stars in movies were still not killed off so casually—further took it out of the realm of light crime-thriller entertainment.

One of the more interesting trends of the forties

CRIME AND PUNISHMENT (1935): A Hollywood interpretation of a Russian detective inspector. Edward Arnold, left, as Porfiri, with Peter Lorre as Raskolnikov, Elisabeth Risdon, Robert Allen, Tala Birell.

was the beginning of an increasing filmic attention to the "crooked cop"—or, at least, the disturbed or neurotic cop. It has never reached the scale on which our myths about the Old West have been denigrated and demolished as a means of creating outlets for personal statements or for implied political propaganda. Of course, there are practical considerations. The 7th Cavalry and the Sioux nation are hardly in a position to lodge effective complaints, whereas too much stress on police corruption and brutality would undoubtedly result in the kind of co-operation (access to files, permits for location shooting, use of police locations and personnel) that Hollywood needs being suddenly withdrawn. Fox's *I Wake Up Screaming* was particularly novel in its use of a psychopathic detective, a sex fetishist who is the killer of the girl (Carole Landis) whose murder he is investigating, and the blame for which he tries to shift to Victor Mature. It was one of a remarkable series of criminal portraits by Laird Cregar, the others including the queasy criminal who orders the killings and is both fascinated and revolted by the details, in *This Gun for Hire,* Jack the Ripper in *The Lodger,* and the demented pianist George Bone in *Hangover Square.*

Later in the forties and early fifties, MGM offered Lloyd Nolan as the resentful, murdering cop in *The Lady in the Lake*—a basically good cop who has made one tragic blunder—and Robert Taylor as the more simply corrupt detective in *Rogue Cop.*

William Wyler's *Detective Story* was a pretentious adaptation of the hit play, rather harmed by too much "method" acting and a censorial toning down of certain key elements, but with an interesting study by Kirk Douglas of an unbalanced detective who has been making too many professional and personal mistakes, and who can expiate them only by deliberately causing his own death in the line of duty.

Perhaps the most gripping and intelligent of them all was Otto Preminger's *Where the Sidewalk Ends* (1950), from a really excellent script by Ben Hecht based on the novel *Night Cry* (by Frank Rosenberg). By a twist of

FEAR (1945): An interesting and unofficial (yet quite accurate, save for a happy ending) "B" updating of CRIME AND PUNISHMENT; Peter Cookson, left, as the student, Ernie Adams, and Warren William as the detective.

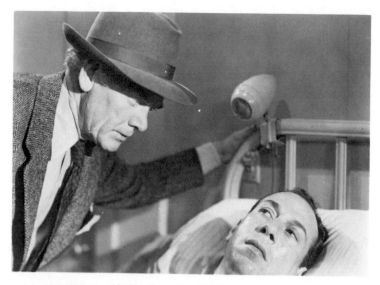

WHIRLPOOL (1949): Detective Charles Bickford and Jose Ferrer.

SCENE OF THE CRIME (1949): Van Johnson, John McIntyre, Leon Ames.

BORDER INCIDENT (1949): Arnold Moss (left) and Alfonso Bedoya (right) suspect that one of their gang, George Murphy, is a Government man.

irony unique to the film itself, Dana Andrews and Gene Tierney of *Laura* are united once more, and Andrews now seems to be playing the same detective a few years later, but no longer the romantic, beaten down by his job, by the cheap crooks, and chiselers he is involved with, and overprone to use his fists to beat information out of those that he has to interrogate. Warned several times, he goes too far, and unintentionally kills a man. The killing is accidental; the victim worthless; yet it is a crime that he knows can break him or send him to prison. Using his knowledge of police procedure, he covers up his part in the crime and plants false clues, but cannot avoid investigating the case himself. The double tension of following the larger case through to its conculusion without implicating himself in the killing which is a small part of it is beautifully maintained and the final solution is both logical, satisfying, and in no way a compromise. *Where the Sidewalk Ends* is one of the best and least known detective films of the fifties, and also one of Preminger's best.

But the last word in crooked cop movies—like the last word in so many movies—has to be provided by Orson

Welles. His brilliant essay in pure (and sometimes impure) filmic style in *Touch of Evil* (1958) has been analyzed so frequently and so extensively as to make comment on the film's structure and photographic fireworks redundant. It does fulfill one of the key (and seldom achieved) requirements of the movie mystery in that the audience—even the audience aware not only of all the rules, but also of the way that Welles will probably break and exploit them—has virtually no chance to deduce or guess the identity of the man who sets the bomb that kills two people in the film's opening sequence.

But seldom has it mattered less: by the time the film has weaved its labyrinth way (accompanied by constantly overlapping dialogue and a roving camera that seems never to come to a standstill) through an incredibly complicated and overpopulated plot, with a lengthy stopover at a motel (with victim Janet Leigh and handyman Dennis Weaver suggesting that here is the embryo for all of *Psycho*), the original crime has all but been forgotten, and we are lucky if we can keep up with the current action. Charlton Heston is the idealistic Mexican official reluctantly investigating the crime, meeting both racial

IMPACT (1949): Ella Raines, Anna May Wong and investigator Charles Coburn.

THE NAKED CITY (1948), directed by Jules Dassin, was the highpoint of the documentary crime films. Don Taylor and Barry Fitzgerald made a good team as the novice and veteran detectives.

149

WHERE THE SIDEWALK ENDS (1950): Dana Andrews, Gary Merrill.

BORDERLINE (1950): Fred MacMurray, Claire Trevor.

150

THE SNIPER (1951): Gerald Mohr, Adolphe Menjou.

C-MAN (1949): This is an excellent example of a really stylish film being turned out on a shoestring budget, imaginatively directed by Joseph Lerner, and with an interesting polytonal score by Gail Kubik. With Dean Jagger, John Carradine.

THE ENFORCER (1951): Zero Mostel and Humphrey Bogart.

I WAS A COMMUNIST FOR THE FBI: (1951): Edward Norris, Frank Lovejoy (the FBI man) Dorothy Hart and James Millican.

THE PEOPLE AGAINST O'HARA (1951): Pat O'Brien, Spencer Tracy, John Hodiak.

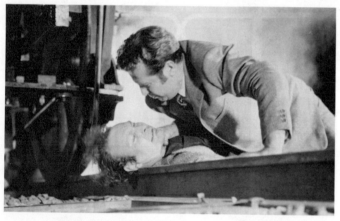

THE TALL TARGET (1951): A period melodrama, dealing with the successful attempt to thwart an assassination attempt on Abraham Lincoln; the pre-FBI detective is Dick Powell, here battling with Leif Ericson.

THE SYSTEM (1953): Frank Lovejoy, Dan Seymour.

prejudice and police antagonism on the American side of the line, specifically from the gross, unshaven, sweaty Orson Welles, and his only slightly more presentable assistant, Joseph Calleia.

Welles, his hatred of all criminals psychopathically motivated by the much earlier murder of his wife, is a "bad" cop in the sense that he accepts favors and graft, frames suspects by the planting of evidence, and cooks up phony witnesses to secure convictions. Conversely, he is a "good" cop in that he is totally dedicated to the ultimate ends of justice—if not to the letter of the law that should administrate it—and in that all of the manufactured evidence he created to secure fraudulent convictions was in a way justified since the men (as his instinct told him) *were* all guilty, but capable of using the law to escape scot free if he didn't stack the cards a little against them.

It's an incredible portrait, repugnant yet fascinating, not without humor and a certain literally soiled charm. One hates the man; yet one still understands him, and feels sorrier for him than for his victims. Joseph Calleia, his aide, is—like Dana Andrews in *Where the Sidewalk Ends*, though less directly—somewhat of a degeneration from a much nobler figure. One is tempted to cast one's recollections back to *Algiers* (1938) in which he played the French/Egyptian detective who, contemptuous of normal police methods, preferred to play a psychological waiting game, assured that in time Pepe le Moko would leave the Casbah and fall into his trap. Now, in *Touch of Evil,* the Casbah has become the equally seedy, smelly Tia Juana and he himself is trapped there. His methods are unchanged: he waits, watches, leaves the police work to others, remains loyal to his profession and to his boss—but could not exist without him, or in another environment. Calleia himself usually played villains; Welles in recent years has certainly enacted rather more than his share. Here he played a typical trick upon his audience by suggesting initially that this unholy pair were crooked detectives; taking it a step further by implying their relationship to the whole world of garish vice which it seems they may well control; and then finally revealing a dedication to duty (if not to fairness and orthodoxy) far greater than that of the hero, who somehow seems to lose a little stature with that revelation. It's unlikely that there will ever be a more obnoxious or repellent crooked detective than Orson Welles' in *A Touch of Evil*—or a more fascinating one.

While this survey of the detective film is intentionally limited to America and Britain, it is worth pausing in this chapter to note in passing the extremely prolific output of such films from France and Germany. Both countries

THE BIG HEAT (1953): One of the best of the later gangster films; directed by Fritz Lang, with Glen Ford and Gloria Grahame.

MEXICAN MANHUNT (1953): George Brent finished his career with a brace of "B" thrillers that were a far cry from his high-powered Warner films of the thirties; with Karen Sharpe.

ROGUE COP (1954): Robert Taylor, Keith Larsen.

BOBBY WARE IS MISSING (1955): Walter Reed, Neville Brand, Arthur Franz.

have paralleled one another in a number of respects: their interest in the genre from the very beginning of the silent period, a serial-like stress on the grotesque in the twenties, a *respect* for the species which has seen their biggest superstars—Hans Albers, Jean Gabin, Jean Paul Belmondo, Pierre Fresnay, Louis Jouvet, Heinz Ruhmann—frequently playing detective roles, and, rather oddly, a concentration on the *official* detective rather than on the private sleuth. Although important domestically, few of these continental mystery films have been seen outside of Europe, and thus it is unwise to attempt to use the limited (and obviously best) few that have been exported to form judgments about them all.

But it does seem safe to say that the interest in private detectives (for example, Eddie Constantine's Slim Callahan and Lemmy Caution roles) and secret agents has been largely a development of the James Bond era, and that hitherto Gallic and Teutonic detectives were essentially rather dull officials. This is especially true of the German films, where, with the exception of Willi Fritsch in Fritz Lang's 1928 *Spies* (itself somewhat lighter than most of Lang's thrillers), the detectives were usually as grim and humorless as the villains—and much less colorful. Detective Wenck, played by Bernard Goetzke in Lang's original 1922 *Dr. Mabuse,* was not even particularly bright, doggedly pursuing his enemy, inconveniencing him at odd moments, but doing little more to bring him to heel than discovering his secret identity (admittedly, not a minor accomplishment in a Mabuse film). But Mabuse's downfall was caused more by his own madness than by police opposition. Apparently, Wenck had no home life, and his whole being was devoted to the unemotional elimination of crime—without any sense of achievement or satisfaction at the successful conclusion of a case.

TOUCH OF EVIL (1958): Orson Welles kills local crime boss Akim Tamiroff, leaving his body draped over the bed of a drugged Janet Leigh.

PAY OR DIE (1959): A powerful and factual account of the Italian detective (played by Ernest Borgnine) who first exposed the workings of the Mafia in 1913.

THE PURPLE GANG (1960): One of the new breed of ultra-violent reconstructions of gangsterism in the twenties; Barry Sullivan is the dedicated detective who breaks up the infamous gang.

THE BOSTON STRANGLER (1968): George Kennedy, Henry Fonda.

THE BOSTON STRANGLER

157

BULLITT (1968): Steve McQueen.

BULLITT: Steve McQueen enjoys fringe benefits (Jacqueline Bisset) denied to movie detectives of less permissive eras.

Cut very much in the same pattern was Inspector Lohmann, the detective in *M* and *The Testament of Dr. Mabuse,* Lang's two early German crime films. Lohmann was played by large and rugged Otto Wernicke, who somewhat resembled a less corpulent Field Marshal Goering. Sound and dialogue humanized Lohmann a little; he was able to indicate wishful thinking for the fishing and sports that crime so often denied him. He was less a stylized figure of nemesis than Wenck had been, but was equally dedicated. And equally outshone by the psychopathic limelight of the master criminals he pursued. When the Mabuse films were remade in the sixties, Gert Frobe quite logically took over the Lohmann role.

France's detectives have included some memorable portraits, some of the best being by one of their finest

Sidney Poitier as Mr. Tibbs in
IN THE HEAT OF THE NIGHT.

M (1931): Fritz Lang's classic thriller, with Otto Wernicke (left) as Inspector Lohmann.

Harry Baur (right) as Inspector Porfiri in the 1935 French version of CRIME AND PUNISHMENT, with Pierre Blanchar (left) as Raskolnikov.

Detective Albert Prejean with Jany Holt and murderer Erich von Stroheim in L'ALIBI (1936).

actors, Louis Jouvet. Even the presence of Erich von Stroheim as a hypnotist-illusionist-killer in *L'Alibi* didn't entirely steal the spotlight away from Louis Jouvet playing the efficient but unglamourized city detective who finally runs him to earth. Jouvet's assistant, the film's romantic lead, was played by Albert Prejean; in a British remake of the early forties, also titled *Alibi,* Hugh Sinclair and James Mason played the same roles, though with considerably less individual style, and with the unmistakable feeling that they were typecast both as to role and as to what "names" the budget could afford.

Outstanding among French detective movies was *Quai des Orfevres* (1947), released in the United States under the title *Jenny Lamour.* It was directed by the cynical Henri Georges Clouzot whose films seemed shocking indeed by the standards of the late forties, and indeed retain their raw power and "nastiness" today, despite the fact that their physical detail is mild and tasteful compared with the explosions of violence and perversion now considered acceptable. *Quai des Orfevres* was a basically familiar murder mystery, its seedy show business background rendered with perhaps a little more realism than was customary, but what made it unique was its exploration of the *people* rather than the plot. All were less than admirable, yet all were somehow touching and real. Most of all, this applied to the detective "hero"; as played by Louis Jouvet, he was hard working and dedicated, appreciated by his department perhaps but never rewarded by it; unable to afford a decent apartment or new clothes, a lonely man living on the memory of a long-ago love, and with a half-caste son whom he dearly loves (but who is occasionally an embarrassment to him) providing the only warmth in his drab and somewhat futile existence. The mystery story itself is intriguing enough, and wrapped up without tricks, though perhaps too neatly and too quickly in the closing reel. (Having plunged all of his key characters into despair through their involvement in the case, Clouzot seems to lose interest in them when the script forces him to remove suspicion from them!) But it is the Jouvet performance that dominates.

Georges Simenon's Inspector Maigret was another "official" French detective, but one with a distinct personality. Without the flair for showmanship or spectacular deduction of his American counterparts, he preferred to wander around the neighborhood of a crime, prying here, poking there, picking up snippets of information over a glass of wine and suddenly marshalling his collection of facts, atmosphere, and suppositions into an intuitive solution. The French have made a number of Maigret films with Pierre Renoir, Heinz Ruhmann, and others; Charles Laughton even played the role in the

QUAI DES ORFEVRES (1947), released in the U.S. as JENNY LAMOUR, starring Louis Jouvet (center, with bow tie).

THAT MAN FROM RIO (1964): A breathlessly fast and very subtle spoof on detective-heroes, with Jean-Paul Belmondo.

PEPE LE MOKO (1937), with Lucas Gridoux as the native detective who finally captures the notorious Pepe (Jean Gabin).

164

interesting if rather untidy American-made *The Man on the Eiffel Tower*. But the best of the Maigrets, and the most familiar, was Jean Gabin, who, though perhaps a little old and a little too portly, did manage to suggest the methods and personality of Simenon's creation. Unfortunately, the films soon became formularized: entries like *Maigret Sees Red* dropped any suggestion of Maigret's home life and played down his unique detection methods, settling instead for a fairly straightforward treatment in which action was minimized and kept within realistic boundaries, but in which there was nothing else apart from Gabin's performance to hold attention.

Something of an offshoot of the Maigret character was a role developed for Erich von Stroheim in the mid-nineteen-fifties. *The Man of Many Skins* was the pilot for a TV series which never materialized. Stroheim himself died two years later. The film cast him (somewhat like

the Old Man in the Corner protagonist of the Baroness Orczy stories) as a detective who solves baffling crimes merely by studying and absorbing every detail of the men known to be involved, and then, by immersing himself in their personalities, is able to predict their moves. Whether the series could have held up for long on such a thin premise is a question; obviously, its main raison d'être was as a showcase for Von Stroheim who played all the roles—well—in convincing makeup. In an egotistical role suited to his own reputation, the film unwittingly provided an appropriately bravura farewell to the screen for one of its most colorful and brilliant personalities. (He did make one more theatrical film subsequent to it, but *Man of Many Skins,* though not productive of a series of its own, was incorporated into another crime series for television, and thus had fairly wide showings throughout the world.)

Heinz Ruhmann, one of the Maigrets, a popular light comedian of German films who had turned to more serious roles, appeared in a minor detective classic of 1960 titled *It Happened in Broad Daylight*. A Swiss-French co-production directed by Ladislas Vajda, it was hampered by barely adequate dubbing for its U.S. release, and perhaps because of that was not received with much enthusiasm. Like Fritz Lang's classic *M,* it dealt with the search for a child murderer. Unlike *M,* with its nightmarish underworld and frightening claustrophobic sets, the new film not only happened in broad daylight as per its title, but in the beautiful pastoral exteriors of mountain village, wood, and meadow.

What atmospheric menace that might have been lost that way was gained back in other areas: the deviate's crimes seemed doubly monstrous when set against a background of such beauty, and in addition so much space made help and interception increasingly difficult. The detective's pose as a workman and his taking up with a widowed mother and child (whom he has pegged as a potential victim) smack of a certain amount of "B" picture contrivance, as does his falling in love with the mother. On the other hand, this too works in its own way, since it furthers audience concern for the child. The rest of the quite long film is strong meat, starting with the suicide of a tramp (Michel Simon) who, suspected of the initial crime, is less upset by fear of the law's penalties than he is by the realization that the townspeople consider him *capable* of such a crime. Then, in the final two thirds of the film, the detective's painstaking methods (depicted in detail) of building up a pattern for the crimes, and systematically narrowing down to a handful of suspects. Both as a film and as a good detective mystery, *It Happened in Broad Daylight* deserves to be much better known than it is.

ALGIERS (1938): The American remake, a more romantic version of the same tale, had Joseph Calleia and Charles Boyer as detective and crook. Sigrid Gurie, right, was Pepe's girl—until the advent of beautiful tourist Hedy Lamarr.

Although the large number of television series with a continuing detective hero have had to be largely ignored in this book, one should perhaps (for the record) make note of the British TV series built around Colonel March of Scotland Yard's Department of Queer Complaints. Not that the series was in any way remarkable, but it does represent the only sustained use of a John Dickson Carr character in any filmed detective series. (Carr, also known as Carter Dickson, is an extremely imaginative writer whose work, apart from a brace of his historical thrillers,

has been ignored by the movies.) Boris Karloff, as the amiable Colonel March, doubtless realizing that he was the main asset of the economically made series, gave his all, often providing the dialogue with more relish and theatrical flavor than it deserved, making the most of every possible gesture and acting nuance. The series, dealing with the peculiar and picayune crimes both beneath the dignity and beyond the scope of the Yard proper, did have some intriguing little plot lines and some interesting casts. Director-to-be John Schlessinger turned up in one of them as a German sea captain. Karloff's gentlemanly behavior—even to the villains—was beyond reproach, though he was sometimes a little foolhardy (as in *The Invisible Knife*) in walking into obvious deathtraps with a Micawber-like faith that something would turn up to divert the situation to his advantage. The murder weapon in *The Invisible Knife* was particularly ingenious—a sliver of glass deposited, right after use, in a glass pitcher of water in full view of the investigating detectives.

Jean Gabin — somewhat plumper — played Georges Simenon's detective hero Inspector Maigret in several French thrillers of the sixties.

10 THE BRITISH

Ralph Richardson as the whimsical detective in Q PLANES (U.S. title, CLOUDS OVER EUROPE) (1938).

The British love detective stories. They read them voraciously, the American ones because they are an exciting escape from the well-ordered (and, to be honest, well-liked) tedium of British life, the British ones because, despite their civilized gentility, they show that murder and intrigue can exist quite comfortably within that rather proper environment. British detective novels tend to make the murder the be-all and end-all of their plots, whereas in the American equivalents, murder is often merely a launching pad to the revelation of much more ambition and far-reaching crime. Most British households maintain some kind of a library, and Agatha Christie and John Rhode can always be found rubbing shoulders with such other nondetective reliables as Ruby M. Ayres, Horace A. Vachell, and Warwick Deeping. Remember the film of H. G. Wells, *The Passionate Friends,* in which Ann Todd, trying desperately to conceal her emotions at a moment of extreme marital crisis, turns to the bookshelves and remarks distractedly, "Oh dear, you've got Aristotle in with Sherlock Holmes again"?

But, because of the profusion of British detective

novels (and in the thirties, at the height of their popularity, they were decidedly expensive in a postdepression and prepaperback era), most British readers preferred to borrow them from libraries rather than buy them outright. The public libraries, the responsibility of local government, were often more concerned with raising literary standards than satisfying public demand, and thus were often quite lax in ordering the latest Dr. Priestley mystery.

So it fell to the commercial lending libraries, with their very nominal charges, to fill the demand for detective fiction. A leader among these libraries was the Boots stores, a chain of chemist shops with a largely feminine, housewife clientele, and most of them included small but up-to-date and well-stocked libraries. Almost every individual in England has been taken as a tot into a Boots store by a mother or an aunt and forced to wait (there being no toy, candy, or otherwise useful juvenile departments to divert him) while his guardian made a choice between the available Christie or Oppenheim, with absolutely nothing to relieve his boredom except for the inhalation of the aromas from bath salts, scented soap, and other toiletries. Thus from childhood he has been reared with a subliminal juxtaposition of the detective novel with the sensual assaults of agents of cleanliness and sanitary well-being. Small wonder that the British mystery novel has always been surrounded by an aura of comfortable respectability.

With such an avid, presold readership, one would expect the British cinema to be full of detailed filmic chronicles of Hercule Poirot and Dr. Priestley. But, actually, such is far from the case. Only totally faithful adaptations of the popular books could have satisfied such a reader audience, resulting in films that would be expensive (because of the story rights involved) and limited very largely to the home market (because of their lack of the physical excitement which foreign and especially American audiences would expect). So, while the British industry probably turned out more detective films (in relation to its overall output) than that of any other country, America and Hollywood not excepted, they were usually fairly economical one-shot films, turned out cheaply and without thought of sequels, so that if one didn't click, there was no loss of investment. Of course, when one *did* succeed, a sequel would be rushed through with a haste almost indecent by British standards.

The detective film (with its overlapping spy genre) was of course well liked in England, particularly in the thirties. The films of Alfred Hitchcock were enormously popular, the detective novels of Edgar Wallace, E. Phillips Oppenheim, and A. E. W. Mason extremely useful as a reservoir of plots and characters, even if they often emerged on screen in almost unrecognizable form.

The only real catalyst for a successful movie *series,* however, was a prior series on radio. Britain having no commercial radio in the thirties and limiting its government-sponsored entertainment to a handful of channels, split up by geographic region and a certain amount of class distinction (lectures, plays of intellectual content, criticism on one channel; music hall vaudeville and thriller plays on another "popular" channel), it stands to reason that any worthwhile radio venture reached an enormous audience, and that same audience could be counted on to back up later filmed versions. (In the early war years, a number of top radio comics—Arthur Askey, Jack Warner, Tommy Handley—became stars overnight through having their highly popular radio shows translated into movie equivalents.)

Thus the semicomedy Inspector Hornleigh radio serial was turned by Twentieth Century Fox's British studios into a trio of extremely successful thrillers. Gordon Harker, a popular British cockney comedian who had already done a number of thrillers, including two Edgar Wallaces *The Frog* and *The Return of the Frog,* was an obvious choice for the lead role of the Scotland Yard inspector. Comedy, however, was diverted to his dumb assistant, Alastair Sim, whose moon face and pantomimic clowning made the comedy much funnier than it often deserved.

In 1948 a British radio serial sleuth named Dick Barton captured the imagination of the public much as Batman became a pop art phenomenon in America in the sixties. Barton was something of an enlargement of Dick Tracy, a supersleuth with lightning reasoning powers (as they needed to be in the 15-minute format of his shows) and a wide range of crime-busting gadgets. The old-fashioned furioso-agitato musical theme (borrowed, surprisingly, from Tschaikowsky!) that introduced each episode set the pace of speed and self-satire which was the series' stock in trade. The episodes were broadcast at a peak listening time, in the early evening, right after the news, and audiences of a still austerity-ridden Britain enjoyed them as much for their extravagances as for their melodrama.

So popular were they that film versions were inevitable, and in quick succession *Dick Barton Special Agent, Dick Barton at Bay,* and *Dick Barton Strikes Back* were brought to the screen by Exclusive Films, the rather smaller scale forerunner of today's Hammer Films.

Unfortunately, the format didn't work as well on film. The lavish gimmicks that sounded fine on radio *looked* like grade Z mockups on screen. The parody of old serial thrills, effective when *heard,* was merely ludicrous when actually shown, and audiences hooted with derision at such scenes as Dick Barton knocking a vial of acid on to his bound hands, the acid eating through the ropes but apparently doing no damage to his wrists. One sequence

Stanley Holloway, music hall comic who proved surprisingly effective in detective roles in
WANTED FOR MURDER and others.

Ronald Howard, among other detectives, a TV Sherlock Holmes.

of a Death Ray operating from the top of Blackpool Tower (an edifice similar in design and purpose to Paris' Eiffel Tower) had some enjoyable melodramatic thrills because the location shooting gave it some semblance of credulity.

Otherwise, the series was crude and clumsy, not once approximating the slick expertise of the Republic Dick Tracy serials that were its inspiration. However, they made a tidy profit for their producers, and later were re-edited into serial form for Britain's Saturday morning kiddie market. Don Stannard, who played Barton both on radio and in the three movies, was good-looking and had an appropriately tongue-in-cheek approach to the role, but was somewhat less than convincing in the fight and other action scenes.

Rather more successful as films (though perhaps less so commercially) were a group of films built around the sleuthing escapades of Paul Temple. Temple was literally

John Mills (TIGER BAY, TOWN ON TRIAL)

John Stuart (NUMBER 17, THE MISSING MILLION)

a contemporary of Dick Barton in that he came to the screen in 1948 (in *Calling Paul Temple*) as a direct result of a popular radio serial written by Frances Durbridge. (Durbridge was an uninspired but extremely efficient mystery writer who always seemed to be able to come up with plots and characters attuned to the public demands of the moment. He worked for radio, the movies, theater, and television, and in 1972 was represented on the London stage with *Suddenly at Home,* an expert if basically familiar exercise in "perfect murder" gambits.)

The several Paul Temple films provide a perfect example of the problems facing the British detective movie. They were based exactly on the style of the radio serials, and doubtless audiences were well satisfied that neither the story nor the characters had been cheapened in the transfer to screen. John Bentley (good-looking, a trifle stolid, but a good actor) and Dinah Sheridan made an enjoyable husband-and-wife sleuthing team, both more sedate and more athletic than the Nick Charleses.

Though quite expensively produced, especially for a

Jack Warner (THE DUMMY TALKS, DEAR MURDERER)

THE RINGER (1931), one of several versions of the Edgar Wallace thriller; Gordon Harker and John Longden.

small company (Butchers Film Service), and well enough acted and scripted to overcome the limitations of a director (MacLean Rogers) who was no specialist in thrillers but an all-around studio director who took everything the studio gave him with a leaning toward comedy, the Paul Temple films presented a commercial dilemma. Well made or not, they were old-fashioned in their appeal: quiet little mysteries perhaps enlivened by an exciting climax which in itself might be old-fashioned too. (One of them fell back on the old chestnut of the escape from the water-filled dungeon!) Domestically, they couldn't hope to compete for top-of-the bill playing time with the latest Bogart and Ladd imports from Hollywood. Therefore, they were limited to second-feature bookings on the big circuits, and occasional top-feature bookings from the independent theaters. Their very length was a liability outside of England, since at 80 minutes they were much too long for the bottom half of double bills, while they were too mild and lacking in star values for anything else. Ultimately, television

sales probably helped recoup their costs and brought in some profit too.

Bentley also starred in a duo of films (*Salute the Toff, Hammer the Toff*) based on John Creasey's gentleman sleuth (with a gentleman's gentleman aide), but they were well below the Paul Temple standards. In fact, though John Creasey was always well in evidence in British bookstores, his books bearing the banner "Creasey for Crime," his stories never attracted the attention of major British film makers. Probably the biggest (and the adjective is merely relative) British film based on one of his books was *Uneasy Terms* (1948), a modestly budgeted film in which Michael Rennie played detective Slim Callahan. Both Rennie's performance and the whole film seemed like a painfully inept imitation of Warner Brothers–Bogart merchandise, and an amateurishly handled fistfight (of which the publicists seemed inordinately proud) merely clinched its inadequacies. Both Slim Callahan and Peter Cheyney were better served by Eddie Constantine's later French-made thrillers.

175

THE GREEN SPOT MYSTERY (also known as LLOYD OF THE C.I.D. 1932): Britain's only sound serial. Despite extensive location shooting in London and an American serial veteran (Henry MacRae) to direct, it was a fiasco; with Jack Lord and Muriel Angelus.

THIS MAN IS NEWS (1938): Barry K. Barnes and Valerie Hobson as Britain's closest equivalent to Nick and Nora Charles.

THE TERROR (1938), another Edgar Wallace adaptation; Richard Bird and Alastair Sim, detectives masquerading as hoboes.

THIS MAN IS NEWS: Barnes with intelligent detective Edward Lexy (left) and dumb one Garry Marsh.

Detective Hugh Williams fights off an unseen killer whose own throat is about to be slashed in a grim scene from DEAD MEN TELL NO TALES (1938).

MRS. PYM OF SCOTLAND YARD (1939), with
Mary Clare.

THE FOUR JUST MEN (1939): A dying
Frank Lawton is aided by Anna Lee.

DARK EYES OF LONDON (1939): Scotland Yard Inspector Hugh Williams, attended by visiting Chicago detective Edmon Ryan, pays a call on possible suspect Dr. Orloff (Bela Lugosi).

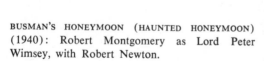

BUSMAN'S HONEYMOON (HAUNTED HONEYMOON) (1940): Robert Montgomery as Lord Peter Wimsey, with Robert Newton.

THIS MAN IS DANGEROUS (1941): Private detective James Mason and his father, also a detective, Gordon McLeod, rescue Margaret Vyner.

ALIBI (1942), remake of an earlier French thriller, starred Hugh Sinclair as the Scotland Yard man (and James Mason as his assistant) with Margaret Lockwood.

ESCAPE (1948), with William Hartnell (right) on the trail of accidental killer Rex Harrison. A good and literate thriller; also shown here, Jill Esmond (left) and Peggy Cummins.

DOUBLE CONFESSION (1950): William Hartnell and Peter Lorre as sleazy underworld types, Naunton Wayne (right) as the detective.

THE FRANCHISE AFFAIR (1950): Nancy Price, Dulcie Gray, Michael Dennison.

CIRCLE OF DANGER (1951): An excellent Hitchcockian thriller directed by Jacques Tourneur, with Naunton Wayne as a jaunty detective, and Ray Milland.

WHISPERING SMITH VS. SCOTLAND YARD (1952): Richard Carlson and Rona Anderson.

Oscar Homolka as Inspector Hanaud in the 1952 version of THE HOUSE OF THE ARROW.

Bernard Lee (right), a familiar figure as the quiet-spoken, utterly dependable British detective: with Cecil Parker in FATHER BROWN, DETECTIVE (1954).

THE HAUNTED STRANGLER (1962): Boris Karloff finally tracked down by Scotland Yard's Anthony Dawson.

Apart from the generous quantity of Sherlock Holmes movies and a series of shorts based on Baroness Orczy's "Man in the Corner" detective stories, Britain made relatively few silent detective films—and for the same reasons, discussed earlier, that Hollywood tended to avoid any sizable concentration on the genre. Paralleling Sherlock Holmes, Scotland Yard's Sir Nayland Smith did put in an impressive appearance, but only in a series of featurettes based (quite accurately) on the Fu Manchu stories. In films like *The Coughing Horror,* however, the stress was primarily on the ingenious methods of murder devised by Dr. Fu Manchu, and they were films of action and mystery rather than detection.

In the sound period, however, detective movies big and small—though mainly small—grew and multiplied from the British studios. Undoubtedly, the mysteries of Edgar Wallace dominated them in terms of quantity if not in quality. Wallace himself was one of the most prolific of all mystery writers, though he had few continuing characters, and many of his novels were frankly lurid

underworld yarns with few pretensions toward intelligent detection.

The Ringer was one of the more interesting Wallace thrillers and three talkie versions were made, the best being the 1938 edition from Ealing Studios under the title *The Gaunt Stranger.* It was a suspenseful yarn about an unsavory but ostensibly respectable businessman who is warned by the mysterious criminal "The Ringer" that he will be murdered at a certain time. Terrified, he calls in Scotland Yard to protect him. However, the murder takes place on schedule and the killer, revealed as one of the Scotland Yard men, is allowed to escape scot free at the end since the killing was morally, if not legally, justifiable.

Another example of Wallace's detectives being "above the law" was in 1939's *The Four Just Men,* likewise from Ealing, one of the best and most elaborate of all British Edgar Wallace mysteries, and a kindred spirit to Alfred Hitchcock's espionage movies. Actually, it bore little plot resemblance to Wallace's original, but it did use his four heroes—men of widely differing backgrounds and talents, but all courageous, patriotic, and dedicated to the downfall of Britain's enemies. Their initiative included the murder of a Member of Parliament (by electrocuting him in his bath) and having one of their group (an actor) impersonate him in the Houses of Parliament, causing England to switch from a policy of appeasement to one of aggression when sabotage in the Suez Canal seems about to start a world war. One of its villains is referred to as "having his fingers in every dirty mud-pie East of Suez," and the story concerns itself with "a plot to destroy the British Empire and place world domination in the hands of one man"!

With the exception of Hitchcock's *Foreign Correspondent,* which came a year later and brought the war into its plotting, *The Four Just Men* was one of the last of the nostalgically simple films about Balkan intrigues and secret treaties. Ironically, it was released just about the time that war was declared, and its climax of an alert, ready-for-anything Britain was hardly backed up by the

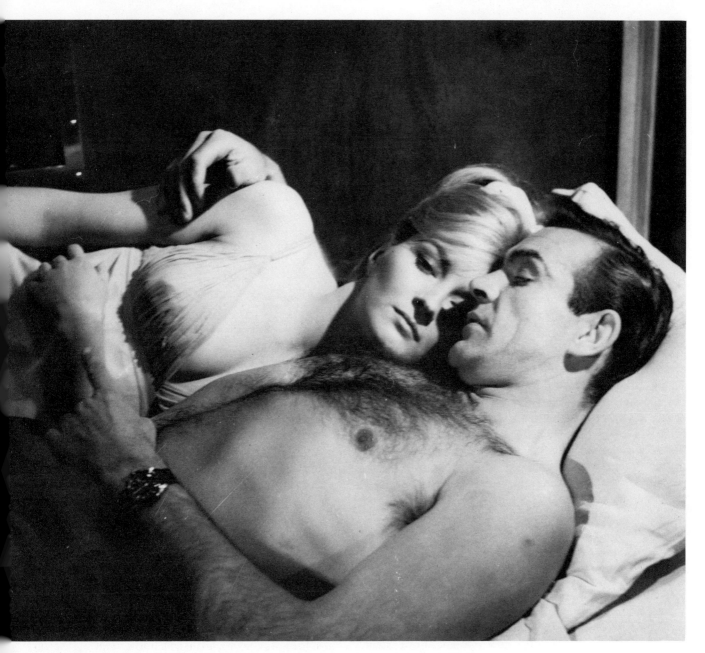

FROM RUSSIA WITH LOVE (1963): The lighter side of spying and detecting: Sean Connery with Daniela Bianchi.

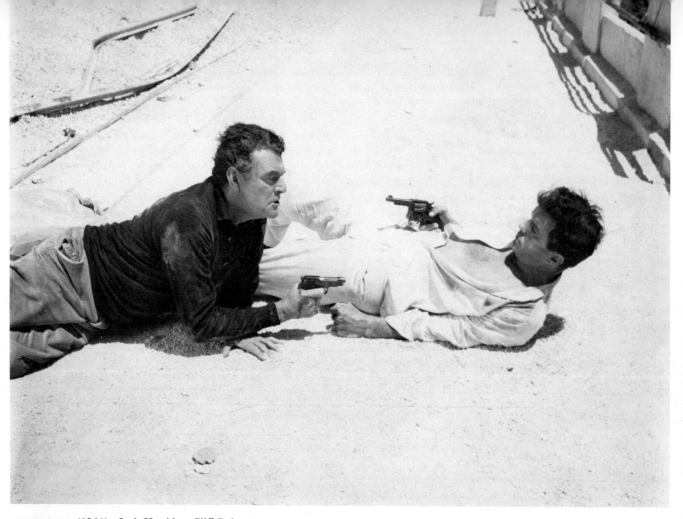

MASQUERADE (1964): Jack Hawkins, Cliff Robertson.

country's actual military status, though it doubtless had a stimulating propagandist effect on British moviegoers. For the American market, a new foreword and an added newsreel montage climax tied it in directly with the war. Francis L. Sullivan, Hugh Sinclair, Griffith Jones, and Frank Lawton played the four patriot-spy-detectives, though Frank Lawton was killed off at the midway point, perhaps to ward off censorial dudgeon at the quartet's somewhat high-handed lack of concern for the lives of politicians. The villains, however, are equally imaginative in their methods of murder: Basil Sydney disposes of his weak mistress by pushing her down an elevator shaft, and kills one of the four by jostling into him at a railroad station and scratching his hand with a suitcase that has been treated with venomous poison!

In *The Squeaker* (1937, released in the United States as *Murder on Diamond Row*), Hollywood's director-star team of William K. Howard and Edmund Lowe went to Alexander Korda's studios to bring Hollywood know-how to a typical Wallace thriller. Unfortunately, a rather

routine script defeated them, although Korda's above-average production trappings and Howard's good camera angling and visual imagination enabled it to remain interesting. Edmund Lowe played a formerly respected detective, down and out through drunkenness, given a chance to redeem himself by posing as an ex-con and joining the organization of a philanthropist who employs ex-crooks for, as the Yard suspects, further criminal activities. Visual highlights included an exciting jailbreak scene, a mysterious encounter between The Squeaker and a jewel thief (with messages exchanged by finger writing on the mist-clouded windows of his car), the final sequence at the Yard where, via a staged tableau and some Germanic lighting, The Squeaker is far too easily tricked into thinking he is seeing the specters of former victims and breaks down and confesses. Such a sequence might have worked in a Fritz Lang thriller where the whole atmosphere was nightmarish and tinged with a suspicion of the supernatural, but it was totally unconvincing in this more realistic modern milieu.

MURDER AT THE GALLOP (1963): Margaret Rutherford as Agatha Christie's Miss Marple, with Robert Morley.

The Missing Million was a more straightforward Wallace mystery with Scotland Yard detective John Stuart on the trail of a master criminal known as "The Panda," while Mr. Reeder—the closest Wallace came to an individualized and unique detective—was played by Scots comedian–character actor Will Fyfe in *The Mind of Mr. Reeder* and *Mr. Reeder in Room 13*. Reeder was an official police detective who, because of his earlier banking experience, was called in primarily for capers involving bank robberies or counterfeiting. Will Fyfe matched Wallace's physical description exactly, except possibly for his Scots accent. The original stories were started by Wallace in the mid-twenties and dropped in the early thirties. Although Fyfe starred in only the two Mr. Reeder films, he carried the characteristics of the role over into two subsequent films, *Missing People* and *They Came by Night*.

Dark Eyes of London (1939) was perhaps the most ambitious British Edgar Wallace thriller, designed to equal the full-blooded horror of Hollywood chillers and to be worthy of Bela Lugosi's starring role as Dr. Orloff. Produced by the normally very proper and genteel Associated British–Pathé, it went overboard in its efforts at physical horror, its grotesqueries sometimes bordering on the tasteless, at other times being merely silly. But for a venture into generally unfamiliar territory for the British, it was well done, and certainly well served by handsome sets and atmospheric photography. Lugosi was in his element in the role of the insurance company executive who leads a dual existence, his "other" self being the apparently kindly and sightless operator of a home for the blind. (Lugosi's makeup was surprisingly convincing for this secondary role, although his accent precluded his convincing anyone he was a Britisher, let alone a kindly one, so his dialogue was dubbed by the character actor O. B. Clarence.) Hugh Williams was Inspector Holt, the dashing Scotland Yard man who wore the latest in sporty overcoats. (Some kind of unwritten class distinction decreed that Scotland Yard men of the rank of sergeant and below invariably wore the standard gray raincoat, while those of higher rank were permitted the luxury of overcoats.) Holding back the action somewhat was the presence of Edmon Ryan as a stereotyped Chicago detective, observing British methods.

If Edgar Wallace was filmed and refilmed constantly, other British detective authors received but scant attention. Until the group of recent Miss Marple mysteries made by MGM, with Margaret Rutherford an amusing and commercially viable lady detective, but a far cry from the Miss Marple of the books (Elizabeth Patterson would have been a closer approximation), the works of Agatha Christie have been limited largely to two versions

BUNNY LAKE IS MISSING (1965): Sir Laurence Olivier, Keir Dullea.

FUNERAL IN BERLIN (1965): Michael Caine, Eva Renzi.

of her nondetective mystery *Ten Little Indians*. Her famous Belgian detective Hercule Poirot was brought to the screen only once, in a rather prosaic adaptation of *Lord Edgware Dies* (1934). Austin Trevor was reasonably close to Poirot in age and appearance, and was able to duplicate some of the charm and all of the egotism which he brought to bear in solving his cases. However, though considerably more ample in physical size, Francis L. Sullivan was a far more acceptable Poirot on the London stage, and it is a pity that he never repeated the role on film.

Another Gallic detective to receive some attention from the British was Inspector Hanaud although curiously, in film, the kindly but not particularly unique detective had grafted on to his character several of the traits of Monsieur Poirot, including conceit and exaggerated self-assurance. A. E. W. Mason (better known for his Empire-building swashbucklers like *The Four Feathers* and *Fire Over England*) wrote a handful of Hanaud mysteries between 1910 and the mid nineteen-forties, but only

the first two (*The House of the Arrow* and *At the Villa Rose*) were ever filmed, each three times, at approximately ten-year intervals. The best were the two made by Associated British–Pathé in 1939–40, with Kenneth Kent admirably cast if one accepts the Poirot-like image. Interestingly enough, the Inspector Hanaud of the 1930 *At the Villa Rose* was Austin Trevor, who would soon play Poirot too. The inspector's last outing on the screen was in Pathé's 1952 version of *The House of the Arrow*, directed by then comparative newcomer Michael Anderson. It was a good-looking little mystery but one with few surprises. Oscar Homolka, however, was totally miscast as Hanaud: his bluff Russian heartiness (and accent) made both his French nationality and his self-esteem totally unconvincing.

Dorothy Sayers' Lord Peter Wimsey also received surprisingly short shrift on the British screen, since his debonair personality could have fitted David Niven, Ray Milland, or a dozen other actors who themselves fitted the Hollywood stereotype of the gay British aristocrat.

His first, and now totally forgotten, film was *The Silent Passenger,* a high-class "B" of 1935 with a good story, some interesting character players (Donald Wolfit among them) and an exciting climax of a chase after the murderer through a shunting yard at a London railroad station. Done entirely on location, this sequence was a real thriller, with good sound effects, excellent photography, and one really classic shock cut in the editing contributing to its effectiveness. However, if the sleuthing was done by Lord Peter, the bulk of the action (and the capture of the villain) was left in the hands of a secondary hero, John Loder. Wimsey was played, largely for comedy, by Peter Hadden who just didn't have the lightness of touch to allow the character to be taken seriously. He did much better as a comic stuffed shirt or as the traditional silly-ass Englishman, for which roles he used the alternate name of Archibald Batty. Though very enjoyable and a genuine mystery, *The Silent Passenger* would have benefited from a good deal less of Lord Peter.

Not so MGM's *Busman's Honeymoon,* based on the last of Dorothy Sayers' stories, and released in the United States as *Haunted Honeymoon.* Produced in England and directed by Arthur Woods, one of the most promising of the newer English directors and a specialist in suspense thrillers (he was killed during the war, unfortunately), it offered an ideal co-starring duo in Robert Montgomery and Constance Cummings. Aficionados of the book felt that the film let them down somewhat, but it was still a most enjoyable light thriller with a particularly distinguished supporting cast (Leslie Banks, Sir Seymour Hicks, Robert Newton, and others).

Some popular British sleuths came to the screen but once. *Mrs. Pym of Scotland Yard,* the heroine of half a dozen books by Nigel Morland, was played on screen by Mary Clare who had the original's toughness but none of her other more endearing qualities. However, Mary Clare has always been much more effective as a villainess; even in her sympathetic roles, her flashing eyes and somehow insincere laugh suggest that she will momentarily be exposed as a maniacal killer.

Gideon of Scotland Yard found a perfect interpreter in Jack Hawkins, reliable, incorruptible, just—and also, when time permits, a family man. However, John Ford's British film based on *Gideon's Day* was neither recognizably Ford nor a particularly good film. It covered far too much ground to be convincing, and prior British semi-documentary tributes to their police and Scotland Yard—*The Blue Lamp,* for example—were much more satisfying. *Gideon's Day,* however, was badly hampered in its U.S. showings by being substantially shortened and released in black and white instead of its original Technicolor. For once, television—much maligned for its cavalier treatment of film—made a partial gesture toward

MODESTY BLAISE (1966): Monica Vitti as the super-sleuth-agent-adventuress, with picturesque but more stable boss Harry Andrews.

its redemption by showing the film in color and in its uncut form.

Josephine Tey's novels have often been cited as the quintessence of the civilized British mystery novels, set in rural surroundings and peopled by polite and for the most part likable characters. Though a lawyer (Michael Dennison) performed the detective function, *The Franchise Affair* was a typical and thoroughly satisfying Tey novel/movie. However, both her detective-hero Inspector Grant and the meaning of the title *A Shilling for Candles* vanished from its 1937 filming by Alfred Hitchcock under the title *Young and Innocent,* somewhat meaninglessly retitled *The Girl Was Young* for U.S. audiences. A gentle yet really suspenseful thriller, it lets the audience know right away who the killer is—and that he has a twitching eye. After a murder in a cliff-edge house during a thunderstorm, the body is discovered in the sea the next morning, its lifeless arm lifted by the surf into a grotesque parody of swimming. The discoverer of the body (Derek de Marney) is naturally blamed for the crime and is kept on the run throughout the film, searching for the killer with an absolute minimum of clues, performing all the detective work himself, while Hitchcock's old Scotland Yard perennial John Longden (from *Blackmail*) is relentlessly on his trail. The climax is still notable for one of Hitchcock's most stunning virtuoso shots. The police hot on his heels, the hero is cornered at a dancehall, where he has reason to believe that the killer with a twitch may be hiding. But how to find him among all these people? In a long crane shot, the camera swoops down from the balcony, over the dancing throng, up to the dance band, into a closeup of the drummer (in blackface), and then into a tight closeup of his eye—which twitches!

George Curzon, who played the twitching killer, was a polished and versatile actor who also made an excellent detective. He was the secret service man in Hitchcock's first *The Man Who Knew Too Much,* and also Britain's best Sexton Blake. Blake was a comic strip and pulp magazine equivalent of Sherlock Holmes, and the line drawings by which he was initially known went to great pains to give him the gaunt, angular features of Holmes. He had no Dr. Watson, but a boy assistant named Tinker combined the functions of Watson and Little Billy. Like Holmes, they enjoyed the services of a solicitous housekeeper, and they had an additional bonus helper in the form of a giant hound. Blake was very much of an intellectual and a scientific detective, yet his adventures were usually serial-like parades of precarious situations which made few demands on his mind. Curzon played Blake in a trio of early thirties thrillers, the best of which was *Sexton Blake and the Hooded Terror,* wherein he opposed master criminal Tod Slaughter, operator of a world-wide crime ring, who had an elaborate snake-filled dungeon built into his London apartment. The Hooded Terror was so efficient that he even managed to escape at the end of that 1938 film, possibly in readiness for a sequel that never materialized.*

Occupying a small role in the film as a lesser agent was David Farrar, who in the early forties took over the Blake role in two films: *Meet Sexton Blake* and *The Echo Murders.* Though quite elaborately done, the films lacked slickness and speed, and Farrar—rugged-looking and a good actor—did not seem at ease in the role. Some twenty-five years later the British revived Blake once more in *Murder on Site Three.* Blake was played this time by Geoffrey Toone, a good actor, but somewhat too stolid and mature for the role.

One of the big surprises of British movies in the late thirties was *This Man Is News* (1938), one of a group of British films made by Paramount and directed by David MacDonald. Intended as no more than a classy little programmer, its speed, wit, and elegance of playing turned it into an immediate "sleeper." British critics enthused about this new native product with all of the Hollywood get-up-and-go—though, later on, American critics were less excited and seemed to find in it most of the vices of more routine British films. Barry K. Barnes, together with John Loder, was one of the very few British leading men of the thirties who projected style, polish, humor, *and* were young, good-looking, and virile. (Most other leading men usually lacked at least two of the vital ingredients—or had been snapped up by Hollywood!) Barnes played a newspaper reporter turned amateur detective, with a charming and intelligent (and more level-headed) wife to help him in his adventures, played by Valerie Hobson. Alastair Sim was a delight as the exasperated newspaper editor, and Scotland Yard was represented by Edward Lexy as the reasonably sensible inspector and Garry Marsh as his dunderheaded sergeant.

Quite unintentionally, the British seemed to have created their own Nick and Nora Charles, and the title even underlined the parallel. A sequel was rushed into production: *This Man in Paris.* It was entertaining, clearly a little more expensive, but somehow it was already a formula picture. The war intervened, Barnes was put into more topical films, and the series was dropped.

The roll call of British movie detectives is both endless—and shapeless—with some of the most intriguing plots appearing early in the sound period in some of the

* Incidentally, another rich Tod Slaughter melodrama of the thirties, *Ticket of Leave Man,* seems to have been the only film to utilize that Victorian forerunner of Dick Tracy, Hawkshaw the detective.

THE BRITISH DETECTIVE—THROUGH HOLLYWOOD EYES

THE MASK OF FU MANCHU (1932): Scotland Yard Commissioner Sir Nayland Smith (Lewis Stone) is threatened by Fu Manchu (Boris Karloff). Oblivious, in the background, Charles Starrett and Myrna Loy.

BLAKE OF SCOTLAND YARD (1936): Herbert Rawlinson, Dickie Jones.

MURDER IN THORNTON SQUARE (1944): Detective Joseph Cotten saves Ingrid Bergman from sinister scheme hatched by husband Charles Boyer.

THE SUSPECT (1944), one of the best acted and best written thrillers of the forties; Charles Laughton as the husband driven to murder, Stanley Ridges as the detective who suspects, yet also pities him.

cheapest of independent films. In 1932, *Condemned to Death* (with Cyril Raymond as the Yard detective) had Britain's Sherlock Holmes, Arthur Wontner, as a judge who is hypnotized by a criminal he has condemned into murdering the jury! When he comes to his senses, he commits suicide—a move that the detective on the case could have prevented, but allows to take place as the easiest way out of an embarrassing situation. Reversing the process, *Twelve Good Men* had the jury themselves turning detective, and forcing a confession from the killer by locking him in a darkened room with a cat. (He had a cat phobia and the sequence—all darkness and suggestion—seemed a real thriller in 1936. It might still hold up for it was written by Frank Launder and Sidney Gilliat, two of the best thriller scenarists in the business.)

I Killed the Count (1939) was one of those films in which a much hated man is killed, and four people all insist on confessing to the crime. The detective-inspector in charge was played by Syd Walker, a cockney comedian and character actor who had achieved considerable suc-

cess on radio as a kind of folksy local Will Rogers. His screen success was less notable, though he died before he had much of a chance to experiment with other roles. The aforementioned John Loder was one of the most over-worked British heroes in the thirties, and one of the best screen detectives. His last British film before leaving for Hollywood was a detective mystery, *Meet Maxwell Archer* (1939), but one of his best was made three years earlier—*Non-Stop New York,* directed by Robert Stevenson.

Next to Hitchcock, Stevenson was Gaumont-British's most reliable action-and-thriller director, and he followed Hitchcock (and Loder) to Hollywood in the early forties. Apart from being a good detective film, *Non Stop New York* is interesting historically in being the last of an unofficial trilogy in which Gaumont-British made some daring (but unfulfilled) prophesies about Atlantic travel. With the idea of transatlantic air travel considered a dangerous impossibility in 1933, they made, as a German co-production, *Secrets of F. P. 1,* dealing with the establishment of a mid-Atlantic floating aerodrome, to refuel

SCOTLAND YARD INVESTIGATOR (1945): Sir C. Aubrey Smith and Erich von Stroheim; it would surely be superfluous to indicate which of them played the title role.

and repair planes, and thus cut the flying distance in half. (The steamship combines tried to sabotage it!) In 1935, considerate of pedestrian traffic needs, Gaumont-British and the Germans got together again for *Transatlantic Tunnel*. (Munitions manufacturers, wary of the world unification and peace the tunnel would bring, tried to wreck that project!) Then, just a year later, *Non-Stop New York* ("It's fictional enthusiasm outstrips science," remarked *The New York Times*) set itself some time in the near future when nonstop transatlantic flights on giant airliners would be possible. Even the giant jumbo jets of the present, while carrying a much larger passenger load then the uneconomical handful of this film, haven't quite caught up to its spacious modern design and observation platform. Presumably, too, in 1938 the prime considerations were space and comfort rather than speed; certainly, detective Loder, performing above and beyond

the call of duty, couldn't have clambered out of the plane and onto its wing at today's supersonic speeds.

For all its fanciful elements, *Non-Stop New York* was a rattling good thriller, with Francis L. Sullivan stealing most of the thunder with his bravura villainy.

John Lodge (ex–Bulldog Drummond) played a French detective inspector in a duo of mysteries, *River of Unrest* and *Premiere*—although in the latter his mere presence at the opening night of a French revue seemed enough to prompt the killer into an unprovoked confession in the last reel, and far more time was devoted to elaborate musical numbers than to investigation. In *Dinner at the Ritz,* an excellent comedy-thriller with much more meat on its bones than its title suggested, David Niven was the debonair sleuth. In fact, virtually every British player of note—star or character actor—has played the detective somewhere along the line. In supporting roles, Jack Raine (a second-string John Williams) was one of the best: business-like, unemotional, polite, wearing his raincoat like a second skin.

The list includes comedians like Stanley Holloway (*Wanted for Murder*), Gordon Harker (*Saloon Bar*), Tom Walls (*Strange Boarders*), Alastair Sim (*Green for Danger*), and Naunton Wayne (*Circle of Danger*); character actors like William Hartnell (*Escape*), Syd Walker (*I Killed the Count*), Alfred Drayton (*The Crimson Circle*), Jack Warner (*Dear Murderer*); stars like John Mills (*Town on Trial*), Alec Guinness (*Father Brown, Detective*), Michael Wilding (*Trent's Last Case*), Ralph Richardson (*Q Planes*), Laurence Olivier (*Bunny Lake is Missing*), Nigel Patrick (*The Informers,* one of the few British detective thrillers to duplicate the pace and convincingly staged action of Hollywood counterparts), James Mason (*Alibi*), Jack Hawkins (*Home at Seven*), and Michael Redgrave (*The Green Scarf*).

All have shared characteristics in common with the true British detective: politeness, evasiveness, restraint, and a belief in the tradition that an Englishman's home is his castle, not to be invaded without a warrant, and then like a gentleman. Those who suspect that the British movie detective may be an idealized exaggeration of actuality, need only listen to the occasional crime reports from police to public via British radio. Whenever the police are seeking a suspect—even one pretty conclusively suspected of murder—they offer a paucity of details of the crime but a maximum of physical details of the man's appearance. The public is alerted to be on the lookout for him, and the man himself is requested to report to a local police station because "the police have reason to believe that this man can help them in their enquiries." Such a broadcast is tantamount to a confession that the police have him pegged as their number one suspect, and naturally he heads for the hills—or the Continent. Still, the gentlemanly charade which fools no one goes on. In 1971 a bank was robbed (during its lunch hour) of several thousand pounds. The teller of that particular department was seen heading for home with a bulging briefcase. Later, still holding the briefcase, he was seen going in the direction of the airport. Yet, with commendable restraint and an understatement that even Naunton Wayne couldn't have bettered, the police issued their standard radio warning that this man might be able to help them in their inquiries!

THE LODGER (1944): In this excellent Jack the Ripper thriller, detective George Sanders shows the Yard's crime museum to Aubrey Mather.

199

THE VERDICT (1946): A heavy-handed, interesting misfire: Sydney
Greenstreet as the Yard detective, Peter Lorre as his friend.
Their Holmes-Watson relationship might have sparked a good
series if the script hadn't disposed of Greenstreet.

HANGOVER SQUARE (1945): A surprisingly effective follow-up film, with George Sanders and Laird Cregar repeating their detective/killer roles.

LURED (1947): Another remake of an original French thriller; detectives George Sanders and Lucille Ball, and smiling, friendly, cooperative Cedric Hardwicke—*one* of the suspects.

LURED: When George Zucco was cast as a detective instead of a villain, he invariably played the role for whimsical charm and comedy. With Lucille Ball.

MIDNIGHT LACE (1960): The best of all of Hollywood's British detectives, John Williams, questions Rex Harrison and Doris Day.

11 THE DETECTIVE AND ALFRED HITCHCOCK

Alfred Hitchcock.

For a man who has made as many great thrillers as Alfred Hitchcock, it is surprising that he has made few mysteries and has also made such little use of the detective figure, a *familiar* figure in many of his movies, but rarely an active participant. However, it makes a kind of sense when one accepts Hitchcock's credo of film making. He doesn't *like* mysteries, particularly those in which the audience has to wait to find out what is going on. He has no objection to the characters in the film being kept in a state of ignorance, but he likes to tip his hand in one

way or another so that fairly early in the film the audience —probably ahead of the hero—is in possession of most of the facts. Given that, it is a waste of time and a draining of suspense to have a detective methodically seek out clues. In any event, there is little logic in the average Hitchcock thriller; to allow the detective (and thus the audience) to examine details would merely emphasize that lack of logic which speed or Hitchcock's own magic has succeeded in covering up.

Sometimes, however, Hitchcock can be quite perverse

in coming up with exact countertheories. He *likes* his heroines, for example, to have something of an air of mystery. For that reason—and his cast lists bear him out—he has never used a voluptuous Marilyn Monroe type for a heroine because (and he says this disarmingly and noncritically) he finds their sex appeal too obvious. From their first scene, there is *no* mystery about them. But the restrained, lady-like types—Madeleine Carroll, Grace Kelly, Sylvia Sidney, Joan Fontaine—appeal to him because they may not be what they seem. As the layers are peeled away during the course of the film, they may be revealed as women of passion (or of ice) but in any event the period of discovery adds zest and interest to the film.

Another curious fixation from a man whose films are literally often *all* chase is a professed dislike for the car (or other essentially *physical*) chase. He was unimpressed by the much-applauded climactic chase of *The French Connection,* feeling that audiences would not accept it as real, that its very expertise would connote faking of some kind.

Similarly, he felt that Peter Bogdanovich missed rich opportunities by not using the element of *total* surprise in his elaborate car chase sequence for *What's Up Doc?* Instead of just missing a plate glass window, Hitchcock suggested that the car should have gone right through it—the surprise being that the window did *not* break. How such a gag could work in a realistic context is a little hard to fathom. Hitchcock's concern in any case (whatever the method) was for relieving audience tension, but by an unexpected route.

Perhaps Hitchcock's reason for disliking the chase is that it is the kind of sequence that cannot be fully pre-planned in the studio. For Hitchcock, all creative film making takes place in the storyboard stage, where every detail, every camera angle, every cut is meticulously pre-planned, so that the actual shooting is a kind of mechanical anticlimax and deviations—even inspired ones—from the original conception are not to be countenanced. It's true that Hitchcock's few traditional chases have been largely studio controlled (*Number 17* with its intricate use of miniatures in a train-bus chase, *Foreign Correspondent* with its studio windmills and carefully cut-in comedy punctuation of the peasant trying vainly to cross the street and finally giving it up as a bad job) and couldn't have worked as well (for him) had they been shot on location.

The most complex detective work in Hitchcock films has always been performed by the innocent hero, sucked into an intrigue beyond his understanding, sought for a murder of which he is innocent, pursued by both villains and the law and (despite other sensible solutions which

Hitchcockian logic never gives us the chance to think about) thus forced to track down the guilty party in order to exonerate himself. Classic and almost identical examples of this are provided by Robert Donat in *The 39 Steps,* Derek de Marney in *Young and Innocent,* Robert Cummings in *Saboteur,* and Cary Grant in *North by Northwest.*

One of Hitchcock's few straightforward uses of the detective as a hero was in one of his earlier British thrillers, *Blackmail* (1929). John Longden played the Scotland Yard man, and Hitchcock can be excused for his orthodoxy on the grounds that he hadn't made many thrillers yet and was still sticking to the rules. Less than three years later, though, in the cheap but marvelously stylish *Number 17,* already a deliberate spoof of the thriller genre that was to become Hitchcock's permanent stamping ground, he gives us a "detective" who turns out to be the villain—and an innocent bystander who turns out to be the detective. Neither do a great deal to substantiate their claims: the bogus detective systematically searches the film's two pretty heroines and rattles his handcuffs, while the real detective explains the case away in a line or two at the end. If it thus can't be considered a "detective film," it can be considered one of Hitchcock's most enjoyable thrillers; the first half all expressionistic shadow and lighting camerawork in an old house, a heritage of Hitchcock's German period, the second half all thrills and chase. John Stuart, an excellent British actor, was the detective—a role he was to play along more traditional lines in many other British films. In the first (and better) of the two versions of *The Man Who Knew Too Much* (the original British 1934 edition), the hero (Leslie Banks) is again forced into the detective role in order to rescue his daughter from a gang of anarchists who have kidnapped her in order to force him to keep silent concerning details of a proposed assassination. The official detective on the case, George Curzon, can do little but appeal to his sense of patriotism and be available with reinforcements in the exciting last-reel roundup.

Sabotage (released in the United States as *A Woman Alone*), made in 1936, is in some ways the best and certainly the most serious of Hitchcock's British thrillers. For once there is little levity; he has respect for his characters, who are real human beings, and not just puppets to be manipulated by Mr. Hitchcock's dexterous fingers to make an agreeable light entertainment. It's a frequently harrowing thriller in which death is presented not as a sophisticated charade but as real personal tragedy. Hitchcock often said that he made serious mistakes in this film and shouldn't have been so uncompromising, but it has real meat on its bones and is one of his most satisfying films. It's also the only one, apart from the earlier *Blackmail,* to feature a detective hero —played in this instance by John Loder. True to his beliefs, however, Hitchcock doesn't slow the film down by any actual detective endeavor. The suspect's guilt has been established for Scotland Yard before the film's opening; it is established for the audience in the very first scene; the hero's role, therefore, is to masquerade as a grocer, spy on the saboteur (whom Hitchcock rather perversely sets up as a cinema manager, with a great deal of realistically detailed "trade" talk to make him doubly convincing), and be on hand for the final showdown—although, as is to be expected with Hitchcock, when it comes it does so with some major unanticipated twists.

It would be a long time before Hitchcock returned to a legitimate detective hero. His second American film, *Foreign Correspondent,* an excellent if overproduced thriller, put Joel McCrea and George Sanders through some energetic sleuthing processes, but in the role of newspaper correspondents. The one seemingly authentic detective in the film (offensively humble Edmund Gwenn) turned out to be a rather nasty hired assassin.

Shadow of a Doubt (1943), one of Hitchcock's very best films and one of his own personal favorites, used detectives again, and with a little more respect than usual. The film was a superbly constructed, beautifully balanced tale of a mass murderer of women (Joseph Cotten) who tires of running, returns to a small California town to hide out with adoring relatives, and gradually decides that he'll have to add the niece who genuinely loves him (Teresa Wright in her subtlest performance) to his list of victims since she is beginning to suspect. Two detectives—MacDonald Carey and Wallace Ford—descend on the town and, virtually convinced of his guilt from prior evidence and masquerading as interviewers for a magazine, work their way into the family's confidence so they can get a picture of the elusive Uncle Charlie. The restraint, doubts, and dislike for their work under these circumstances are realistically portrayed and they are refreshingly nondramatic in their behavior.

In *Notorious,* Cary Grant was a kind of super-scale, upper-echelon detective—but, again, knowledge of the criminal's guilt was established prior to the film's opening, and the plot was concerned more with the attempts to trap him than with attempts to *prove* him guilty.

In *Stage Fright,* Michael Wilding was the official Scotland Yard detective—personable, charming—but little more than a figurehead, with most of the work being done for him in semicomedy manner by Alastair Sim and Jane Wyman.

Dial M for Murder (1954), however, featured one of the most delightful and engaging of any of Hitchcock's

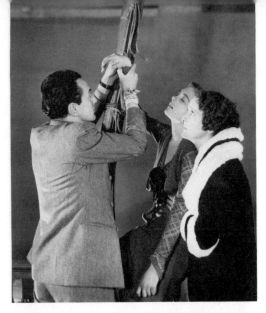

NUMBER 17 (1932): Detective John Stuart and Ann Casson (centre) saved from a tricky situation (tied to a collapsing stairwell bannister) by Anne Grey.

THE MAN WHO KNEW TOO MUCH (1934): Leslie Banks (centre, with Nova Pilbeam) as the prototype Hitchcock hero: the disinterested observer forced into becoming an amateur detective. At left and right, political assassins Frank Vosper and Peter Lorre.

Another example of the unwilling hero: Robert Donat in THE 39 STEPS (1935) must find the killer of Lucie Mannheim (sprawled over his bed, bread-knife in her back) before the police find him.

THE 39 STEPS: Scottish detective Frank Cellier refuses to believe Donat's story.

SECRET AGENT (1936): Peter Lorre, John Gielgud, Robert Young, Madeleine Carroll.

detectives, although Hitchcock had less to do with the shaping of the role than usual. The film was based on the phenomenally successful Broadway play by Frederick Knott, one of those intricate "perfect crime" essays where there isn't a great deal of actual mystery (since the audience is informed every step of the way) but a great deal of two-way suspense in wondering how the criminal is going to slip up and how his victims will escape his net. It was a precision-made jigsaw puzzle on stage, and there was little need to change it for the screen, other than for getting bigger name stars and using color and 3-D film. Hitchcock was not in favor of the latter device, and the film's content and limited settings did not seem to justify its use. He carefully avoided the usual stunt effects of 3-D, limiting himself to a few in-depth shots of the telephone, a key prop in the vital attempted murder scene. However, when the film was released, flat prints were used and none of the film's effectiveness was lost.

A major part of that effectiveness was the retention from the stage version of the play's two leading supporting actors: Anthony Dawson as the seedily aristocratic hired assassin and John Williams as the Scotland Yard inspector—dapper, sporty, a bit bored by crime, much more astute than he appears, yet also dedicated to an abstract kind of justice, not really caring too much whether the heroine (Grace Kelly) is a murderess, but caring very much on an impersonal level that the truth be established. It was a beautifully played performance, providing the light relief that the story needed while carrying it forward at the same time. Williams' polished perfection did occasionally suggest, in its use of effective bits of stage "business," that this was a role he'd played so many times that he could do it in his sleep. But, on the other hand, off-screen, Williams had exactly the same kind of personality (fortunately, this traditional "stage" Englishman is a reality too, and far from a disappearing breed) so that personal spontaneity constantly shone through the well-oiled mechanics of the smoothly written role. Williams had been in films and on the stage for a great many years, but his great personal triumph in this role boosted his stock and of course made repetition of the role (in such films as *Midnight Lace,* a Doris Day–Rex Harrison thriller of suspiciously similar design) a foregone conclusion. It also introduced his English aristocrat to the lucrative world of television commercials.

John Williams was the last really memorable detective In the remake of *The Man Who Knew Too Much,* James Stewart took over the amateur detective work of Leslie Banks and officialdom, in the form of Ralph Truman, repeated its watch-and-wait process. Martin Balsam's detective in *Psycho* was murdered rather quickly, his presence less important for its contribution to the plot than for the setting up of one of Hitchcock's most unexpected and wholly effective shock sequences.

SABOTAGE (1936) (U.S. title: THE WOMAN ALONE): Britain's most over-worked movie detective, John Loder, takes Sylvia Sidney to lunch.

At one point it seemed highly possible that Hitchcock would direct the screen version of *Sleuth,* which would have given him, for the first time, a film in which the major figure was a detective. However, Hitchcock's films are more infrequent now, and he works only on those that interest him personally and give him a chance to put his own imagination and puckish sense of humor to work. *Sleuth,* obviously not a property to be tampered with, was not that kind of a vehicle, and was made by Joseph Mankiewicz with Sir Laurence Olivier in the lead.

Even assuming that the question of Hitchcock directing *Sleuth* ever got past the conjecture stage, it was fortunate indeed that he didn't, for it left him free to make 1972's most enjoyable thriller, *Frenzy.* A remarkably fast and sprightly film for a director in his mid-seventies, it was a refreshing return to the style (albeit on a more sophisticated level) of such earlier films as *Young and Innocent.* The critics' ecstatic raves were perhaps a *little* generous; it is by no means a great film. But their enthusiasm was indicative of something else: their hunger for (and delight with) a modern thriller that played down ugly sensation and played *up* humor and, in addition, was a thoroughly professional film—beautifully edited, paced, photographed; with a beginning, middle, and end; no pandering to flashy technique, zooms, and jumpcuts or the fashionable and overworked flash-forward and flashback cuts.

For once in a rare while with Hitchcock, the detective figure was not only a major one but a stabilizing one. Most of the other characters in the film are the usual rather tricky Hitchcockian people: one has little sympathy for the hero and a certain amount of sympathy for the villain (once you're sure which is which), while one's feelings for the apparent heroine(s) are somewhat abused since they have a habit of being killed off just as soon as one has accepted them and learned to like them. The detective, however, does play at least an equal part with the hero in running the psychopathic killer to earth. Moreover, he is an extension of John Williams' amusing detective of *Dial M for Murder,* except that he is less theatrical, a butt for most of the humor rather than its purveyor. As played by that fine actor Alec McCowen (as yet, not as well used in film as on stage), he is the traditionally methodical, rather unemotional Yard man, quite as adept as Williams at throwing away the witty line, but a far less stereotyped character. One is delighted with him right away when one gets to know him as he attacks (in his office) a Technicolorful plate of eggs, bacon, and sausage, explaining the while that in order to survive in England one has to eat "a good English breakfast three times a day." The film's running gag (his wife insists on serving him ghastly gourmet dishes with beady-eyed fishheads floating in an uneatable French stew) provides a useful clearinghouse for infor-

SABOTAGE: Yard men Mathew Boulton and John Loder investigate the wreckage of a bus blown up by the saboteur.

SHADOW OF A DOUBT (1943): Killer Joseph Cotten, his adoring niece Teresa Wright, detective MacDonald Carey.

207

mation. As he eats (or delays eating), he brings his wife (and the audience) up to date on the case. There are constant sight and sound counterpoints in black humor, the wife snapping breadsticks in punctuation just as her husband describes the killer's breaking of a victim's fingers that have hardened by rigor mortis. It's one of the most delightful—and dramatically valid—uses of the detective in any Hitchcock film. Since the film has also come full circle, a triumphant return to his English style but with the addition of all the Hollywood know-how that he has acquired in the intervening thirty years, it would form a perfect climax to his career in the (unlikely) event that he should decide to retire and rest on his laurels.

THE MAN WHO KNEW TOO MUCH (1956): Doris Day, James Stewart.

STAGE FRIGHT (1950): Amateur detectives Alastair Sim and Jane Wyman, and professional Michael Wilding.

DIAL M FOR MURDER (1954): John Williams, Grace Kelly, Ray Milland.

NORTH BY NORTHWEST (1959): Cary Grant, in much the same position as Robert Donat in THE 39 STEPS, has to outwit spy James Mason to prove his own innocence.

FRENZY (1972): Alec McCowen as a Chief Inspector of Scotland Yard.

FRENZY: McCowen arrests suspected sex killer Jon Finch, later has second thoughts and helps to prove his innocence.

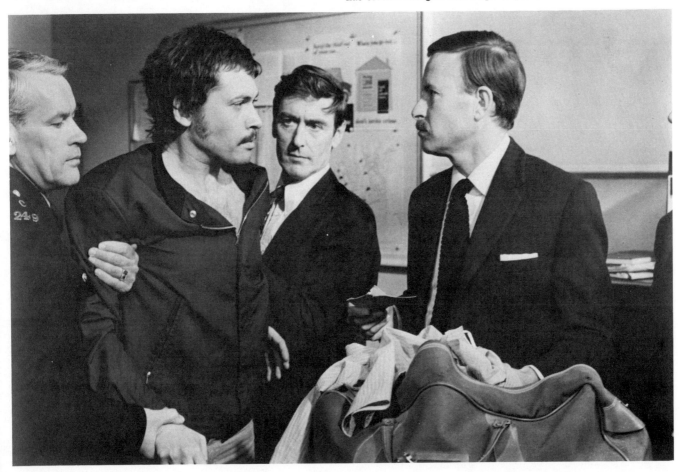

12 COMEDY AND CAMP

THE BIG NOISE (1944): Laurel and Hardy.

The detective film has never lent itself too readily to satirization or to utilization by established comedians. With its direct-line development and its emphasis on dialogue, it is the antithesis of the average comedy, which needs both speed and visual sight gags. Other genres have generally proven much more adaptable to the comedy treatment. The "old house" thriller (*The Cat and the Canary, The Gorilla, The Ghost Breakers*) is an ideal format. For one thing, audiences will accept a comic coward as a hero far more than they will a noncomic coward. The formula for this kind of thriller is for an atmospheric and visual depiction of terror, into which the scared comic hero can fit quite naturally. He doesn't need to drag his own comedy routines in because the format already provides enough alternatives. Sometimes the horror content can even be increased because of the safety valve of frequent laughs; Bob Hope's *The Ghost Breakers,* for example, has moments that are more chilling than similar sequences in straight chillers.

The western, on the other hand, with its familiar props,

clichés, and settings, has produced surprisingly few genuine satires. Laurel and Hardy, Abbott and Costello, the Marx Brothers, Martin and Lewis, Bob Hope, and others have all tried, with varying degrees of success, to spoof the western. One that did it best was Allan Dwan's *Trail of the Vigilantes* (1940) and its method was to play the clichés—and the villains—totally straight, and to make only the heroes bumbling and inefficient, so that the menace lined up against them was more one-sided than ever. Too often, the western (and the detective) spoof seems merely a matter of established comedians trotting out their familiar routines against a new background, making little or no attempt to satirize a specific kind of film. The genuine satire has to succeed on two levels: it has to be subtly funny, without ridiculing its inspiration, and it also has to be a good enough example of the genre it is kidding to stand up to the particular demands of that kind of film.

One detective film that succeeded superbly well in this respect was the British *Bulldog Jack* (1935), a spoof of the then currently popular Bulldog Drummond films. It got off to a good start by a traditional set of credit titles, with appropriate agitato music, but punctuated by a pistol shot and a scream halfway through. The villainy was in the experienced hands of Ralph Richardson (a wonderfully satiric portrait, yet one fraught with real menace too), a topheavy opposition to the zaniness of Jack Hulbert, who replaces the real Bulldog Drummond in a case involving kidnapping and the looting of the British Museum.

Hulbert was a song-and-dance comic (though wisely keeping musical interludes out of this particular film) who followed the Harold Lloyd technique of combining comedy with thrill. He had a breezy, cheerful personality and good diction which made him far more acceptable to American audiences than many of the regional comics from Britain with their heavy local accents. His films were always solidly produced, with good sets, camerawork, and well-staged action scenes.

The dialogue in *Bulldog Jack* is not only pithy and amusing, but some of it seems to play in direct parody of recognizable scenes. The confrontation between detective Hulbert and master criminal Richardson—apologizing in mellow, cultured tones for the unavoidable necessity of killing him—has an exact parallel in that same year's *The 39 Steps* from Hitchcock, with its identical confrontation between Robert Donat and Godfrey Tearle.

The action scenes carry real thrill too because, despite the comedic punctuation, they are tense and so carefully staged that even with the use of some meticulously constructed miniatures, they look like the real thing. The

SHERLOCK JR. (1924): Buster Keaton as the movie projectionist turned detective; with Kathryn McGuire.

DETECTIVES (1928): Karl Dane (bowler hat in hand) and George K. Arthur (smiling).

211

final third of the film is virtually all chase: up and down the spiral staircases of London's subway system, around the darkened exhibits of a museum at night, a frighteningly realistic fight adjacent to the third (electrified) rail on the subway tracks, and finally a splendidly edited chase and fight aboard a runaway subway train, heading for the end of the line and disaster. With brother Claude Hulbert backing up Jack, and Fay Wray playing the lady-in-distress with all the earnestness she displayed when being chased by Lionel Atwill or King Kong, the film is a little gem, a perfect example of the well-done detective spoof: a good vehicle for the personality of its star (but with inappropriate elements, such as his tapdancing skill, eliminated), a good comedy, *and* a rattling good thriller.

Almost as good, though less well received, was a Universal Deanna Durbin vehicle devised by "Saint" mystery

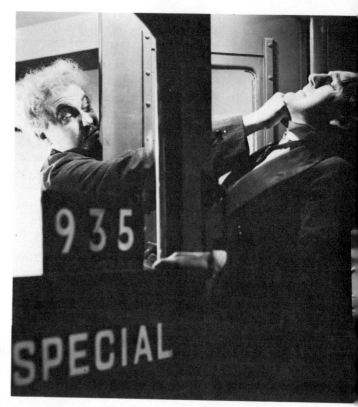

Jack Hulbert in a showdown battle with master-criminal Ralph Richardson in the subway train climax of BULLDOG JACK (1935).

THE GRACIE ALLEN MURDER CASE (1939): Dumb amateur detective Gracie Allen muddies the waters for equally dumb professionals Donald McBride and William Demarest.

writer Leslie Charteris. Although it undoubtedly made money, *Lady on a Train* (1945) was dismissed by both audiences and critics of the day and generally regarded as no more than another misfire in the then slipping career of Deanna Durbin. While, to a degree, one can understand the reception it got in 1945, it is hard to understand why (like, for example, *Beat the Devil*) it didn't at least acquire a belated reputation. Perhaps it might have if some of the creative personnel attached to it had later graduated to an "in" hierarchy, but none of them did. The reasons for its comparative rejection at the time aren't too hard to fathom. Durbin still had her faithful following, and fans reared on *Three Smart Girls* and *Spring Parade* didn't take kindly to their girl being given a sexy buildup and dumped into a murder mystery. Also, Deanna was undeniably pleasantly plump, and neither her earlier image nor her current shape really suited her new sexpot buildup.

Second, and more important, the film itself seemed out of step. It was a throwback to the gaily lunatic comedy of the thirties—the mixing of madcap murder and cocktails, as in *The Thin Man* and *Remember Last Night?* At this point in the forties, murder was being taken very seriously in all the tough and violent crime/private eye melodramas with Bogart, Ladd, Raft, et al. Even so, it's such a lavish and entertaining frolic that it's hard to see why it failed especially as, like *Bulldog Jack,* it succeeds both as a comedy *and* as a thriller. It's certainly good enough not to need judging as a Durbin vehicle; take away the songs, take away Deanna, put lovely little Peggy Moran into the lead, and you'd still have a delightful film.

The plot premise is an intriguing one that had worked well earlier in a French film and in its British remake, *A Window in London*—a murder glimpsed through an open window from a passing train, with just enough clues taken in during that brief glimpse to launch the heroine's private investigation—and to cause the killer enough concern to try to get rid of her before she tracks him down. Unusual care seems to have been taken in all aspects of production. The sets (especially the nightclub and the inevitable old mansion) are quite remarkably lavish for economy-conscious Universal. The camerawork (Woody Bredell) is first-rate, with Deanna the recipient of grade A glamour treatment via intricate back lighting and a mobile camera that literally caresses her in soft closeups and gliding dolly shots.

The dialogue is snappy and bright (especially from Edward Everett Horton) and the cast well chosen. The fairly intelligent shifting of suspicion from character to character is adroit and well above normal Hollywood mystery levels, and is let down only by infallible type-

THE BANK DICK (1940): with W. C. Fields.

THE BIG STORE (1941): The Marx Brothers vs Douglas Dumbrille.

WHISTLING IN THE DARK (1941): Radio detective "The Fox" (Red Skelton) and Conrad Veidt.

MY FAVORITE BLONDE (1942): Bob Hope, Madeleine Carroll and friend.

SO'S YOUR AUNT EMMA (1942): Zasu Pitts and Tristram Coffin.

WHO DONE IT?: Abbott and Costello in the hands of detectives William Gargan and William Bendix.

WHO DONE IT? (1942): Abbott and Costello with Ludwig Stossel.

casting which gives the game away as soon as the killer appears in all his smiling, solicitous charm. But doubtless Universal felt that Miss Durbin's particular following would not have seen enough mystery movies to be suspicious of so amiable a gentleman as Ralph. (The surnames of Morgan and Bellamy were interchangeable: it always turned out to be *one* of them!)

There's a lot of Hitchcock in the film, particularly in the use of innocent (yet not common) settings as a background to scenes of menace; piles of white grain take on a nightmarish quality when a murder attempt is played out against them. And the film really *moves;* the fights are brisk and energetic, there are constant changes of location; melodramatic sequences frequently have neat and unexpectedly comic wrapups. And, as in *Green for Danger* and *Bulldog Jack,* the overall levity does not intrude into episodes of genuine menace, which are all the more effective for the sudden change of mood. Deanna Durbin, plump or not, still looked very lovely and sang a trio of deliberately varied songs very effectively. An attempt was obviously made to return, in adult framework, to the same kind of character that she projected in *A Hundred Men and a Girl* and other earlier vehicles: overly energetic, intrusive, a bit bothersome. Her own charm and a stable of reliable veterans kept her youthful ebullience in check in earlier days, and the same necessary check works here. Incidentally, her final fadeout closeup is an effective period to a comic-erotic gag that belongs to the earlier Lubitsch period, and was quite rare in the forties.

The film is so enjoyable on so many levels that one regrets all the more that it was the only major American film of Frenchman Charles David—who had worked in French films throughout the thirties, had come to Hollywood during the war as an assistant to Alexander Korda, Jean Renoir, and René Clair, and finally turned to directing himself. His unusual "B" *River Gang* (more interestingly titled *Fairy Tale Murders* originally, with kindly old stereotype John Qualen turning up as a homicidal uncle!) was made in the same period as *Lady on a Train.* But if David's Hollywood career got nowwhere, there was some consolation in that he walked away with Miss Durbin as his bride.

Super Sleuth, an RKO Radio programmer of 1937, almost makes it into the elite list of comedy-detective thrillers that really work. In 1937 it *did* work; today it seems a little arch, Jack Oakie's hard-working fast-talking comedy not quite as funny as it was then, its restriction of setting too indicative of its stage origin. Nevertheless, it has an interesting premise and again allows the villain (Eduardo Cianelli) to ply his trade without any concessions to comedy. The plot concerns a movie de-

COSMO JONES CRIME SMASHER (1943): Richard Cromwell (left) and Frank Graham.

LADY ON A TRAIN (1945): Dan Duryea, Ralph Bellamy, Deanna Durbin.

HARD BOILED MAHONEY (1947): One of the Bowery Boys series, with Leo Gorcey, Huntz Hall, Betty Compson.

DICK TRACY (1937): First of the Tracy films and serials: Smiley Burnette, Francis X. Bushman, Fred Hamilton and Ralph Byrd as Tracy.

DICK TRACY RETURNS (1938): Ralph Byrd in a scrap with Charles Middleton and henchmen; 2nd of the four serials.

DICK TRACY (1945): First of the Tracy features; Morgan Conway as Tracy, Lyle Latell as Pat, Joseph Crehan as the Chief, Anne Jeffreys as Tess Trueheart.

tective so assured of his own astuteness that he guarantees to bring in a mysterious "Poison Pen Killer," basing his investigations on the kind of formula situations that his writers dream up for his screen character. Edgar Kennedy played his own traditionally dumb detective in support. It certainly had some funny moments and a really exciting climax with the hero trapped in the killer's mansion, all tricked up with Buster Keaton-ish mechanical gadgets. RKO remade the film, much less effectively, in the forties, as a heavyhanded Wally Brown–Alan Carney comedy in which all the honors were stolen with no effort at all by Lionel Atwill as the villain.

The same kind of plot premise had seen service earlier in the thirties in *Whistling in the Dark,* with Ernest Truex as a meek little radio actor who plays the daring and all-knowing private detective "The Fox." He, too, gets mixed up in a real life murder case. MGM remade the film, at considerably more expense, in the early forties under the same title. It was now a vehicle for rising comic Red Skelton, and Conrad Veidt played the villain. So successful was this glossy comedy-thriller that MGM made two follow-ups, *Whistling in Dixie* and *Whistling in Brooklyn,* both fast and funny, before Skelton was considered worthier of much bigger (and, as it happened, much less funny) vehicles. All of the "Whistling" films had the sense to let a well-knit story dominate and to absorb Skelton (and sidekick Rags Ragland) into it, if not logically, at least with restraint.

Such was rarely the case with other established comics spoofing detective films. Laurel and Hardy got off some interesting satire in their early silent short *Do Detectives Think?,* but their much later sound feature *The Big Noise* was merely a rehash of their old routines, and their roles as detectives were largely incidental to a loosely connected story line. Abbott and Costello's *Who Done It?* was a slick comedy set against the background of a mystery program on a radio show, but too many of the Abbott and Costello routines were basically unconnected to the detective theme.

One can hardly expect logic from the Marx Brothers, yet it does seem a shame that their *The Big Store,* in which they played lunatic private eyes, did so little toward totally demolishing the clichés of the genre, as only they could. There was a hilarious vaudevillian interpolation in which Groucho convinces harassed Italian papa Henry Armetta (who has somehow lost six of his brood of twelve children in the store) that he could not possibly have so many children. and proceeds to prove it by quoting the statistics for a man earning Armetta's salary. That kind of surrealist reasoning (and the rambling yet somehow logical incoherence of so much of their dialogue) could have made a satire of Holmesian deduction devastatingly funny. But, apart from an open-

Stuntman David Sharpe doubling for Ralph Byrd in action scenes from DICK TRACY VS CRIME INCORPORATED (1944).

THE SPIDER'S WEB (1938): Warren Hull as one of the most colorful of all masked detectives.

ing sequence kidding the seedy office of the Philip Marlowe type of investigator, there is little real genre satirizing, merely the expected Marx Brothers routines and their musical specialties, leading to a remarkable acrobatic chase through the store.

Martin and Lewis followed the same route; Harold Lloyd with his comedy plus thrill formula made *The Cat's Paw* (1934) rather pleasing; the British, in such films as *Seven Sinners* (Edmund Lowe in a good Launder and Gilliat script) and *Bulldog Sees It Through* (with Jack Buchanan), came up with enjoyable examples quite frequently. Of the major comics, only Charlie Chaplin never ventured into the field, but obviously his Tramp character could never be diverted to the more extroverted role of a detective.

The popular silent comedy team of Karl Dane and George K. Arthur did, however, as part of their late twenties series for MGM, make a film called simply *Detectives*. It was directed by Chester Franklin, who seemed to be up to the same tricks he had employed in *The Thirteenth Hour*. Once again, he used the framework of the detective film for something quite different: the two comics played a house detective and a bellhop in a large hotel, and most of the film consisted of purely physical and visual comedy as they pursued a burglar.

JUNIOR G MEN (1940): A serial in which Ken Howell (well-dressed, centre), younger brother of a G-Man, spent much of the time rather priggishly instructing the Dead End Kids in the art of scientific investigation and the importance of good citizenship.

SPY SMASHER (1942): One of the slickest and best of all Republic serials; with Kane Richmond, Marguerite Chapman.

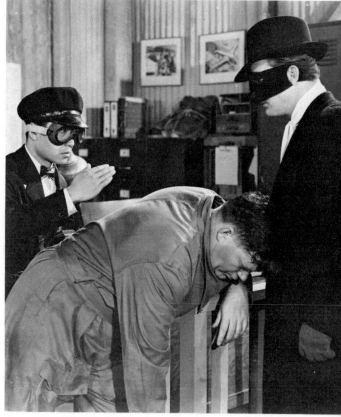

THE GREEN HORNET (1940): Keye Luke and Gordon Jones.

CAPTAIN AMERICA (1943): with Dick Purcell in the title role, a colorful alternate personality to his regular job as District Attorney!

Undoubtedly, the last word in the silent detective comedy was provided by Buster Keaton's *Sherlock Jr.* of 1924, although the cleverness of the whole concept and the brilliance of the technical tricks (Keaton, a would-be detective, is employed as a projectionist in a movie theater and, daydreaming, enters a detective film, is ejected by the actors, reenters, and thereupon assumes the role of detective himself) often takes one's attention away from the bite of the detective satire itself. Top-hatted and elegant, Keaton kids the immaculate, intellectual detective—a latter-day Holmes, and a forerunner of Philo Vance—and takes potshots at the traditional movie handling of attempted murder, interrogation (his "thorough" search of the heroine consists of keeping a proper distance and chastely looking into her apron pockets), chase, and rescue.

Since it is designed purely as comedy, one cannot say of it that, like *Bulldog Jack,* it could succeed as a thriller too. But its invention and pace are such that its constant movement and surprises could enable it to work purely as an action film, quite divorced from its comedy content. One of its sequences—Keaton playing billiards, not knowing that one of the billiard balls is a bomb—was repeated *seriously* as the climax of a 1933 crime film, *Blood Money*. Doubtless, in 1933, Keaton's gag had been forgotten by audiences. Today, with the Keaton films so fresh in their wit and so widely circulated, the gag has rather become his property again, and it is impossible to take the situation seriously in the otherwise intelligent and offbeat *Blood Money*.

"Camp" is a virtually meaningless and derogatory term, but it does provide a kind of instant identification for the "superhero" detectives who were born in the comic strips and spent the majority of their movie lives in the celluloid equivalent, the serial. For all of its facile absorption into contemporary language, the word camp still denotes a rather complex form. It is almost impossible (except, perhaps, for a really subtle performer) to create camp deliberately; it has to be achieved unwittingly and over a period of time by changing standards both within the art form and within the audience, and can only come out of something that originally was meant to be taken relatively seriously. Invariably, attempts to make a camp film deliberately become self-conscious and artificial, as the commercially successful (but quickly forgotten) "Batman" television and theatrical movies of the sixties soon showed.

Bonafide detection played a small part in the makeup of the movie superheroes and, in fact, only Dick Tracy, conceived in Chester Gould's comic strips, was a straightforward detective who eschewed the melodramatic effects of a gaudy costume. Tracy, who found a perfect visualization in Ralph Byrd, first came to the screen in a 1937 Republic serial, *Dick Tracy*. It was not very good,

being extremely slow, cheaply made, with a maximum of back projection and other studio economies and with a dearth of imaginative chapter endings. It did have a good cast, however, including veteran Francis X. Bushman as Tracy's superior, some interesting story twists (Dick Tracy's brother transformed into his enemy by a brain operation), and a goodly assortment of villains, headed by the supposedly unknown "The Lame One" (whose hidden identity was all too obvious) and a hunchbacked henchman named Moloch.

Republic's subsequent three Tracy serials—with Ralph Byrd starring in all of them, and the villainy in the thoroughly efficient hands of Irving Pichel, Ralph Morgan, and Charles Middleton—were a tremendous improvement, full of fast action, slick production values, and the imaginative melodramatic climaxes for which Republic was famous. On the detection level, however, the scales were always loaded very much in Tracy's favor. A typical plot gimmick would be for Tracy to find a specific clue, perhaps a fragment of some rare mineral. A rapid check would invariably reveal that such a mineral was handled only by one specific company and, knowing that the villain needed it for some current infernal machine, off Tracy would troop to the warehouse where it was stored, either to forestall the villain's acquisition of it or to give chase if he was too late. Such gimmicks would be good for milking for a couple of episodes, and then something else would crop up: a captured pair of boots encrusted with the kind of clay which could be found only in a specific region, tipping Tracy off to the fact that the villains were obviously setting their sights on the one gold mine in that area.

With a few and sometimes more elaborate variations, this was the kind of sleuthing modus operandi that permeated all of the Tracy films and, backed up by more spectacular gadgetry and computerized information banks, it was also the basic extent of the "detection" work in the Batman films. Its sole purpose was to enable the hero to anticipate the plans of the villain, and keep the action moving constantly. After the serials, Dick Tracy moved into features for RKO Radio. Morgan Conway was a rather dour Tracy in the first two films and then, fortunately, Ralph Byrd took over again. These were quite elaborate "B" films, well mounted and making a serious attempt to capture the larger-than-life action and characters of the comic strips. Most of the basic characters— Tess Trueheart, Junior, the Barrymoresque ham actor Vitamin Flintheart—were brought into the films and the villains were physically repellent with such Gouldian nom-de-plumes as Splitface, Cueball, and Gruesome (a role played to perfection by Boris Karloff).

Cheerfully sadistic and sometimes a strange mixture of action and self-satire, they were enjoyable films but confusing to audiences (especially European ones) who might not know the comic strip or the spirit in which the films were intended. Tracy also encompassed television via a regular half-hour series, and by a group of animated cartoons. An extremely funny "black" cartoon from Warner's titled *The Great Piggy Bank Robbery* (with Daffy Duck starring as Duck Twacy) was also an amusing satire of Tracy and his colorful villains, and of the whole private eye cycle so popular in the forties.

The caped and masked heroes—The Spider, The Green Hornet, The Shadow, The Green Archer, Captain America, and the others—rarely had time for more than pursuit and bone-shattering fights, although The Shadow did have a nominal career in some pleasant little Monogram "B"s, enacted by Kane Richmond. Usually, these worthies were too much above the law to need their suspicions confirmed by the detection method. Captain America (Dick Purcell), in his Republic serial, was a one-man army of destruction, slaughtering villains right and left on the slightest provocation. Possibly in serial form the appalling death rate among his enemies passed unnoticed, but if the serial were ever revived as a feature (as many of them were) the pileup of corpses at his hands would be seen to reach astronomical proportions. The donning of grotesque disguises by these superheroes (and by their supervillain opponents, The Gargoyle, The Octopus, The Scorpion) always seemed to be a most impractical form of attention-getting conceit, especially for the villains who often had to affect a limp or a twisted back in order to live up to their uncomfortable-sounding names. Apart from making their wearers unduly conspicuous, the capes got in the way during the fight scenes, the flowing robes hampered escape and/or pursuit, and the masks cut down on the field of vision!

Best of this brand was probably Columbia's *The Spider's Web,* in which private detective Richard Wentworth also masqueraded as Blinky McQuade, a rather obnoxious-looking underworld stoolie who managed to look constantly in need of a bath, a shave, and dental treatment (despite his quick changes from the clean-cut Warren Hull). Blinky ferreted out the information, Wentworth absorbed it and mulled it over, and then The Spider went into action. Helping him to a very minor degree was Joseph Girard, that most inefficient of police inspectors, who in picture after picture displayed the dull wits that suggested he was long past the retirement age. One classic moment in *The Spider's Web* had him capture a villain (seen in shadow on the other side of an office window) and call out, "Come out with your hands up!" No sooner had the miscreant raised his hands obediently than Inspector Girard blasted away with his gun, shattering both the window and the villain on the other side of it!

The two Spider serials, and in fact most of the Columbia serials of the late thirties and early forties, were directed by James Horne, a former Laurel and Hardy director, who deliberately aimed at the frenetic and the grotesque, kept his serials rolling at a furious pace, ridiculed heroes and villains alike by exaggerated situations and gestures, and seemed to encourage all concerned to regard the whole thing as a gigantic lark.

In such serials as *Holt of the Secret Service,* he didn't allow detective hero Jack Holt, or his female agent Evelyn Brent, even the luxury of a change of clothes. Through an endless series of fights, chases, falls, and escapes from fire, flood, mud, and oil, they survived in the same simple and durable clothes which became increasingly soiled and crumpled and, presumably, were prevented from becoming offensive to the rest of the cast only by their frequent immersions in water!

BEHIND THE MASK (1946). The Shadow was a popular masked detective hero of pulp magazines, and movie serials and features. In this 1946 feature, Kane Richmond is behind the mask.

13 THE PRIVATE EYES:
2. Marlowe to Klute

DR. BROADWAY (1942): MacDonald Carey and Jean Phillips.

Although the term "private eye" was absorbed into common usage by the moviegoing fan primarily from the early forties, and is thus associated mainly with the Philip Marlowe school, it was used casually in movies throughout the thirties—often in a derogatory sense. The tough private detective in fiction effectively dates from Sam Spade of 1930, although there are certainly earlier examples: done not so much in the hope of instigating new trends, as a kind of protest by the individual author against the basically artificial form of detection practiced by the dilettante intellectuals.

Between the aggressively gentlemanly conduct of the Philo Vances of the thirties and the deliberately pugnacious and often antisocial behavior of the Marlowes and the Spades in the forties, a few neutral private eyes have become somewhat lost in the shuffle. Brett Halliday's Michael Shayne was created in 1939, and came to the movies before the big Marlowe-Spade cycle of the mid-forties. In direct competition with the rather bloodless Saints and Falcons, he was a refreshingly realistic type, played with self-confidence and good humor by Lloyd Nolan in a series of seven for Fox. All were "B" products,

221

FOG OVER FRISCO (1934): Donald Woods, Margaret Lindsay, Hugh Herbert.

REMEMBER LAST NIGHT? (1935): Robert Young and Constance Cummings as another Nick and Nora derivation.

though the last one (*Time to Kill*) was based on Raymond Chandler's *The High Window,* which they would remake in time as an authentic Marlowe. Hugh Beaumont —a Lloyd Nolan type, but a duller personality with little humor—also made five (cheaper and much inferior) Shayne mysteries in the later forties.

In Bill Crane, writer Jonathan Latimer created a cynical and liquor-fancying detective who, especially in his sleazy clients, seemed to predate Philip Marlowe. Crane was well portrayed on screen by Preston Foster in three late thirties Universal programmers: *The Westland Case, The Lady in the Morgue,* and *The Last Warning.* All were part of Universal's "Crime Club" series, based on popular but decidedly non-best-seller detective novels. The "Crime Club" label indicated subliminally a kind of endorsement for the films, though it was commercially less of a success for the films than it had been for the publishing house. (*The Black Doll,* a non–Bill Crane mystery, was another good entry in this series.) On film Crane was a little more conventional, but the plots were intelligently worked out and the casts above average. However, since Preston Foster made so many crime "B"s in that period—either as official detective, private eye, or newspaper reporter turned amateur sleuth—at both Universal and Fox, it was difficult for his Crane series to retain much of an identity of its own.

The Ellery Queen mysteries (Queen was both the detective hero and the pen name for the authors) were enormously popular from their inception in 1928, and some are regarded as minor classics of detective fiction. On film, however, they have never risen out of the "B" programmer category, and none have achieved the ingenuity of the original stories, although the first one (*The Spanish Cape Mystery*) did offer the novelty of having Queen (Donald Cook) *fail* to solve the case, which is then wrapped up by a lesser character. Eddie Quillan was the most unsatisfactory Queen of all in *The Mandarin Mystery,* although it was hardly his fault since the casting was monumentally inept and automatically caused the film to be played for comedy rather than thrills. These two Republic "B"s of 1935–36 did nothing to establish Queen as a popular movie detective, and he disappeared until Columbia reactivated the series with *Ellery Queen, Master Detective* in 1940. Ralph Bellamy was a sensible approximation of the novels' conception of Queen, and Margaret Lindsay (as Nikki Porter) and Charlie Grapewin (as Inspector Queen) made good teammates.

Apart from well-above-average casts, however, the films had little to recommend them: production values were merely adequate, and the "mysteries" less so. Bellamy made four Queen films before handing over to William Gargan who made three more with Lindsay and

REMEMBER LAST NIGHT?: Amateur and professional sleuths— Robert Young and Edward Arnold—investigate the murder together.

MEET NERO WOLFE (1936): Edward Arnold as Wolfe, Lionel Stander as his aide Archie, Victor Jory, Joan Perry.

LADY IN THE MORGUE (1938): with Bill Elliott, left, and Preston Foster, right.

LEAGUE OF FRIGHTENED MEN (1937): Walter Connolly as Wolfe, with Eduardo Cianelli.

In the mid-thirties, Frankie Darro and Kane Richmond made a lively series of minor detective thrillers, with the accent more on action than deductions.

THE SHADOW STRIKES (1937): Rod la Rocque (right) as The Shadow, with Kenneth Harlan.

Just the opposite was a series that Frankie Darro (seen here with LeRoy Mason and Mantan Moreland) made for Monogram in the early forties. Light on action, the scripts presented Darro as an amateur detective with a flair for deductive reasoning.

THE BLACK DOLL (1938): Nan Grey, Donald Woods, C. Henry Gordon.

SHADOWS OF CHINATOWN (1936): Bruce Bennett and Joan Barclay.

DEATH OF A CHAMPION (1939): One of the most enjoyable mystery "sleepers" of the period; Lynne Overman and Donald O'Connor.

Grapewin continuing in the same roles. Detective aficionados have few good words to say for the Gargan Queens, but purely as program actioners they were a big improvement. They *moved,* and they retained the distinguished cast lists. William Gargan may have been a more orthodox Ellery Queen, but he also seemed a more relaxed one. He was an actor well versed in the role of the screen detective—from *I Wake Up Screaming* and *The House of Fear* (Universal's interesting remake by German director Joe May of German director Paul Leni's silent *The Last Warning*) to his very popular "Martin Kane" private detective series on television.

Although Edward Arnold is regarded primarily as a character actor, and his relation to crime usually thought of in connection with his villain roles, he has quite a remarkable career in movie detection to his credit. He was the screen's first and best Nero Wolfe in 1936's *Meet Nero Wolfe,* made by Columbia. Rex Stout's super-intellectual Wolfe was a well-to-do, lazy, and very fat detective—but a shrewd one. Most of his cases he solved at home, with his faithful handyman Archie doing all the necessary footwork. He was also devoted to two basic hobbies: raising hothouse orchids and eating gourmet food. Obviously, the role was made-to-measure for Arnold, since the personality traits not only overlapped into Arnold's own, but also into some of his previous movie roles.

The film was a thoroughly satisfying mystery, unusually generous in its supply of suspects, and in those days of relaxed, pre-Marlowe detecting, was able to milk even the simplest ingredients for maximum suspense. The arrival of a ticking brown paper parcel (which may or may not conceal a bomb) was a beautifully built sequence of tension which in these days of ultra-shock and sensation wouldn't be considered worthy of inclusion. Walter Connolly took over from Arnold in a second Wolfe film, *League of Missing Men,* which had a better plot but lacked the magnetism of Arnold. (Connolly was an excellent actor, particularly in exasperated comedy, but he was not the right personality to attempt Nero Wolfe.) In both films, Lionel Stander was ideal as Archie, one of those rare roles which provides the (allegedly) necessary comedy relief while keeping the plot moving forward.

In 1933, in *Secret of the Blue Room,* Arnold played the detective inspector in a middle European community who comes to investigate mysterious murders in Lionel Atwill's chateau. Unfortunately, he didn't arrive on the scene until *after* the first murder; had he, like the audience, seen the first reel he could have predicted the whole plot *and* the murderer's identity well before the mayhem was under way. His abilities were more severely tested in *Remember Last Night?,* a 1935 Universal film (based on Adam Hobhouse's *The Hangover Murders*) in which he,

FAST AND LOOSE (1939): Robert Montgomery investigates; Alan Dinehart, John Hubbard, Don Douglas, Frank Orth.

TELL NO TALES (1939): Melvyn Douglas.

as a New York City detective, and Robert Young and Constance Cummings, as husband-and-wife socialite amateur detectives, are confronted with a genuinely baffling plot and a multiplicity of motives and characters, all of whom somehow tie in neatly for the final denouement.

Although the film was obviously inspired by *The Thin Man,* the director (James Whale) brought to it many additional ingredients, including his own macabre sense of humor, a photographic and lighting style reminiscent of his great horror films for Universal, and a zany, almost surrealist sense of speed and comedy. *Remember Last Night?,* virtually forgotten today, was one of the most enjoyable mysteries of the thirties, and Arnold's detective—tough, irked by the superficialities of the playboy crowd, liking them as friends yet knowing that one of them is the killer he must arrest—managed to make its subtlety felt despite the razzle-dazzle of production technique and almost constant noise and movement. Since neither Ralph Morgan nor Ralph Bellamy were on hand, the lineup of suspects (including Robert Armstrong, Reginald Denny, Jack la Rue, George Meeker, Gregory Ratoff, Sally Eilers, and Gustav von Seyffertitz) was an honestly puzzling one, although since they began to be killed off with some regularity, the accusing finger did begin to point in the right direction by the last reel, if only by a process of elimination.

Another notable, if more prestigious, "official" detective of Arnold's was Inspector Porfiri in Josef von Sternberg's adaptation of Dostoyevsky's *Crime and Punishment.* Like Sternberg's adaptation of Dreiser's *An American Tragedy,* it was much simplified (particularly in the person of the hero-victim) and the unstressed updating of the story (contemporary language, clothes, décor, yet a strict avoidance of automobiles and other symbols of modernity) made it a confusing and uneven film, interesting only for Sternberg's pictorialism and for Arnold's thoroughly professional (and human) if not very Russian detective, who works on Raskolnikov's conscience and finally gets the confession of murder from him. As representative of a different kind of officialdom, Arnold was one of the ruthless detective chiefs in William Wellman's *The President Vanishes* (1934), one of several films of the period advocating police state tactics to combat crime.

In the forties, Arnold returned to a Nero Wolfe–like role in *Eyes in the Night* and *The Hidden Eye,* two MGM mysteries in which he played a detective who was mobile as little as possible—in this case not because of lazy self-indulgence but because he was blind.

Some of the most enjoyable mysteries of the thirties were without official detective heroes, though otherwise fulfilling all the requirements of the best detective stories. *Fog Over Frisco,* a 1934 Warner Brothers film directed by

FAST COMPANY (1939): One of three second-string Thin Man-type thrillers that MGM made one after the other with different leads; here, Melvyn Douglas and Florence Rice.

TELL NO TALES: The Negro wake sequence.

William Dieterle, was such a film and, incidentally, one of the most complex of all movie mysteries until *The Big Sleep*. Not only did it have as many characters and interweaving subplots, but it was only half as long, literally giving audiences no time to think.

It is probably the *fastest* film ever made, even though its physical action is limited to a well-done car chase through the San Francisco streets, and a brief fistic scuffle at the end of it. Everything in the film (from the initial script stage through to the final editing) is done to promote nonstop motion. Dialogue overlaps, key information is revealed only partially or while characters are moving, the film's opening scenes start with a plane landing, a passenger being rushed to a waiting cab, and speeding to a nightclub, the camera restlessly following or preceding him, never stopping long enough to give us even a hint as to what the haste is all about, and when he does finally come to a halt in an office, he punctuates his remarks to a fellow crook by pounding his fist onto walnuts and cracking them.

We are constantly cut into the middle of scenes, and yanked away before they are finished; characters walk (or run) slightly faster than they would under like circumstances in life, and they talk at a staccato speed faster than that of everyday reality. The mathematical precision of the editing and the constant use of swish pans makes the already fast pacing even faster. The camera is constantly on the move: at one point it tracks Margaret Lindsay up the stairs, pauses while she meets the butler en route, follows him for a moment or two in the opposite direction, catches up with the girl as she reaches the top of the stairs, follows her to her room, prowls restlessly with her as she paces up and down, darts with her to the telephone, and, via an optical iris effect, literally places her in her automobile and ejects her from the screen! The use of optical effects is most ingenious in its geometric rhythm and symmetry. Characters aren't so much introduced as *revealed,* Bette Davis making her appearance giggling behind a screenful of balloons, which she pops with her cigarette until her face is visible, and when they exit they seem to be pushed off-screen by wipes or dissolves which follow them agitatedly, the next scene already struggling to take over the screen!

One character, a Chinese manservant, seems to exist in the film *only* so that he can provide a dual plane of action, moving from foreground to center screen to answer the telephone which is intercepted by somebody from the background moving *forward;* or moving across the screen from right to left when the basic action of the scene is going from left to right!

The sound track is often equally creative. In one scene where Margaret Lindsay has been abducted in a freight-yard, her screams are duplicated by the wail of a passing train, which both echoes and mocks her cries. It's a fascinating exercise in style, of speed artificially grafted onto a nonaction subject, and as such is as worthy of serious study as the more profound works of Eisenstein. The fantastic speed is maintained until the very end when, after a last-ditch attempt to make a red herring out of Henry O'Neill, the extremely enterprising villain is finally revealed and his complex machinations explained by hero Donald Woods in a couple of breathless and detail-crammed lines. Instead of calling for a lawyer and bluffing it out, the exposed villain produces a gun, holds everyone at bay, and escapes through the door. Barely has the door swung behind him than a barrage of shots rings out, a woman's scream is heard, and we cut to the corridor and a policeman, smoking machine gun in hand, who explains apologetically, "Well, he tried to shoot it out!", although for such quick action the cop must have been poised and ready, his gun waiting to blast the first face that appeared!

Donald Woods is the newspaper reporter hero who does much of the detecting although, as a pleasant novelty, *not* at the expense of the official detectives. For once they are bright and hard working; headed by Alan Hale (using a curious Irish accent), Robert Barrat (another ultrasuspicious red herring who, to nobody's surprise, turns out to be an undercover man), and Charles Wilson. However, it is the comedy relief—Hugh Herbert as the newspaper photographer—who turns up the one clue that finally cracks the case.

Not all Warner films of the thirties were as distinguished, but they did keep up a steady stream of ultra-efficient and fast little thrillers ranging from *The Second Floor Mystery* (a 1930 adaptation of Earl Derr Biggers' *Agony Column*) and *Murder by an Aristocrat* (one of several "B"s in which Lyle Talbot, before he became portly, made a handsome and dashing romantic sleuth) to 1938's *When Were You Born?* (in which detective Charles Wilson is beaten to a solution of the murder case by Chinese Anna May Wong, who uses astrology charts as an aid to deductions!).

"Gimmick" mysteries of the thirties included *The President's Mystery* (1936), an idea suggested ostensibly by detective fan President Roosevelt and employing the combined efforts of a number of detective writers (S. S. Van Dine and Anthony Abbott among them), and *The Woman Accused* (1933) in which ten writers did anything but collaborate. The idea (in the publicity, if not in actuality, although the film does tend to substantiate it) was that one writer begin, build to a climax without solution, then hand over to another writer for immediate solution plus predicament number two, and so on. It was an intriguing idea, although the end result had a kind of formularized unity even though the internal sections were a bit arbitrary and lacking in cohesion. Perhaps writer number ten was given a roving commission to tidy up after his nine predecessors! One rather overworked gimmick, in an attempt to get away from the traditional detective or reporter hero, was to make the hero or

FAST AND FURIOUS (1939): Ann Sothern, Franchot Tone.

Ralph Bellamy, the Ellery Queen of Columbia's early forties series.

William Gargan, who assumed the Queen role following Bellamy, and Margaret Lindsay who played throughout the series as Nikki Porter.

Charles Grapewin, cast as Inspector Queen, Ellery's father, in the same series.

DRESSED TO KILL (1941): William Demarest, victim, and Lloyd Nolan as Michael Snayne.

MURDER IS MY BUSINESS (1946): A later Michael Shayne, Hugh Beaumont (centre) with Lyle Talbot, left, and Pierre Watkin.

ALIAS BOSTON BLACKIE (1942): Adele Mara, Chester Morris.

heroine a detective story writer caught up in a real crime (or, in later years, the writer of detective scenarios for radio or the movies). Films in this category ran the gamut from 1930's *Midnight Mystery,* in which writer Betty Compson (stranded in one of those convenient island castles on a weekend party) seems able only to uncover evidence that her husband (Lowell Sherman) is the killer, to the serial *Shadows of Chinatown,* with Bruce Bennett as a somewhat unlikely mystery writer pitted against the evil Bela Lugosi, an archcriminal whose ambitious designs are explained thus: "He wants to wipe out the entire Occidental and Oriental races, and start a new race of his own"!

In the early forties, the big detective film was a rarity and crime, having been diverted from detection to gangsterism and the espionage thriller, was limited largely to the "B" films. Chester Morris was the last of a not very long line of Boston Blackies (the character featured in a number of silent films), the reformed jewel thief turned amateur detective, making a series of thirteen enjoyable but minor "B"s between 1941 and 1949, all held together more by the Morris personality than by Columbia's scripts, production values, or interesting casts.

In 1943 Columbia also put Warner Baxter (the sophisticated sleuth of 1933's *Penthouse*) into the interesting but meagerly budgeted "Crime Doctor" thrillers in which the noticeably aging Baxter was, like Morris, the only feature of sustaining interest.

One extremely enjoyable one-shot mystery was Paramount's *Dr. Broadway,* with MacDonald Carey as a medico-sleuth in a film that played like a highly polished and noncomic reworking of Damon Runyon situations and characters.

MGM, still looking for a parallel to *The Thin Man,* tried out Gracie Allen and William Post, Jr. in 1941 as *Mr. and Mrs. North* (who didn't catch on in the movies, but *did* much later on in television). In 1950 the studio was *still* trying, but Marjorie Main and James Whitmore as *Mrs. O'Malley and Mr. Malone* didn't turn the trick either.

Republic, in 1941, made a brace of extremely enjoyable thrillers based on radio detective "Mr. District Attorney." Dennis O'Keefe and Peter Lorre starred in the first, bearing that title; the second, much less ambitious but in mystery content quite superior, was called *The Carter Case* and starred James Ellison. It must be unique among all detective films; in picking the least suspicious character to be revealed as the killer, it went beyond all bounds of audience expectations and against all movie tradition and cliché. Further breaking from the norm, the last-reel climax was devoted to a Mack Sennett slapstick chase!

Another decidedly offbeat little work in this period was

229

THE CRIME DOCTOR'S STRANGEST CASE (1943): Lynn Merrick, Lloyd Bridges, Warner Baxter, Constance Worth.

MURDER MY SWEET (1944): Otto Kruger, Mike Mazurki as Moose Malloy (the inevitable brutal psychopathic giant, a fixture in mystery thrillers of the day) and Dick Powell as Philip Marlowe.

MURDER MY SWEET: "Tell your husband I went home; tell him I got bored!" Dick Powell, Claire Trevor.

1942's *The Mystery of Marie Roget,* an unusually carefully made little "B" with good suspense and characterization, even if motivation was a little vague. It was a much more faithful screen adaptation than Edgar Allan Poe was accustomed to, and Patric Knowles (as Dr. Paul Dupin) and Lloyd Corrigan (as Inspector Gobellin) made a good team that could profitably have been put into a whole series—but wasn't.

Obviously, with the detective film so severely restricted to the programmer level, the genre was in need of a massive jolt to restore it to boxoffice favor. The jolt came somewhat unexpectedly with *Murder My Sweet,* produced primarily at the urging of Dick Powell who saw (quite rightly) in the Philip Marlowe role a chance to establish a new image and bolster his flagging career. *Murder My Sweet* was made in late 1944 and, although it has never become the "cult" favorite that *The Big Sleep* has (due primarily to that film's Bogart-Bacall teaming and the presence of Howard Hawks as director), it remains by far the best of the Marlowe films and, indeed, second only to *The Maltese Falcon,* the best of the private eye films. This is all the more surprising in that its director, Edward Dmytryk, is a rather placid and unexciting film maker, usually adding little to his films not already indicated by the script and overprone to imposing social comment onto stories with the slightest encouragement. *Murder My Sweet,* taking the sleazy underbelly of glamorous Hollywood as its setting and a complex mystery peopled by weaklings and savages, generally unworthy of Marlowe's help, but worth no more than the "$25 a day and expenses" he charges, established a whole new mood for the "detective film *noire*" of the forties. Unlike *The Maltese Falcon,* which avoided the seedy back alleys of life (though they were Spade's normal habitat), *Murder My Sweet* was dark, full of hints of degeneracy, drugs, a nightmare world as enclosed and as escape-proof as that of Fritz Lang.

Purely as a thriller, with a complicated yet logically worked out plot, *Murder My Sweet* was near perfect. Powell—because the realistic conception of the private eye was relatively new, and because Powell was totally new to it—*became* Marlowe far more easily than Bogart, who had several other competing images working against him: the gangster image, Sam Spade, Rick from *Casablanca.* Powell tossed off the tired, contemptuous, yet biting Raymond Chandler wisecracks and insults with superbly underplayed style. The drug delirium scenes, though simple in design and conception, are still among the most convincing ever filmed. The film was just the right length (long enough to explore the labyrinth story lines, short enough not to stretch tension past the point of no return) and was beautifully cast, the only really "nice" people (the simple heroine, Ann Shirley, and the honest cop, Don Douglas) also being the most ineffectual.

The private eye cycle that *Murder My Sweet* started overlapped into the end of World War II, and was obviously affected by it. The extreme physical violence of the war films was sublimated, quite naturally, into the private eye films which got increasingly *more* aggressive and sadistic in the postwar period. The western, too, absorbed much of this violence-without-a-home, although it probably acquired it directly from the detective films since suddenly the "B" western heroes began talking in the staccato, big-city-menace phrases of Philip Marlowe.

The postwar period also produced the psychopathic war veteran, returning with combat fatigue to track down his own identity (if he was suffering from loss of memory) or the murderer of his wife. The psychological bent of so many of the new thrillers fitted in well with the black outlook of the private eye films. Although often realistic in characterization, they were rarely realistic in milieu; their world was a nightmarish one of police interrogation rooms, third-rate bars or restaurants, morgues, psychopathic wards, small private hospitals run by quack doctors. Sunlight was rare; sleek black oversized limousines were used not as modes of escape or pursuit but as agents of death or for observation. The lack of dependence on the automobile as a means of speedy escape was stressed by the number of shots in which large limousines maneuvered slowly and clumsily through constricted studio-built streets.

A far cry indeed from the detective world of Alfred Hitchcock—the theater, gay public restaurants, busy railroad stations, or an open roadster on a sunny afternoon. Even the crimes were limited in these films: crimes of passion, of petty greed. In *Somewhere in the Night,* Fritz Kortner (in a marvelous performance) complains somewhat petulantly, "I'm just a *cheap* chiseler"—indicating that the time for grandiose crime has gone, if only temporarily, perhaps dwarfed by the war.

The most commercially successful of the Marlowe follow-ups was obviously *The Big Sleep.* That no one could understand much about it except its title (a metaphor for death) hardly mattered; the book was complex enough and, in order to whitewash it for the screen and launder the pornographic book racket which provided one of its plot lines, it became even more obtuse since explanations were not diverted, they were just ignored! It had speed, the usual enormous Warner efficiency, Howard Hawks' stylish direction, and a thundering Warner score. What I suspect made it such a cult film later on was that it had what the cultists could never get enough of—Bogart and Hawks.

Lady in the Lake, MGM's 1946 Marlowe film, was a courageous experiment that made quite an impression for

MURDER MY SWEET: Los Angeles police detective Don Douglas and Marlowe compare notes.

THE BIG SLEEP (1946): Humphrey Bogart as Marlowe, Lauren Bacall, Martha Vickers.

THE BIG SLEEP: Trevor Bardette, Humphrey Bogart, Bob Steele.

THE BIG SLEEP: Lauren Bacall, Joe Downing, Bogart.

its novelty alone, but which quickly evaporated on subsequent viewings, and now seems a *bad* film (an unthinkable reaction when the film appeared initially). Directed by and starring Robert Montgomery, it was an interesting attempt to use the subjective camera throughout, seeing the whole investigative process through the eyes of the detective, who is seen only when reflected in a mirror (a device that would be artificial, and which is wisely not used too much) or, at the beginning of the film, when he addresses the audience directly. Unfortunately, it is a *technical* device rather than a dramatic one, since the camera cannot approximate the movement of the human eyes or add that sense of intuition of people or things present to the left and right of the field of vision. The scenes of the hero slugged by a heavy fist or seductively kissed by the heroine (Audrey Totter in her considerable prime) had a certain novelty but were unsubtly underlined, like the objects heaved at the camera in the early days of 3-D.

But, more important, the whole pace of the film was artifically slowed by the process. When the ears pick up a sound, the head does not have to swivel to meet it; sometimes a mere shifting of the eyes is sufficient. Or if the head moves, it does so in one swift movement, picking up no detail on the way. But certainly the head does *not* move in a smooth panning shot, registering every detail in focus until it reaches the object of its attention. Nor, when one walks (whether stealthily or briskly) does one walk in the measured, ritualized gait necessary for a heavy camera being pushed along by a crew. Since the whole concept is unreal, the story (a good one) becomes unreal too, creating neither suspense for its situations nor concern, pity, or hate for its characters.

Lady in the Lake was an interesting experiment but its subjective camera explorations were done much better, on the basis of individual sequences, by Huston (in *The Maltese Falcon*), by Hitchcock (in *Stage Fright*), and by Edgar Ulmer (in *The Black Cat*).

232

LADY IN THE LAKE (1947): Robert Montgomery as Marlowe, Lloyd Nolan, Audrey Totter.

THE BRASHER DOUBLOON (1947): George Montgomery as Marlowe.

THE BRASHER DOUBLOON (1947): George Montgomery as Marlowe.

MARLOWE (1969), with James Garner.

THE HIDDEN EYE (1945), with William Phillips, Edward Arnold as a blind detective, Frances Rafferty.

The fourth of the initial Marlowe films, *The Brasher Doubloon* (1947, from *The High Window*), was also the least ambitious, an enjoyable programmer with some typically pithy dialogue, but with an imitative performance from George Montgomery as Marlowe.

During the mid-forties, the private eye (or related) thrillers prospered, their common denominator being an increasing lessening of action and a parallel increase in violence (specifically, the beating up of the hero by goons) although, by contemporary 1970's standards, this violence is still restrained. The film concentrating on crime rather than detection (*Double Indemnity, The Postman Always Rings Twice*) also made an appearance in this period, though it never dislodged the private eyes.

Among the best detective thrillers from this period were *The Dark Corner* (Mark Stevens as a very effective detective hero), *The Blue Dahlia* (written directly for the screen by Raymond Chandler, it holds up less well than the others of the group, but is still one of the best Alan Ladd vehicles), *Out of the Past* (a film almost as complicated as *The Big Sleep,* but directed with real style by Jacques Tourneur and with a private eye performance from Robert Mitchum that is one of his best), and, above all, *Somewhere in the Night,* written and directed by Joseph L. Mankiewicz. Too long by about 20 minutes, it is still a model of its kind: literate, witty, evocative of its period, well knit in its plotting, and with a fascinating array of characters. If it had a detective hero (John Hodiak is the amnesiac war veteran trying to discover his identity, constantly uncovering evidence which indicates that he was a criminal; Lloyd Nolan, in a small but very effective role, is the detective who befriends him), it would be one of the best of all detective movies. But, even with that technical shortcoming, it ranks with *Murder My Sweet* as the best and most representative of the "film *noire*" thrillers of the forties.

Naturally, the boxoffice success of these films inspired a flock of imitations on both programmer and "B" levels. The popular radio series "I Love a Mystery" was turned into a short-lived two-picture series by Columbia with Jim Bannon as the private eye hero. Both *I Love a Mystery* and its follow-up *The Devil's Mask* tried too hard to live up to the series title: there was so much mystery and such a diverse array of characters that one could read three different reviews of each film and find each one giving a different plot line! Lesser private eyes like Frank Gruber's Simon Lash turned up in one-shot mysteries at Monogram and PRC, specializing in that kind of fare. Richard Arlen played Simon Lash in PRC's *Accomplice,* above average for the studio, but concerned more with action than detection and afflicted with an artificially prolonged climactic chase. Lash was a surly and unattractive hero.

THE HIDDEN EYE: A trio of suspects: Byron Foulger, Morris Ankrum, Ray Collins.

THE BLUE DAHLIA (1946), written directly for the screen by Raymond Chandler, was the best of the Ladd-Lake vehicles. Here Ladd conducts a test to prove that William Bendix is not the shell-shocked psychopath (and probable murderer) that detective Tom Powers (extreme right) believes.

ALAN LADD and VERONICA LAKE were a popular starring team in mystery thrillers of the mid-forties which flirted with the private-eye genre, but never quite embraced it.

CRACK UP (1946): An involved mystery starring Pat O'Brien (right) as an art expert suffering from amnesia, turning detective to determine his own identity and bring some art thieves to book at the same time. With Margaret Sheridan, Claire Trevor.

The private eye cycle reached its zenith in 1946–47, with films like *Out of the Past, The Web* (a slick and enjoyable mystery with Edmond O'Brien and Vincent Price), and *The Runaround*. The latter, starring Rod Cameron and Broderick Crawford as competitor private eyes, was something of a free-wheeling putdown of the entire genre, with all problems solved via hectic chases and virtually nonstop fisticuffs.

The private eyes had descended not just into fodder for the "B"s made by the major companies, but into the "B"s made by the independents (Screen Guild, Lippert) as well. The same thing had happened to the gangster film in the thirties. Films like Grand National's incredibly cheap series with Conrad Nagel (*Bank Alarm, Yellow Cargo,* etc.) were clearly poverty-row copies of *G-Men,* but at least they had the saving grace of a certain amount of fast physical action. The cheap private eye melodramas, however, *without* the dynamism of a Bogart or the superior writing of a Chandler, were sorry films indeed. Only in the action-oriented and slick "B"s at Republic—one of the best being 1946's *Passkey to Danger,* directed by Lesley Selander with Kane Richmond as the detective—did the films really work on this economy level.

By the tail end of the forties, interest in the species was petering out. Although short-lived, the move toward location-filmed documentary thrillers—exemplified best perhaps by Jules Dassin's *The Naked City* (itself productive of many imitations, including Dassin's own London-based *The Night and the City*)—made the studio-shot private eye films seem a trifle old-fashioned. Too, the gangster film seemed to be returning, spearheaded by *White Heat,* and bolstered by an increasing craze for nostalgia and the twenties.

The only new private eye (the equivalent word of "shamus," used occasionally in the films themselves, never came into common usage) to cut much mustard at the boxoffice was Mike Hammer, the hero of Mickey Spillane's tough (and very sexy) novels. Hammer was very much a product of the McCarthy era. The earlier private eyes were sometimes not too bright, their basic assets dogged persistence and a strange kind of integrity, a pride in their work, and a responsibility to their clients. Hammer had no such integrity, and few scruples. He was more ruthless (at least in the books) than the underworld hoods he fought and he was particularly inflamed by his self-appointed role as crusader against Communists. A latter-day but less exaggerated Captain America, he started where Marlowe and Spade left off; occasionally, they bent the law a little; he took it boldly in both hands and defiantly broke it, the end apparently justifying the means. A quartet of Spillane films hit the market quite profitably in the fifties and early sixties: *I the Jury* in 1953 cashed in also on the 3-D cycle, and starred Biff Elliott as

235

THE DARK CORNER (1946): Mark Stevens, Clifton Webb.

THE DEVIL'S MASK (1946): A complicated entry in the "I Love a Mystery" series. Jim Bannon and Southern-accented Barton Yarborough (at right, flanking Anita Louise) were the two private detectives, Thomas Jackson (centre) represented the official law once again, and Mona Barrie (left) was the apparent villainess who turned out rather differently.

THE RUNAROUND (1946): Rod Cameron, Broderick Crawford, Ella Raines.

ACCOMPLICE (1946): Richard Arlen as Frank Gruber's Simon Lash; with Veda Ann Borg.

JOHNNY ALLEGRO (1949): George Raft as a Government man; Nina Foch.

Hammer; *Kiss Me Deadly* (in 1955) was much better, starred Ralph Meeker, and became something of a cult film due to Robert Aldrich's direction; *My Gun Is Quick* (1957) with Robert Bray seemed to finish off the series. An unexpected one-picture revival of Mike Hammer in 1963's *The Girl Hunters* was rather a pleasant surprise. Not only was it an enjoyable return to the Marlowe brand of mystery (with a sexy femme fatale villainess coming to a spectacular end), but Mickey Spillane himself, playing Hammer, was quite effective. In addition, the film was a fascinating (and successful) exercise in illusion: apart from a very few establishing shots of New York, the whole film was made in England, yet the intercutting of those few authentic shots with matched-up British sets, plus the use of familiar American faces, gave the film the wholly convincing veneer of an American-made film. Darren McGavin played Hammer in a fairly successful TV series, although he was less effective than Brian Keith, who played the role in a single TV pilot. But, the isolated renaissance of the private eye through Mike Hammer excepted, the genre did seem to be in semi-retirement, replaced by a merger of the gangster film with the austerity of documentary techniques in such films as Bogart's *The Enforcer* (1951).

Interestingly enough, it was nostalgia—the same quality that had brought the gangster film back—nostalgia for the forties and the vanished Bogarts that led to a tentative return to the private eye film. *Harper* (1966, directed by Jack Smight) starred Paul Newman as its private eye hero and was a serious, intelligent, well-done return to the old tradition, played completely straight and updated only by its commercially necessary utilization of color. Harper's office and his modus operandi remained those of Marlowe, and there was a Chandler-like attention to detail, as in the hero's second use of stale drip-grind coffee as a time-saving breakfast in his office.

Unfortunately, the film was played *too* straight: though it did well, it didn't do well enough to revive the species, as reviews enthusiastically predicted it would. Audiences, it seemed, either wanted "camp" rehashes or totally "mod" contemporary equivalents, as in John Boorman's *Point Blank*. That particular film, allied with much relaxed censorial supervision, marked another turning point in the move away from the detective hero, through the antihero, to what can only be described as a non-hero. The acceptance of the "sympathetic" racketeer came first; now, in films like *Prime Cut* (1972, with Lee Marvin in a weird extension of his *Point Blank* role), we have a film in which all the protagonists are mobsters, engaging in the most explicit and revolting forms of brutality and vice, and it is only halfway through the film that one realizes with some horror that Lee Marvin is in fact the *hero!*

THE BIG STEAL (1949): A particularly fast and enjoyable minor thriller: Robert Mitchum, William Bendix.

MANHANDLED (1949): Dan Duryea as one of the few private eyes of the forties who was also the villain of the piece.

237

The private eye, in trying to find a new and commercial identity, has used extensively all of the screen's new permissiveness—sex, nudity, extreme brutality, perversion, the coarsest of gutter language. The route via the initially objectionable *The Detective* and *Tony Rome* (quickly rendered tame and relatively inoffensive by the excesses that followed) is a violent and ugly one. The nudie-quickie, emboldened by the acceptance of out-and-out pornography, moved in on the private eye film too. Ginger Caffaro, a well-endowed but singularly unattractive and hopelessly inept actress, played a kind of female James Bond, and parlayed boudoir tactics into an acceptable substitute for detection. (Curiously, she chastely withheld herself from the advances of her detective boss, who apparently loved her quite sincerely, but went all the way with a minimum of persuasion with the villain of the piece!) Detection was at a minimum in *The Abductors,* but full and total female nudity was at a maximum and, if it stopped short of the clinical revulsion of hard-core pornography, that was its only concession to taste. There was some genuine if unintended amusement in the dialogue of the villains who—although engaged in an international vice racket and presumably men of the world—uttered such words as "strip" and "panties" with all the tremulous excitement of nine-year-old schoolboys scrawling their naughty words on toilet walls! The word "abduct" seemed to hold some special fetishist excitement for the writers, as though it were the most obscene and sexually provocative word in the English language, since it is repeated ad nauseam in every possible situation, and is the key word in about every fourth sentence!

Free-wheeling sex (but handled for humor and eroticism, usually rather tastefully) had come to the detective genre via the James Bond and spinoff spy films. Although initially extremely enjoyable, these films had more of a kinship with the old-time serials and to the Fu Manchu thrillers than to the detective field. James Bond, backed by semifantasy gadgets, operating more on hunches and intuition than anything else, was even less of a detective than Sir Nayland Smith, and the many secret agents that followed in his wake need no consideration here, other than a recognition of the change that their popularity wrought in the detective film, causing it to be infused more and more with sexual content and to be taken less and less seriously. *Marlowe* (with James Garner), based on Chandler's *The Little Sister,* was the sexiest of the Marlowe films—and the weakest. More and more, the detective film came to be played for shock, for comedy, or for dramatic gimmicks.

In the Heat of the Night introduced Sidney Poitier as a black detective working against the opposition of a white world, and was followed by a stereotyped sequel, *They*

CRAIG STEVENS: (seen here in a publicity pose for MURDER WITH-OUT TEARS, 1953) knocked around in "B" mysteries through the forties and fifties before hitting the jackpot with his Peter Gunn, an interesting and well-written private eye series for TV that was later transferred to the movie screen too.

I, THE JURY (1963): Biff Elliott, right, as Mike Hammer, with Preston Foster.

LADY IN CEMENT (1948): Frank Sinatra in the second of his Tony Rome mysteries; with Raquel Welch.

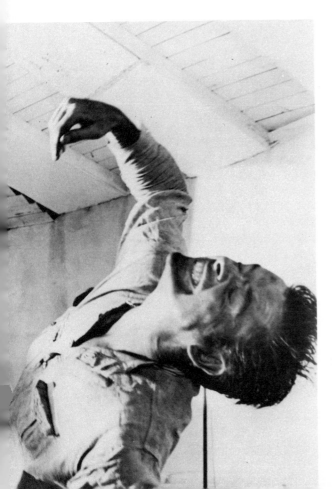

HARPER (1966), with Paul Newman.

COTTON COMES TO HARLEM (1970): One of the first and best of the increasing number of all-black detective (and mystery/action) movies of the seventies; Raymond St. Jacques and Godfrey Cambridge are the detectives.

Call Me Mr. Tibbs. With the expanding commercial importance of the Negro market, the theme has been expanded to the idea of black detectives working in an almost exclusively black world, either for comedy (in *Cotton Comes to Harlem* and its sequels) or for straight melodrama (*Shaft* and its sequels). *The French Connection* goes *Bullitt* and all the other car-chase-highlighted detective films one further by making the climactic chase ostensibly the chase to end them all, and a talking point guaranteed to bring audiences into the theater.

Klute (1971) perhaps shows how far we have come—or fallen. Jane Fonda deservedly won an Academy Award for her realistic interpretation of the call girl—but she was no more convincingly a bitch for her free use of four-letter expletives than Claire Trevor had been in *Murder My Sweet*. The plot itself provided an excellent premise for a good detective thriller—offbeat, multilayered, constantly but not predictably moving toward a solution, intelligently nonsatisfying in its climax in the manner of *The Maltese Falcon*. Yet its infatuation with "mod"

European-introduced techniques robs it of much of the simple pleasure that goes to make up the classic detective film. The heroine's lengthy interviews with a psychoanalyst (dull, repetitive, shot without imagination from a single angle, as though a hasty afterthought, designed and shot after the film was completed, and cut in quickly to add "depth" to the film), plus the film's erratic and confused visual style, combine to minimize its excitement potential. In contemporary jargon, it has become "meaningful"—but has stopped being a film. While it may seem terribly fashionable and up-to-date for a year or two, it will probably seem incredibly old-fashioned and unviewable by 1980—whereas Hitchcock's *Frenzy* will doubtless seem modern and up-to-date when they start televising old movies to the first moon colonists!

Perhaps no film more sums up the detective film's current loss of identity than the British *Gumshoe* of 1971. Part *Secret Life of Walter Mitty,* part imitation *The Maltese Falcon,* and part satire, it winds up as a "whole" nothing. Albert Finney plays a contemporary failure,

240

KLUTE: Donald Sutherland, Jane Fonda.

KLUTE (1971), with Donald Sutherland.

a dull little man leading a dull life, who wish-fulfills himself into a Sam Spade involvement in contemporary crime. What it lacks most of all is consistency: Finney is at times far more efficient than such a character could be, and he uses stereotyped forties dialogue, not as a for-effect attention getter, but as a matter of course. While the film fails as an imitation *Maltese Falcon* (which, after all, it did not set out to be), it also fails as a parody and as a commentary on the impossibility of trying to make the dreams and hopes of an earlier era work when transposed to a contemporary social environment. Perhaps the detective film was the wrong framework for such an idea: it had more validity in *Billy Liar* or *Morgan.* In any event, it is never clear whether *Gumshoe* is trying to revive the Bogart tradition, satirize it, or demolish it.

Fortunately, *Gumshoe* isn't an important enough film to do more than illustrate an uncertainty that is widespread within the industry, a hit-and-miss attempt to discover what will click with contemporary audiences.

GUMSHOE (1971), with Albert Finney.

Luckily, *The Maltese Falcon,* more than thirty years old, continues to be a major attraction on television, a cornerstone for film study at universities, a boxoffice attraction of increasing rather than diminishing returns at revival houses. And if one tends to be smug and jaded, to feel that the great detective films are in the past, one has only to look at *Frenzy*—possibly 1972's most accomplished film—to be reassured. As for the future: some of our best directors—Stanley Kubrick, Sam Peckinpah, Ken Russell—have not yet embraced the genre at all. We need not be greedy: in seventy years, after all, the screen has given us only a handful of unquestioned detective classics. If Messrs. Kubrick, Peckinpah, and Russell give us merely one apiece, and old maestros Hitchcock and Welles turn their hand to it occasionally, we shall have much to look forward to. And when the current stress on ugliness, sex, and violence abates—as it has to, in time—we shall have an extra bonus perhaps in a return to the *civilized* mystery in which once more the only major question of importance will be "Who Done It?"

INDEX